DECONSTRUCTING HIGHER EDUCATION REFORMS IN INDIA

DECONSTRUCTING HIGHER EDUCATION REFORMS IN INDIA

K.S. Chalam

GYAN

Deconstructing Higher Education Reforms in India

Rs. 750

ISBN: 978-81-212-1089-8

Published in 2011 in India by
Gyan Publishing House
23, Main Ansari Road, Darya Ganj
New Delhi-110002
Phones : 23282060, 23261060
Fax : 011-23285914
E-mail: books@gyanbooks.com
Website: www.gyanbooks.com

Laser Type Setting by: Rudra Computer Graphics, Delhi
Printed at : Chawla Offset Printers, Delhi

"A university stands for Humanism, for tolerance, for progress, for adventure of ideas and for the search of truth. It stands for the onward march of the human race towards ever higher objectives. If the universities discharge their duty adequately, then it is well with the nation and the people."

-Jawaharlal Nehru

Contents

List of Tables 9

Prologue 11

1. **Higher Education Policy and Reform** 15
2. **Knowledge Outcomes and Evaluation** 29
3. **Equity and Quality Syndrome** 43
4. **Competencies for Good Teaching** 55
5. **Crisis in Professional Education** 71
6. **Inclusive Education and Social Empowerment** 77
7. **Productivity of Higher Education and Economic Reform** 99
8. **Financial Strategy for Educational Reforms** 109
9. **Addressing Inequity in Human Capital Under Foreign Universities Regime** 131
10. **Emerging Dichotomies during Economic Crisis** 143
11. **Deconstructing Dichotomies through Public Accountability** 153

Annexures 161

Bibliography 297

Index 305

List of Tables

1.1. Higher Education Indicators 23
2.1. Optional Subjects taken by Civil Service Examination Successful Candidates 39
2.2. Top 10 Optional Subject Combinations as per the Number of Candidates Recommended 41
4.1. Learning Objectives and Teaching Methods 66
6.1. Educational Development of Scheduled Castes at School Stage 1980-81 to 2006-07 96
6.2. Stage -wise Drop Out Rates 2006 97
6.3. Enrolment of SC/ST in Higher Education 2006-07 98
8.1. Trends in Social Service Expenditure by Central Government 2009-10 129

Prologue

Higher education policy and reforms in India have been shaped by several elements. The social history, the economic structure and international relations seem to have contributed more to the character and content of education than the needs and aspirations of the masses. Though higher education is an important component of the education system, it has never shown any predilection for other stages like primary and secondary levels. Each stage is developed as an autonomous unit. Therefore, Indian higher education is perceived to be more concerned about the elite, the ruling classes and the upward mobile groups. It is always an outward looking process with minimum emphasis on internal requirements. Ever since the establishment of the first three universities in the country with English characters, higher education, it is alleged never bothered about its Indian identity. This attribute is not found in most of the neighbouring countries nor in some of the erstwhile common wealth states. The post-colonial urge for national identities did not influence our higher education much despite of the recommendations of Radhakrishnan and Kothari Commissions. Thus, the system is simply absorbed in the West after liberalization and internationalization of higher education.

The development of higher education and research in the country, it is alleged, is not directly related to the requirements of a post-colonial economy. Even the development of Agricultural Universities was broadly associated with PL 480 and the associated conditions. The cultivation of science and technology and the advancement of applied research were sponsored by the state through CSIR and DRDO laboratories. The criticism that universities have contributed very little on their own however is not totally based on facts and history. In fact, the university system and other institutions in the country were used as stepping stones to get the minimum credentials to go abroad, mostly to the best. The brain drain was a gain for countries like the USA where institution like NASA, Silicon Valley and several laboratories are increasingly swarmed by Indians. The trend was never discouraged though the students and scholars were totally subsidized and encouraged by the state. There seem to be some weakness present in the policy formulation particularly in its implementation. Therefore, it was allowed to continue till the so called OBC reservation came on the horizon. Thereafter, higher education was given importance in the budget allocations first to satisfy the competing groups and finally attempts are being made to open up the system for external investment. Several policy changes in the structure of education have been initiated in the form of Bills, pending before parliament. Indian corporate sector is exalted for their resilience in capturing foreign companies. But, it never occurred to the business houses first to capture a Harvard or MIT or Oxford so that their branches could be opened in India. Is internationalization a one way process?

I have been reflecting on our education system ever since I started teaching Economics of Education and Human Resource Development in Andhra University from 1976. In fact one of the papers included in the volume was submitted at an UNESCO conference in Frankfurt as far back as in 1983. I have been publishing books and articles to express my opinions on education before I joined the Commission in 2005. There was some gap in my academic endeavours. But, now my interest in the subject is renewed by AIU and some universities in the South by asking me to write and deliver lectures on higher education policy and reforms. This has helped me to produce some publications. Already some unpublished material was available with me which I thoroughly revised for the present publication. The publisher has brought to my notice the pending bills before the parliament. We have included them in the Annexure as they relate to the proposed reforms in higher education. The opinions expressed in the book are to be treated as perceptions of an academic scholar. They are not related to my present position in UPSC. Some of my former colleagues and friends have proded me to bring out a book in view of the contemporary debate on higher education in India. Mr. Raj Kumar has typed the manuscript for submission to the publisher. Gyan Publishing House, New Delhi took interest in the book and personally collected the script from me. I am grateful to all of them.

PROF. K.S. CHALAM

1

Higher Education Policy and Reform

The concept of policy is as old as the foundation of an organized state. Policy is generally alluded to a line of argument specified by a state or authority. There are several definitions on policy. We are concerned here with education policy. Although, educational policy is considered as that of any other policy, it is not uniform and is found to differ on the basis of the orientation of each state or country. The popular educational policies of Romans and Spartans are quoted to indicate that one was concerned with combat skills while the other on oratory accomplishments. Each state and government has formulated its own policy to realize the goals for which education was imparted. It is a well known fact that German education policy during Hitler was significantly different from Russian education. Therefore, there is no universally accepted meaning of education policy. But a historical rotund about the educational policies followed in different countries of the world indicate that a policy is a plan of action and a direction indicated by an authority. The policies are generally taken through a legislative action or decision arrived at by an authority empowered to do so. They are in principle guided by the constitutional objectives or preamble. The policies are formulated by people or agencies who are specifically nominated for that. In a modern democracy with an elected government in position, it is bureaucracy that assists the state in formulating policies. Bureaucracy is in place in all modern governments to implement the rule of law and the constitutional mandate where education is considered as an important item of public policy. Education policies are always pursued to achieve some social goals.

Educational Reform

Reform is attempted by every government that comes with an agenda to achieve certain social, cultural and economic objectives. Reform as a concept is defined by Oxford dictionary as, "the amendment or altering for the better, of some faulty state or things esp., of a corrupt or oppressive political institution or practice, the removal of some abuse or wrong". Education reform always presupposes an existing system in place. It means that already an education system was operating and found incapable of delivering the expected goals. It may be due to faulty policy or due to corrupt practices that made the system invalid. Most of the educational reforms brought out by governments are due to change of ideological moorings of the incumbent. Educational reforms are generally attempted after a review of the existing policies. For instance, in the USA a report on 'A Nation at Risk' in 1983 looked at the low comprehension and high drop out rate of school children. Therefore, the government has embarked upon a reform in the system. A new concept of 'charter school' thus came into existence in USA in 1990. Though, the charter school was permitted to operate in the private sector with state financial support, they are made to accountable on a five point performance scale approved by the government. In other words, reforms are always attempted after a review of the existing system.

Reform and policy are closely related concepts. They are always used in tandem to convey that one follows the other. As far as educational reform is concerned, it is always attempted on ideological considerations. The policy or policies are formulated to reform education. There can be several policies within education such as admission policy, recruitment policy, financial policy, curriculum policy and so on. While the policy in each sector is framed, the ideological Orientations such as, socialist, humanist, fundamentalist etc., remains always behind them. According to some educational policy analysts, ideology has played an important role in formulating educational policies of Margaret Thatcher or Tony Blair or Bush or Obama. Similarly, educationists in India have analyzed the educational policies of NDA or UPA governments under this approach. In fact, the class or group interests play a very significant role in formulating and implementing most of the policies concerned with people. The debate on the ideological or political underpinnings of new economic policy or economic reform in India is well known. We are not going to discuss it here as educational policy according to some educationists has remained to be some what independent of economic policy. There is however, some continuity or a status quo in the broad educational policy of India ever since the first policy was formulated on the basis of Woods dispatch of the East India Company in 1854. Democratization of education seems to have been started from this policy in India[(1)].

A Brief History of Educational Policy

There are several scholarly studies on the history of education in India emphasizing that the modernist project in education was ushered in through the so called Anglican or English education[(2)]. But seem to be very few studies to indicate that education was available to all castes or social groups during different periods of Indian history. Except the "beautiful tree" of Dharmpal that recount the spread of universal education in 18th century, no study has supported the argument that education was universal in pre-British India[(3)]. It is strange that no critical study on the educational policy of ancient period particularly with reference to Buddhist principles of equality of access to viharas and the Muslim education of madarasas for common folk vis-à-vis the unlettered classes or castes has been made available. Though, the study of Radhakumud Mookerji mentioned about the availability of knowledge of Samkhya and non-Vedic agamas to all castes and women, it was based on evidences from scriptures and studies of scholars like Keith A.B.[(4)]. They are not based on historical data. According to the travelogues of Hiuen Tsang and I-Tsing, admission into university education was based on entrance examination of high standard. It was secular education and therefore no distinction of caste was observed at Nalanda. We have evidences from medieval period that great saint poets like Ravidas, Kabir, Vemana and others from lower castes have composed great libertarian poetry[5]. They were all literate emancipators and educators. Then, why the literacy rates of non-Brahmins particularly the so called scheduled castes and backwards was found to be low during the British period and thereafter?

The educational policy of the East India Company was primarily aimed to educate Indians in English to be interpreters between the company and the people they governed. This has created a modern educated class. But social reformers like Phooley Jothi Rao had to contest this policy before the Hunter Commission as it was not made democratic. The British India government had tried some changes. But the re-organized education had neither destroyed the oriental learning nor provided a restrictive curriculum for the elite particularly in the colleges and institutes of higher learning sponsored by them. The curriculum and syllabus used in most of the colleges during the period consisted of both the traditional Vedic education and English education that was prevalent in contemporary England. Several leaders and Scholars including Ram Mohan Roy, Gandhi, Nehru, S. Chandrasekhar, Jagdish Chandra Bose, C.V. Raman, Tagore, Meghnad Saha and several scientists were trained by them.[6] It was this system that has produced the first three Indian noble laureates. Interestingly, some scholars while appreciating the liberal education of the British critiqued it by saying that it was introduced to exploit India. If that was so, why the policies and reforms that were attempted by the government after independence have not substantially overhauled the system? The state has invested in public higher education at the cost of primary and secondary education. It is clear from the allocation of funds for different levels of education during the plan period 1951-2000.

National Policy of Education

The major concern of the post-independence period was to rebuild India. The University Education Commission (1948-49), the Secondary

Education Commission (1952-53), and the Kothari Commission (1964-66) made several recommendations to realize the socialistic pattern of society. A national policy of education was declared in 1968[7]. The policy has deliberately proclaimed that it was for national development. The first sentence of the report had emphasized on the future of India would be shaped in the class rooms. The Commission spoke about free and compulsory education, equalization of educational opportunity common school, Science education and research, education for agriculture and industry, establishment of new universities with adequate funds, education of the minorities, distance (correspondence) education, examination reforms and above all a new educational structure of 10+2+3. This was for the first time a comprehensive review of education from nursery to university research covering almost every aspect of education was made. The Commission has utilized the services of great educationists of the time involving both American and Russian experts. It was in this report a progressive direction of investing 6 percents GDP on public education was made. The commission report was extensively debated in all forums throughout the country. Intriguingly, it is still debated indicating how the sage advice of the commission was trivialized.

The emergence of 21st century was considered by all developed societies as an opportunity to reform their existing systems of education. India has also reflected and introduced the challenge of education in 1986. A programme of Action based on the recommendations of the 1986 policy was formulated. Thereafter, two review committees headed by Acharya Ram Murty and N. Janardhana Reddy made about 100 suggestions for implementation. The 1986 policy document has honestly looked at every weakness of our system and made comprehensive recommendations for a technological society. The recommendations and advice of the committees were kept aside while the Ambani and Birla committee was made to recommend privatization of Higher Education in 2000. A knowledge commission was appointed under the chairmanship of a technocrat Sam Pitroda in 2006 to make recommendations to reform higher education for a knowledge-based economy. The planning commission has incorporated in its Eleventh Five Year Plan some programmes for an inclusive education. Finally, the Right to Education Act was prepared in 2009. The implementation of the Act will have farreaching consequences for massification of higher education in future. Thus, the national policies of education in India have a long list of expert advice almost on every aspect of education during the post independence period. Therefore, we cannot say that there was no intention or policy to reform education in India. It is always available in print.

Westernization of Higher Education

Sociologists have developed the concepts of modernization, Westernization and even Sanskritisation to describe how the Indian society has undergone the process of change. M.N. Srinivas has brought in the concept of westernization in 1962[(8)]. It was noted by him that English as medium of instruction and opening of schools to all with the secular orientation of education among other things has brought westernization. He has elaborated the concepts of westernization and sanskritisation as opposite notions in understanding the process of social change. The concepts can be applied to education. But, the system of higher education that was prevalent during the East India company, 1960s-1980s and 2010 has almost remained the same. In fact, the use of English as a medium of education and the clamour for American slang is widened today than ever before. A number of courses like Business Management, Fashion technology, soft skills, ICT and other courses that are popular and in great demand in the USA, Australia and other english speaking countries were introduced not only in the private sector and in non-formal educational institutions, but even in university departments and in deemed universities. A cursory look at the courses designed by the deemed universities and in private institutes and the twining programmes of western universities with Indian institutes clearly indicate the deep involvement of Indian higher education with American sentiment. The state has remained helpless spectator if not a facilitator. The issue is how these reforms or developments are taking place in education if there is already a national policy? Do the above mentioned developments and the declared and undeclared policies that are forthcoming correspond with Indian ethos or western sentiment or a continuation of the East India company project of modernization? Those who are interested in Indian education or at least indigenization of education have ever tried to change the trend? It appears that all those who are benefited by the system either in the past or in its present form have facilitated it to continue while debating vociferously against it. The elite and the governing classes or social groups who are benefited by English education have perhaps taken the education to its logical end-westernization?

Emerging Dichotomies

Dichotomies or contradiction is a dialogical concept used to analyse a social or cultural phenomenon. Higher education in India and the policies pursued by successive regimes in power seem to have paid little attention to the emerging contradictions that are erupted into the system. There is very little that we have learnt from the radical policy reforms made in the USA in its higher education system, though we are very fond of imitating them. India can favorably be compared with the 'melting pot' of USA's plural culture. They have systematically provided various incentive schemes to bring equality of opportunity in higher education. The data from the official web site of education (NCES) department of USA indicate that the enrolment of whites in higher education was 61 per cent in 1975. The blacks with 41.7 percent and Hispanics with 58.0 percent were lagging behind. But the gap between whites and blacks and whites and Hispanics was reduced; blacks reaching 66.7 percent and Hispanics reaching 64.0 percent in 2007. We have similar situation and the government policy of reservation for OBCs in 2007 has received violent protests. The gap between general and OBCs and general and Adivasis and dalits will continue if the present trend remains the same. This will result in social tensions.

The economic down turn in USA in 2008 made the American Association of state colleges and universities to reflect on state policy issues in 2009. They have identified declining state revenue due to negative economic conditions. The association has projected reduced appropriations for public post-secondary education. This will have an impact on the tuition prices of public colleges due to insufficient or declining state appropriations. It was projected that the operation of Higher Education Opportunity Act 2008 will put pressure on states' part in financing post-secondary education as the Act emphasize on the responsibility of the state for higher education. Despite of the financial constraints, the competitive edge of the US in the global economy through strengthening of higher education with new initiatives shall continue. The US is seriously thinking about the right to higher education of the so called undocumented students (non US citizens) to offer in state tuition benefits. Therefore the association hinted that the institutions must concentrate on innovations so as to improve cost efficiency and productivity. It seems, no such exercise was attempted by our policy makers to apply principles of efficiency to overcome the negative effects of budget constraints on the programmes of higher education in India.

The UNESCO has produced a document on the "Trends in global higher education: Tracking an Academic Revolution" in 2009[(9)]. After a careful survey of the trends in higher education in different countries of the world, the document has listed out the following. They are cited here to find out what dichotomies will emerge if they are applied to our situation in India.

1. Changing Patterns of Enrolment

It is noticed that there is a continuing massification of higher education world wide. The demand for higher education will come from separate sectors. However, the expansion has not resolved persistent social inequities. Further more, socio-economic background and parental education all too often influence the level of education an individual will achieve. The underlying causes of inequalities are pernicious and not easily resolved.

The data in Table-I indicate enrolment trends in India vis-à-vis other countries. China with an investment of 1.9 per cent of GDP on education has achieved 52 percent enrolment in higher education while India with 3.2 percent of GDP has only 12 percent. Much worse, the researchers working in R&D are found to be 708 per 10 lakh population in china and it is almost 7 times less in India with 119 researchers. The data relating to our Eastern neighbors like Thailand, Malaysia, Korea and Japan are far ahead of us. However, our enrolment in technology courses

Table-1.1
Higher Education Indicators

Country/rank		*Gross Enrolment Ratio % in H.Edn*	*Science & Tech. Enrol-ment % to Total H.Edn*	*Research in R&D per 10 lakh population*	*Public Exp on Edn % oj GDP*
Australia	1	75	22	4587	4.7
Canada	2	59	20	3759	5.2
Sweden	3	75	26	3597	7.4
Japan	4	58	19	5287	3.6
France	5	56	--	3213	5.9
USA	6	82	16	4605	5.9
UK	7	59	22	2706	5.4
Germany	8	--	--	3261	4.6
Korea Rep	9	95	40	3187	4.6
India	10	12	22	119	3.2
Pakistan	11	05	24	75	2.3
Kenya	12	03	29	--	6.7
Malaysia	13	30	40	299	6.2
Thialand	14	48	--	287	4.2
China	15	52	--	708	1.9

Source: Human Development Report 2007-08 and UNESCO.

(perhaps due to ICT) is 22 percent comparable to that of any of the developed countries. It is instructive here to bring in the recent Human Development Report 2009 on Human mobility to find out the trends of educated out migration[(10)]. It is found that 51 percent of the migrants from India have higher education qualifications, while Japan has only 1 percent and U.K. 10 percent. Our neighboring countries like Pakistan and Malaysia have less than 30 percent. It means that we are subsidizing manpower requirements of advanced countries like USA. Will the remittances of our migrants outweigh the costs including opportunity costs of using the human capital to exploit our own resources for development?

2. From Mass Access to Completion

It is reported that mass enrolment has opened access to previously excluded population groups like women. It is shown that these groups have made progress. But, this does not mean that these cohorts will complete the courses. Traditionally, students collected credits, sat for examination to get degrees or certificates. Now, greater emphasis is laid on the 'education value added' as a result of academic study. But, there is little consensus how to measure this outcome.

3. Diversification

The increasing enrolments have diversified academic systems to provide education including the strong contender private sector, while most private institutions will serve a mass clientele, some may emerge as semi-elite or even elite research universities, 'Quality will continue to be a major preoccupation'. The universities and colleges in the private sector in particular and public institutes in general have not shown any innovation in experimenting with diversification of the class rooms as in India where diversity of caste, language, religion and region are very wide.

4. Privatization and Funding

Tuition and other fees charged to students will increase and become more ubiquitous world wide. The emergence of neo-liberal attitudes and propaganda will make public financing for higher education decline. As a result, cost of tuition fees will emerge as a big barrier to access even if students have intellectual capacity. This will severely impact socially and economically disadvantaged groups in India.

5. New Technologies and Quality Concerns

Information and communication technology through the operation of email, blogs, wikis and pod casts, the rapid expansion of distance education, electronic publication etc., have impacted higher education. The impact on the communication of the teacher may not replace her immediately. But, the teacher quality and competencies should include skills in ICT. The growing international mobility of students with different qualifications earned will create problems of comparison of standards. The present quality assurance programmes with many elements of measuring and monitoring remain problematic.

6. The struggle for the Soul of Higher Education

Universities, traditionally, seen as key cultural institutions to be responsible for public enlightenment. The 'commercialization' of higher education has placed considerable strain on its social mission. The oft cited Nehru's qualification for a university that stands for "humanism etc" need to be replaced with profit, market, manipulation, control, authority and so on. This will create challenges of uneven distribution of human capital and finds that it will allow some nations and groups to take full advantage of new opportunities while others drift further and further.

7. Corruption and Ethics in Education

It is brought out by a UNESCO report that corruption and unethical practices are as much present in education sector today as in any other commercial activity [(11)]. There are several economic activities like production of Text books, construction of buildings and other infrastructure activities that invoke corruption particularly in the projects funded by external agencies. The more serious problem of corruption is identified in the manipulation of merit through examination frauds, private tuitions, diploma mills, distance education paper certificates etc. It is also indicated in the report that the expansion of ICT facilities has multiplied the academic fraud. For instance, with internet, one can produce project reports, research papers through cut and paste facility. There is also a perceptible change in the ethical and codal practices of teachers eroded at all levels of education leading to corruption, fraud and malpractices in education.

8. Policy and Social Sciences

The policy of any sector depends upon the amount of knowledge available about the society and economy. It is also necessary to understand the stage of development of the economy and the preparedness of the society to receive a particular policy including science and technology. All the efforts of our scientific and technological endeavours are ultimately utilized for the use of the individuals and human society. Therefore, the effective implementation of the policy depends upon the social sciene knowledge gathered through research and development. It seems teaching and research in the universities of developing societies like India are being neglected in the mad rush for scientific and technological advancement. The university departments of social sciences in many of the universities are at the verge of closure due to lack of students, teachers, scholars and support from state.

Deconstructing the Dichotomies

Deconstruction is being used by scholars as an analytical approach to study the contingent origin of the binary hierarchies as envisaged by Derrida [(12)]. It is being used in literary criticism, philosophy, political policy and other social science discourses as an approach. Many deconstructive arguments revolve around the analysis of conceptual oppositions like presence –absence dichotomy. The binary of the opposites will provide a clear understanding of the phenomenon in a meaningful way to judge the issue at hand. We have at hand the educational policy of India. Indian scholars, philosophers and policy makers are very intelligent beings and have solved several problems in metaphysics. But, the empirical realities will always remain contrary to what has been elucidated in theory or policy statement. This is true even in the case of higher education policy. Therefore, we have tried to bring out the dichotomies in different educational policy issues here. The purpose is to find out a meaningful solution to resolve these dichotomies. Once these dichotomies are identified and specified, the resolution is simple. We have tried to provide some solution at the end of the book through deconstruction.

Notes and References

1. Chalam K.S. **Modernization and Dalit Education,** Rawat Publications, Jaipur, 2008.
2. **Challenges of Higher Education**, Anmol, New Delhi, 2005.
3. Dharm Pal, **The Beautified Tree**, Biblia Impex, Delhi, 1983.
4. Radhakumud Mookerji, **Ancient Indian Education: Brahminical and Buddhist**, Macmillan, 1947.
5. Omvedt Gail, **Seeking Begumpura: The social vision of Anti- caste Intellectuals Navayana**, New Delhi, 2008.
6. Kochar, R.K. "**Science in British India**" Economic and Political Weekly 17, August, 1991.
7. Govt. of India, **Education and National Development** (Report of the Kothari Commission (1964-66) NCERT, 1968.
8. Srinivas M.N., **Social Change in Modern India,** University of California Press, Berkley, 1966.
9. Philip G. Altbach and others, **Trends in Global Higher Education: Tracking an Academic Revolution**, UNESCO, Paris, 2009.
10. **UNDP Human Development Report 2009 : Overcoming Barriers: Human mobility and Development**, Oxford University press, Delhi, 2009.

11. Jacques Hallak and Murical Poisson, **Ethics and Corruption in Education**: Results from the Expert workshop, UNESCO, Paris, 2002.

12. Derrida J, **Of Grammatology**, www.en.wikipedia.org.

2

Knowledge Outcomes and Evaluation

Teaching, learning, research and evaluation are considered to be inseparable functions of higher educational institutions. The first 3 Universities in India were established to set up examination bodies to certify the knowledge transacted in various colleges and schools. The concept of university itself was developed by the British and it was different from what the Indians understood since the time of Nalanda and Takshasila. However, the establishment of the university system of education formally in 1857 facilitated the knowledge base of the Indians to be evaluated by the western standards. The university as an institution was conceived as a universal category accessible to all and to impart broad-based knowledge. But, slowly the university has become sub-versity without any emphasis on diversity by the end of 20th century. There are several other institutions that are offering courses at higher level and are considered to be deemed universities, institutes of national importance etc. The contemporary debate on whether a single discipline based university is worth considered in a world of transcendental knowledge explosion is well taken. We are not going to discuss about the concept of university here. We shall discuss about the methods of evaluation and the tools used to evaluate the knowledge of students here. There are several orgnisations in place to conduct examinations in addition to the university examination wings and boards of various Government and Quasi-Government Organizations. Public Examinations have also been organized to test the knowledge and competencies of students so as to shortlist them to select and serve certain bureaucratic and developmental functions in Government.

Knowledge Outcomes

The basic function of any examination system is to test the intelligence of a person. Intelligence is to be considered here as an important critical ground for explaining cognitive performance. We are all aware of the fact that the classical concept of intelligence as good thinking, correct judgment and successful learning is supplemented by new concept of multiple intelligence, practical intelligence, social intelligence, emotional intelligence and so on. Higher educational institutions are considered to be concerned with the creation and dissemination of knowledge that promotes intelligence.

The outcomes of knowledge in higher educational institutions have been certified by the university system. But, there is no agreement among educationists as to constitutes the outcome. One view is that the three domains of educational activates identified by Benjamin Bloom (1956) as knowledge, attitude and skills as the outcome of learning process. Later, educationists have also incorporated precision, articulation, perception, skilled movement etc. as parts of knowledge outcomes. The university systems have been examining the students to find out the above knowledge outcomes through different assessments and certify them in the forum of a degree/certificate. The development of Science and Technology and the expansion of manufacturing sector by using technology have facilitated the development of different fields of knowledge. There is a difference between general world knowledge measured by vocabulary tests of memory, learning, ideas, mental speed etc. and is distinguished from that of specialized knowledge. The specialized knowledge is developed to meet content specific demands and provide domain related skills. Therefore, the universities and specialized institutions have developed several methods of evaluation to test the knowledge outcomes of the students whether specialized or general. There is a growing body of literature on the methods and the limitations of such methods of measuring academic achievements. The Association of Indian Universities (AIU) has initiated a project on modern trends in evaluation methodology and in fact has pioneered the question bank series in several subjects. In 1972 the UGC has brought out a document on Examination Reforms a Plan of Action. The UGC in this document has insisted upon internal assessment with semester system to be implemented in all the Universities and Colleges. By 1990 it was found that about 50% of the Universities have shifted to internal assessment. The concept of autonomous colleges in the 90s and the great demand for deemed University status in the 21st century made the system of evaluation as an important issue for debate. In the meanwhile, the country has feverishly seized with the global virus of internationalization of higher education. This has several implications. One of the important changes that has taken serious root in our education system is the entrance test mechanism. In fact, the American system of higher education when shifted to management mode desired to provide opportunities to the students who have pursued different disciplines but craved to enter into business. The Harvard Model of Business Management came into existence. The MBA syndrome has entered the country through the first programme at Andhra University in the 50s. Later the Indian Institutes of Managements have been established to train business managers to manage various activities of the industry and the business. These developments have also influenced the methods of evaluation and assessment. Though some academics use these concepts interchangeably, they are not the same. Assessment is how the teacher gathers information about the students in the class, whereas evaluation involves making judgement about the performance of the students. Measurement relates to quantification and assigning a number to performance while test is a formal systematic procedure to obtain the information about the student. Let us look at the experience of the West with these tests as they have profound influence on our system.

Admission Tests

In order to provide admission to various graduates into MBA, the US has introduced the GMAT to test the basic verbal, mathematical and analytical writing skills of those who are willing to take up management courses. The GMAT does not measure business knowledge, job skills, nor assess the qualities like motivation, ability etc. Though, it was designed in the early 20th century, the GMAT has undergone changes to capture the developments in management education. It is now conducted every year through out the world with a maximum score of 800. The scores are valid for five years and several management schools both in USA and India are making use of this scores for admission into MBA. Since, most of the graduates who studied in our educational institutions aspire to enter the American and Western Labour Market, the business schools in India have been proliferated with the help of regulatory authorities for quite sometime. The IIMs under this background wanted to take the best from the clientele and have started CAT examinations, which is being conducted under the control of an IIM. The CAT examination is conducted to test the qualitative abilities, the data interpretation skills and English Language Comprehension of the candidates. Similarly, the GATE is being conducted by an agency under the MHRD for entry into PG Courses in Science and Engineering in various universities, IITs and other institutes. The examination is conducted to test the knowledge content of several identified disciplines and carry 150 marks divided into objective and the Essay Type Questions. The examination is for three hours. The DRDO conducts Scientists Entry Test in engineering subjects for recruitment as Scientists in DRDO. The test relates to analytical and qualitative skills with some emphasis on Current Affairs and General Awareness.

The college admissions in USA are based on Scholastic Aptitude Test (SAT). The test is conducted to test the critical reasoning, literacy aptitude, numeracy and writing skills. The test is conducted 7 times in a year for 3 hours 45 minutes carrying 2400 scores. The test scores are used by the candidates to get admission with scholarship into various graduates' programmes in the USA. It is reported that the SAT has facilitated a lucrative business in USA as it provided opportunities for various companies to prepare books and tests. There are several limitations in using the test scores of SAT. It is alleged that it is a tool for the privileged to maintain the statuesquo. There are 7 other standard college level tests in use in USA. There are several agencies in India now conducting aptitude tests and providing services for certification of qualifications and competencies of candidates.

We have explained above, the evaluation methods that are being employed in USA and have been adopted in India to provide scores on the abilities and aptitudes of graduates. However, it is found that majority of the tests are being conducted to test the knowledge of the candidates which are already tested by the Universities and other Boards of Examination. The major lacunae in all these tests appear to be that these tests are used to test the content specific competencies and or proficiencies. There appears to be a problem with the academic value of these tests as none of the agencies is serious about the relevance of the knowledge to the Indian conditions.

Educational institutions particularly in the higher education sector are using scarce national resources to develop competencies and skills so that they will be effectively used for the development of the nation by using the resources available in the country. But, the trend so far appears that the students who have undergone training in these institutions get content specific competencies and skills to get opportunities in the labour market outside the country. In fact the NPE, 1986 has emphasized on this point particularly with reference to our IIT's and IIMs. The relevance of the knowledge has never been put to test in the Indian conditions. In fact, evaluation of the knowledge content of the students is done based on the taxonomy of educational objectives as developed by Benjamin Bloom. According to Bloom, the domain of cognitive behaviour relates to knowledge, comprehension, application, analysis, synthesis and evaluation. Several scholars who have worked in the area of evaluation and examination have raised doubts about the tests that are being conducted without taking into consideration the Blooms taxanomy of educational objectives and without standardization of the tests with reference to the socio-economic background of the students. This is true in the case of the so-called aptitude and entrance tests that are being conducted in our country. As we have already pointed out in the above, most of the tests that we have cited here are conscious about the knowledge outcome of the students who have undergone training in the universities and institutes. In fact, the test scores given by the agencies and the marks obtained by the students in their academic examinations are often positively correlate. Then where is the need to conduct innumerable tests spending millions of rupees in organizing and administrating these tests? Instead, these agencies can test the relevance of the knowledge that the students have obtained from the institutions to take up various professions in the country for which these institutions are supposed to have trained them.

Validity and Reliability of Tests

It is pointed out by scholars that a good assessment or test lie in its validity, reliability and consistency. The validity of a test depends upon the decisions that are made using the assessment information such as the scores and not necessarily the assessment approach itself. The assessment information collected for one objective for a group of students is not necessarily valid for other decisions of another group. The validity itself is a matter of degree such as highly valid, moderately valid or invalid and it is not considered as valid for all times. Of the three important components of a good evaluation, reliability is considered to be very important. The reliability refers to stability or consistency of assessment information and its appropriateness. Reliability is a necessary condition, but is not sufficient, for validity. An assessment or test that provides inconsistency results cannot be relied upon to provide information to take useful decision. The consistency of a test depends upon its capacity to withstand in its assessment information at different places and time. This is very important for countries like India which are training students to provide various knowledge based competencies so that they can utilize them within the country to match the available natural resources. It means that the knowledge must be made to address the requirements of the people of the country and not elsewhere. There is a classical example given by an educationist P.H. Coombs, that if Eskimo children are taught about tropical agriculture effectively, it may not be relevant to their conditions and situation despite of the valid assessment. Here, the evaluation technique must be made in such a way that the test score should be relevant to the conditions of the Eskimos. In other words, the tests are to be designed in such a way that the students knowledge or competencies are to be tested not only in its content areas but also its application to the conditions in which it is supposed to apply. In most of the tests, it is generally found that the candidates are tested about their analytical abilities and reasoning, assuming that with the help of the analytical reason he will be able to apply the knowledge to the given situation. This is not proved to be valid based on any empirical evidence. Therefore, the UNESCO world declaration on higher education made in October, 1998 under Article-6, specifically mentioned about relevance of education. It is said that, "relevance in terms of the fit between what society expecting of institutions and what they do. The relevance of a course is based on the long term societal aims, needs and environment". If, it is translated into our conditions and the kind of evaluation methods that we employ to provide the test scores to educational institutions and sometimes to recruiting agencies, it is often found wanting. The test scores provide basic information about the knowledge of the candidate in certain areas of study while the recruiting agencies look at the knowledge content of the candidate only (if they wanted to train him to suit their needs and conditions). If, we look at the efforts of our educational institutions during the last few decades, it is very distressing to note that they are over emphasizing on the content part of the knowledge in demand elsewhere and are not serious about the relevance of the courses to our conditions. I have already written about the implications of economic downturn vis-à-vis ICT professionals. (See Chapter-10)

Test Scores and Design of Courses

The design of a course in a higher educational institution must be grounded not only on the content and its application, but also the relevance of the content to solve practical problems in our own situation.

In fact, most of the exercises of the curriculum design in our higher education system relate to course outlines with content selection based on some topical approaches of the course originator. It is also found in some specialized institutions that narrow fields of specialization are indicated based on the knowledge developed by the originator without examining its relevance. There is no doubt that in certain fields we need super specialty experts. But, their number is to be limited depending upon the demand for such experts. The personality of the expert who accumulates knowledge and skills in a narrow field of specialization is also very important as it is through him that it is delivered to the customers. Further, most of the institutions are not taking sufficient care in developing the personality traits of the students and do not design courses in relation to the personality of the students. Often, we find a mismatch between the knowledge base of the candidate and his/her personality traits that ultimately lands him/her in frustration due to unsuitability of the candidates' character to the job.

There are basically five dimensions of the personality that can be incorporated as a part of each course. The five dimensions are: 1. extra version, 2. emotional stability, 3. agreeableness, 4. conscientiousness and 5. openness to experience. The five important dimensions of the personality of an expert need to be systematically guided by the educational institutes through a process of developing special courses or incorporating such content as part of the course structure. It is also necessary that such courses are to be evaluated not only for the knowledge content but also the personality of the students. A course evaluation is different from student assessment. There is some confusion among the test developers between the two. It is noticed that there are several deficiencies in our aptitude tests, admission tests and university examinations as they are not serious about the personality of the individual/student and relevance of the courses.

Experience of Recruiting Boards

The experience of some of the recruiting agencies like the Union Public Service Commission, State Public Service Commissions and various

Recruitment Boards are hardly taken into consideration while designing courses or making the courses relevant to the jobs. It is indicated in one of the recruiting agencies that the mental caliber of a candidate is not only assessed in terms of his intellectual qualities but also in terms of his/ her social traits and knowledge about current affairs. It is listed that mental alertness, critical powers of assimilation, clear and logical exposition, balance of judgment, authority and depth of interest, intellectual and moral integrity and leadership qualities are considered as important to select a candidate for an administrative job. It is increasingly noticed from the results of the UPSC that majority of the candidates are qualified in subjects in which they were not basically trained. This is true particularly with reference to Engineering, Science and Technology Graduates who are from the premier institutes with good academic records but do not qualify in their own subjects in the Civil Services Examination. The details are given in Tables. This trend seems to be an indication that most of the courses that are offered in our higher education institutions are not related to our requirements, not necessarily to occupy positions of power but even to act as technocrats. Therefore, there is a need to rethink over the design of courses and their evaluation.

The academic courses are to be designed in such a way that they should be able to train the young minds in specific content and apply the content to solve the practical problems in our own situation. This is possible not just by offering courses in Humanities and Social Sciences for Engineers and Technocrats and courses of Science and Technology for humanities and social sciences students. They are to be creatively designed by making use of the experience of the experts from academics and administration. There are hundreds of institutes and experts who are working in labs and institutes in Government departments who are hardly consulted/used by our institutes. They can be put to use by relating the content of the courses with that of the evaluation methods. The evaluation methods that we have so far been using are useful to test the knowledge outcomes of the institutions and to test the absorption capacity of the students in a discipline through the method of recall at the time of examination. This is not going to solve the problems of our country with limited resources. In a country like USA where full employment is supposed to have prevailed so far, the candidate can fit into any job through a process of acquiring the required competencies. There are agencies and institutions that will take care of the frictional unemployment by providing paid training to impart skills. It is reported that the recruiting firms conduct about 600 assessments for jobs. In some countries a separate vocational qualification framework is established to take care of this. Evaluating students in certain competencies that are required by the labour market, without providing first the opportunities in the educational institutions, will be a mockery. For instance, we can train a student as an engineer but cannot test him for his suitability for administration, without first offering him the relevant curriculum in the institution. The teachers must also be trained to transact such competencies with students through curricular and co-curricular activities. I remember how difficult it was to convince the teachers about the importance of social relevance of courses in Academic Staff Orientation courses in Andhra University. It is also not correct to treat the human being as a resource and then fragment him/her to extract whatever competencies and skills the organization needs/wants. This will lead to early burnout. Educational institutions cannot do this function. They are supposed to humanise knowledge and work. We hope that the academics, technocrats and experts interact and reflect on these issues on a continuous basis to arrive at a creative solution for the universities of the 21st century.

Table – 2.1

Optional Subjects taken by Civil Services Examination Successful Candidates

Sl. No.	*Academic Discipline*	*2005*			*2007*		
		Different Subject	*Same Optional as studied*	*Total*	*Different Subject*	*Same Optional as studied*	*Total*
1.	Humanities and Social Sciences	101 (22.10%)	40 (8.75%)	141 (30.85%)	145 (22.73%)	64 (10.03%)	209 (32.76%)
2.	Commerce	39 (8.53%)	1 (0.22%)	40 (8.75%)	54 (8.46%)	6 (8.53%)	60 (9.40%)
3.	Science	82 (17.94%)	6 (1.31%)	88 (19.26%)	101 (15.83%)	12 (1.88 %)	113 (17.71%)
4.	Engineering/ Technology	130 (28.45%)	9 (1.97%)	139 (30.42%)	180 (28.21%)	5 (0.78%)	185 (29.00%)
5.	Medical	39 (8.53%)	1 (0.22%)	40 (8.75%)	54 (8.46%)	2 (0.31%)	56 (8.78%)

(Contd.)

(Contd. Table 2.1)

Sl. No.	*Academic Discipline*	*2005*			*2007*		
		Different Subject	*Same Optional as studied*	*Total*	*Different Subject*	*Same Optional as studied*	*Total*
6.	Management	7 (1.53%)	0 (0.00%)	7 (1.53%)	6 (0.94%)	0 (0.00%)	6 (0.94%)
7.	Others	2 (0.44%)	0 (0.00%)	2 (0.44%)	8 (1.25%)	1 (0.16%)	9 (1.41%)
	Total	400 (87.53%)	57 (12.47%)	457 (100.00%)	548 (85.89%)	90 (14.11%)	638 (100.00%)

Table – 2.2

Top 10 Optional Subject Combinations as per the Number of Candidates Recommended 2007

Sl. No.	*Optional Subject Combination*	*Appeared*	*Written Qualified*	*Finally Recommended*
1.	Geography – Psychology	381	113	48 (42.5)
2.	Geography – Public Administration	661	158	45 (28.5)
3.	Sociology – Public Administration	291	83	32 (38.5)
4.	Psychology – Public Administration	235	75	28 (37.3)
5.	History – Public Administration	541	85	28 (33.0)
6.	History – Political Science	298	54	26 (48.1)
7.	History – Philosophy	671	104	23 (22.1)
8.	History – Geography	604	71	21 (29.5)
9.	Psychology – Sociology	133	40	20 (50.0)
10.	Anthropology – Public Administration	93	37	20 (54.0)

Notes: Figures in brackets indicate % to the Qualified.

3

Equity and Quality Syndrome

Once the knowledge is created and imparted to the student, subsequently the question of its Quality arises. The method of evaluation to test the quality was discussed in chapter-2. Equity and quality in higher education are projected as dichotomous in India. It appears that there is very little truth in it. They are not two different issues of a problem. They are not one against the other. In fact, they are complimentary to each other, if, we look at the recent literature in Social Sciences. Interestingly, the World Development Report 2006 is titled as 'Equity and Development' and the Human Development Report 2005 concentrated on equity(1). Both the reports have emphasized on the need for providing equality of opportunity to achieve development. It is necessary here to draw from these reports to understand the present predicament of higher education in India, which is suffering with a phobia of equity and quality. The real issue here is about the historical conditions under which higher education was developed in the country and its achievements. It seems that those who are involved in the policy making have failed to use the intellectual inputs provided by the World Bank, UNDP and other independent thinkers on this issue to resolve the so-called dichotomy of equity and quality.

Equity and Development

The World Development Report has referred to a number of influential thinkers including John Rawls, Amartya Sen, Ronald Dworkin and John Roemer to provide a theoretical background to show how equity promotes development[2]. The thinkers referred to above have shifted their focus of social justice from outcomes to opportunities. It is brought out in the World Development Report, 2006, that the inter-connection and resilience of some of the inequalities imply that some groups have consistently inferior opportunities—economic, social and political-than their fellow citizens. Most people feel that such flagrant disparities violate a sense of fairness, particularly when the individuals affected can do little about them. It is conveyed that markets often work imperfectly in many countries, whether because of intrinsic failures- such as those associated with asymmetric information- or because of policy imposed distortions. Micro-economic case studies suggest that an inefficient allocation of resources across productive alternatives is often associated with differences in wealth or status. Therefore, the World Development Report emphasized that redistribution from richer and more powerful groups to poorer groups that face more limited opportunities should be pursued. It is also indicated that when considering policy trade-off between equity and efficiency, the full long term benefits of equity including the development of better and more inclusive institutions need to be taken into account. These arguments are applicable to achieve the objective of equality of opportunities in education because they influence the investments in human capital. It is pointed out that the perceptions of discrimination, conscious or not can affect investments in human capital. Those who expect to be discriminated against in particular labour market-rightly or wrongly, consciously or otherwise-will tend to invest in less in acquiring the type of human capital that the market rewards. This could perversely generate self-reinforcing behaviour. If members of the discriminated group invest less in their own education, or in searching for employment, others might use this underinvestment to confirm their prejudice against that group.

In order to substantiate the argument, the Report has quoted from studies to show how stereotypes influence behaviour. It is instructive to quote from Karla Hoffmann and Priyanka Pandey study for the World Bank in the year 2004, which has established that caste system in India is influencing the performance of the students in the classrooms. In the experimental study of Hoff and Pandey two groups composed of three low caste (untouchables) and three high-caste Junior High School students were asked to solve mazes and were paid based on the number of mazes they solved. "In one condition, no personal information about the participants was announced. In a second condition, caste was announced with each participant's name and village. In a 3rd condition, participants were segregated by caste and then each participants' name, village and caste were announced in the six -person group. It was found that when caste was not announced there was no caste gap in performance. But increasing the salience of caste led to a significant decline in the average performance of the low caste, regardless of whether the payment scheme was piece-rate or tournament. When caste was announced, the low caste children solved 25% fewer mazes on average in the piece-rate treatments compared with the performance of subjects when caste was not announced. When caste was announced and groups were composed of six children drawn from only the low caste, the decline in low-caste performance was even greater. It is concluded by the scholars that cognitive limitations may prevent others from judging stigmatized individuals fairly. If such beliefs persist, it will generally be rational for those discriminated against to underinvest in the accumulation of skills for which, the return is likely to be lower for them. The study is cited here to show that how parents underinvest in education from the families belonging to the socially and educationally backward classes in India. Therefore, it is inevitable for the state either to invest in those in whose education there was an underinvestment or take measures to restore equity. As the state is responsible for social investment and rightly so, the recent debate on equity and quality need to be understood in a correct perspective in the overall development of the country and not for the development of a few individuals or groups here and there.

Educational development of the western countries particularly the USA is cited as an example in most of our discussions to show that how quality is maintained in that country through the process of promoting merit. But the facts of the matter as revealed in a recent study are different. It is reported in the Economist that Daniel Golden has published a book "The Price of Admission: How America's Ruling Class Buys its way into elite colleges- and Who Gets Left Outside the Gates". The contents of the book show that less than 60% of the places in elite universities are given to candidates who have some sort of extra 'hook', from rich or alumni parents to 'sporting prowess'. The number of whites who benefit from this affirmative action is far greater than the number of blacks. It is reported that Harvard admits 40% of legacy applicants compared with 11% of applicants overall. The author has quoted such discrimination practices in several universities in favour of the rich that is devoid of any merit. The content of the article are mentioned here to indicate that the quality of education in a university and the students who are admitted in the institutes need not directly be related. On the other hand, if the institutional standards and traditions are so strong they can even promote equity and development. The discussion that the policy of equity affects quality of higher education therefore, has a very weak argument. Prof. Anand Krishna's study of Tamilnadu for the Moily Committee has also proved this point[3].

The quality of higher education in India has been discussed in different forums as it is really a matter of grave concern. It is surprising to find that everyone who is interested and commented on quality of higher education have very little to offer in the debates on equity. In fact, in a country like India both the issues need to be discussed as they are going to influence the quality of life. It is universally recognized that those who are admitted in higher education are academically bright. There is no doubt that those who are intelligent and possess the necessary eligibility conditions alone will be admitted into post-secondary education (which is called as higher education). But higher education in our country consisted of several streams and categories. Each stream of higher education is developed on a different historical setting. Some of the post secondary educational institutions were brought under the aegis of the university system after the establishment of the three universities in 1858.

But, some of the institutions continue to maintain their identity and quality. Though the University Grants Commission came into existence in 1953/1956 to maintain standards of higher education, it is, however, not given the mandate to maintain standards of all categories of higher education. Unlike the USA where land grant system has helped to strengthen higher education, in India each category of the institutions has a unique history. Religious and social groups have mobilized their resources to educate their own community or group. The inequalities were built in within the system from the very beginning in India. This needs to be recognized while examining the issues of quality and equity in education.

After the introduction of the programme of action 1992, UGC is limited to maintain standards of general higher education. AICTE, ICTE, AICME, Pharmacy Council and several other organizations have been given the mandate to maintain standards of their own disciplines without an overall coordination among them. An institution called NAAC was created to assess and accredit general higher education institutions, which come, by and large under the ambit of UGC. There are also similar organizations to assess quality in other streams of higher education. But the fact remains that the standards of higher education are different from that of quality. It is alleged that both are deteriorating in India.

Quality and Standards of Education

The concept of quality is related to the inherent character or property of an institution. The concept, standard on the other hand takes care of the attainment or agreed level of quality based on some tests. These concepts are even interchangeably used in the literature to indicate the performance of educational institutions in the country. But economists have been using the concept of productivity and efficiency to test whether the education skills used as inputs in the process of production are contributing to positive outcomes. One of the earliest studies on the productivity and efficiency of higher education in the country was attempted by the Author in 1986 (Chalam, 1986)[4]. It was found that higher education in Andhra Pradesh according to the Author was internally productive but externally unproductive indicating the relevance of the skills or knowledge obtained by the students to the economy and society. In fact, those who are concerned about quality of higher education have been looking at it only from its internal functioning by using their own yardsticks like Marks, Publications etc, and some academic attributes to qualify some people as meritorious. But, the industry and other sectors of the economy that make use of the students in their processes are not concerned about the marks obtained or the merit certificates awarded. They are basically concerned about the skills, the attributes of knowledge etc., based on the students' performance in certain functions to produce the expected outcomes. Therefore, they look at the standards or qualities from a practical perspective and not necessarily on the academic knowledge base of the students. They are concerned about overall quality of the individual as an input in the production process. Therefore, we find that there are two different approaches to understand quality of higher education. One, the educational institutes' perspective, which is concerned about the education value-added, the skills imparted to a student on the basis of structured curriculum, Two, the perspective of a producer who makes use of a student as an input in the process of production and to entrust him with a specific function to be performed and looks at the quality from his own perspective. Therefore, these perspectives seldom concur with each other. The industry has realized the lacunae in higher education and introduced a strategy called on-the-job training to convert the raw graduates into useful inputs.

The quality of education is now looked at from an international perspective after the emergence of global labour markets. The recruiting agencies are now doing an intermediary function of recruiting raw graduates and converting them into 'packaged labour' (body shopping) with necessary inputs of training to suit the requirements of the industry. This has created the scope for mushrooming of training institutions in the private sector that are doing the short-life functions of higher education leaving the long life functions to established universities and colleges (see Chalam K.S. 2005). It is very difficult to assess the quality of an educational institution in a complex situation of this kind where the established educational institutions are producing students with given set of objectives. Except, a few disciplines like IT & ICT, majority of the courses offered in the universities and colleges are designed to produce a graduate with a specified amount of knowledge and skills. If, the quality of these products is evaluated from the perspective of the needs of the industry, it is very difficult to arrive at a conclusion about their relevance. Similarly, the institutes, the colleges and universities which are assessing their qualities on the basis of their internal functioning, may not meet the quality requirements of the industry. For instance, the criteria used by NAAC to assess the quality of colleges and universities consisted of a set of 7 items, such as (a) curriculum aspects, (b) teaching, learning and evaluation,(c) research, consultancy and extension, (d) infrastructure, (e) students support, (f) organization and management and (g) healthy practices. The above criteria was used to assess the quality of institutions. The industry on the other hand is interested in a person, as mentioned above, who can deliver the goods. Therefore, the quality of education (or standards) that he expects from the student is measured in terms of his own parameters.

There is also another challenge that has emerged in recent times, the cross border education and distance education. The parameters of quality here depend upon the origin of the institutions where they belong. They are expected to operate in a host country/state with their own parameters. Therefore, it is difficult to assess the quality here as the requirements of the host country are different from that of the native country. It is exactly here that the quality of education needs to be defined in terms of specific functions for which they are produced. It is also necessary that the knowledge base or the skills imparted must be related to the needs and requirements of the nation with social and cultural dimensions of the knowledge. Measures like TQM, ISO etc. have limited application to higher education, as they are not concerned about the internal process and its socio cultural relevance to the nation. The quality (standards) of higher education here needs to be comprehensively defined, so that the institutions must be made to care not only for the internal process of education but also relate the products with their effectiveness outside the institution.

In the recent debate on the provision of additional seats to the 27% OBCs in the so-called quality institutions, a lot of discussion was generated on the availability of infrastructure without any reference to the internal process of higher education. There is no doubt, we need good infrastructure, sufficient and competent faculty, laboratories, libraries and good administration etc. But, these facilities alone do not ensure quality. In fact, most of the so-called quality institutes take their inputs after a lot of screening. Naturally the best brains go to these institutes and it is relatively easy for them to maintain standards. What is essential of these institutes here is to compare the educational outcomes after the students get exposed to these institutes. It can be measured in terms of the comparison of entry standards and outcome standards. For instance, if a student is admitted with 80% marks and gets 85% at the end of the course, one can say that it is not a big achievement. If, the institute can admit a student with 50% marks and the students can turn out to be a graduate with 80% marks, definitely it is a great achievement (keeping all assumptions). In fact, we have not fixed our standards in relation to the academic, social and cultural and family background of each student of these institutions. It is also necessary to define the functions for which these groups of students are produced and need to be assessed about their performance after they enter the job. There are several such studies available in the literature on economics of education. Unfortunately, our institutions have not taken the social responsibility of reducing inequalities that exist between students and groups of students as a challenge. It should form one of the important objectives of our education and should go also as one of the indicators of quality of higher education. In a country like India where there are several diversities, the opportunities are not equitably distributed. It is necessary that the institutions are made to take the responsibility of bringing equity as equity brings development as per UNDP. On the contrary, there is no evidence that equity has ever suppressed development.

It is imperative that the educational institutions be provided with teachers who are capable of dealing with the problems of diversity. It is not the knowledge base that alone makes a good teacher; it is his ability to communicate and relate himself with the students that makes him an effective teacher. A good teacher is always an asset to an institute and he will be able to overcome the deficiencies of infrastructure, curriculum etc, to turn the students as quality products.. But, unfortunately teachers in most of the higher education institutions are not given due recognition and their security is in peril. It is very difficult for a teacher to concentrate on the quality of education if he is not permanent and is not motivated to do research and take the results to the classroom. In fact the educational institutes have another laudable function. The so called knowledge (whatever imperfect or useless it may be) cannot be offered as courses in the colleges and universities as some policy makers think. It requires a different process to convert knowledge into a course. The quality of teachers, students and internal process make significant contributions to achieve this. It is a challenging task to the system. This happens in an atmosphere of collective process of learning without any prejudices. Unfortunately, there are several unhealthy trends that are emerging now in our higher education system particularly in the professional stream of higher education that causes a concern for educationists.

How to Ensure Quality

Thus, higher educational institutes as distinguished from coaching centers, MNC HRD units have several responsibilities to attend to. It is not just providing knowledge excellent and universal. It is more than this. Further, the challenges of higher education in the 21st century are not limited to meet the requirements of the country. As the system of education is now globally exposed, it has both opportunities and also limitations. We cannot think about the quality of higher education and its quantitative expansion from the perspective of the Western Society and its requirements. The history of higher education in the Western Society is different and the present conditions and the scope are also different from that of India. The country has sufficient unexploited resources both material and human. The education system should be designed and expanded creatively on the basis of our own strength to make use of these opportunities. At the same time, we can also learn from others and introduce new institutional structures to manage and enhance quality. It is appropriate that a national coordinating Agency is created to bring together the efforts made by different agencies of higher education, to ensure quality. The agency is necessary now because of the fact that there are several areas of research and study that traverse across narrowly defined fields of study due to trans discipline research. For instance, Biotechnology, it goes in to Pharmacy, Zoology, Biology etc, and therefore needs a forum to discuss issues that help to improve quality and facilitate to lay down certain standards applicable to all branches of study.

The UGC was created to maintain 'standards' of higher education. In order to ensure these standards, the quality of the inputs and the process are put to routine inspection regime. It seems it has failed to a large extent in our affiliating college system. It is to be evaluated whether the process of NAAC has overcome this problem. The standards of higher education in the country cannot be ensured without improving the quality of education in the vast majority of rural colleges and mushrooming of the colleges in urban centers. It appears that a new dimension is emerging with the advent of deemed universities as autonomous institutes with their own agenda. The standards of higher education can be ensured with the help of strengthening the quality of teaching with innovative methods of teaching as universities in our country have remained by and large teaching universities. Though Chalam K.S has studied and established for the first time that the cost of university research is several times lower than that of research in institutes, universities have remained by and large teaching universities[(5)]. The Government of UK in its white paper on higher education 2003 has emphasized on improving the standards of teaching and is investing more on improving teaching standards to establish a cutting edge over others. As the investment in R&D in the private sector in India is slowly increasing, it is possible to have collaborative work so as to reduce the cost of research commitment of the universities. It is also possible to introduce the scheme of adjunct professorship in universities to invite teaching inputs from industry and from abroad. There are several such ideas that have been already generated under university industry-interaction scheme that can be used to strengthen standards of higher education. Except Academic Staff colleges (which need to be further strengthened) there are very few schemes for the development of quality of education in unaided affiliated colleges. The bulk of the PG students are now coming from these so called unaided colleges, particularly in the vocational stream. It is necessary to bring them under the aegis of the UGC, as these colleges do also train students for the university degrees and the standards of higher education in the country in future depends upon these colleges.

In the area of quality higher education, it is necessary to identify some of our own contributions to the world of knowledge and by capitalizing on this; it is possible to expand it into other areas. It is pointed out by scholars that, India had a relative advantage in disciplines like Mathematics, Space Science and Technology, Biotechnology, Nano-Technology, Pharmacy, Economics and several other fields. It is possible to identify and strengthen these fields of specialization with our own resources and with the help of support from outside. There is a need to establish a permanent group of experts in UGC to identify the emerging areas of study and research. This will definitely help to improve the quality of education and provide opportunities to exploit unexploited resources for the development of the country.

Notes and References

1. UNDP, **Human Development Report 2005,** Oxford University Press, New Delhi, 2005.

2. *Op. cit.*

3. Anandakrishnan M paper in, **Veerappa Moily Oversight Committee Report on OBC Reservations in Higher Education**, Government of India, Delhi.

4. Chalam K.S., **Finances, Costs and Productivity of Higher Education**, Inter India, New Delhi, 1986.

5. Chalam K. S., "**Cost of University Research: A Case Study of Andhra University**". University News, October, 1982.

4

Competencies for Good Teaching

India is known for its traditions of great teachers like Vishnu Sarma and sages like Viswamitra ,Vasista, Tagore, Radhakrishnan and several others Savants. But, these customs and practices utilised by them have become obscure today under the hegemony of Anglo-Saxon traditions of education. It is in this context that we may draw lessons from the two important events that have occurred in the Western World during the year 2006 that have direct bearing on the future of teachers in the world. It was reported in the Economist, that a student leader of the University of California Los Angeles Campus declared a cash incentive to be given to those who produce a tape consisting of a Professor who just can't stop talking about President Bush, about Howard Dean and about the war in Iraq. It is said that, "If, you can help UCLA Profs. Com, collect information about abusive one sided or off-topic classroom behavior" you will get a cash award of $100. Quite contrary to this, the Labour Party MPs in the UK in 2006 have signed an 'alternative white paper on education' wherein they have emphasized on the return to more traditional teaching methods and school discipline. The incident in the so called liberal democracy of USA speaks about the kind of informal censorship let loose on the teachers who are known to have enjoyed full freedom in the classroom from time immemorial. In the latter case, the Labour Party which is known for its 'fair' play in school reform is insisting on better status to teachers and diversity in school admissions. It appears that India is not going to learn anything from their past or present patrons. The status of the teachers in India particularly those who are working in the private sector either in the Engineering Colleges or in the so called Public Schools now remains to be that of despair and decadence. Teaching as a profession in higher education sector is becoming more complex than ever before. The age old 'guru shishya parampara' is replaced by the technology supported teaching. At present, there is no need to learn directly 'anything' including music and mantra from the mouth of a pious teacher. There are now several alternative sources of knowledge that are readily available to provide various depths of learning. The virtual class room is within the reach of everyone who possesses access to internet. Thus, technology is making the class room available to the learner and teacher for 24 hours not only to teach and learn but also to give and take hand outs, assignments, tests etc., on line. This has revolutionized the process of learning particularly in higher education. However, there are still certain important functions like mentoring, inter personal relationships, research and scholarship etc; that are to be performed by an enlightened teacher in person. Virtual classroom, web based learning, on line teaching and other forms of teaching learning exercises can definitely improve the efficiency of teaching and enhance the capacity of the teacher to impart knowledge. But, they are short of providing the human element of the collective joy of learning that both the learner and teacher can enjoy in the direct one to one interaction. This is the basic element of teaching that needs to be strengthened in the era of globalization and worldwide web.

The teachers are at crossroads today. It is because of the high expectations of the students in the classroom on the one hand and the teachers are expected to teach and test isolated skills on the other. It is said that, "universities will maintain their competitive edge against knowledge industries through the maintenance of their core values—including research based teaching and a curriculum that provides for the long term needs of individuals". Therefore, each University will be developing its own identity on the basis of developing more complex design of courses to provide skills rather than depending upon the universally accepted methods of imparting knowledge. It is envisaged that there will be fewer universities in future that will be interested in imparting analytical abilities or problem solving competencies than the ones who will concentrate on short duration soft skills and industry specific tailor-made courses. These courses and the learning resources will be patented to create artificial scarcity of skills etc, so as to restrict the access of other educational providers to enter the business. It is this situation that makes the art of teaching very impervious. It has several implications for teaching profession in general and higher education in developing countries in particular. It is already found that there is a dearth of good teachers in all important branches of knowledge throughout the world.

School Education whether it is early childhood education or the primary education is now often debated in public. Some in the metros focus their attention on how the parents are interviewed for the admission of their children in pre-school, while many others in the country debate on the national curriculum frame work. But interestingly, the participants of the debate, most of them are experts and well meaning people do generally focus their attention on the ideological underpinnings involved in the content of the curriculum rather than the practical difficulties involved in implementing the framework, the outcomes of a centralized structure at the grass roots etc. Further, the fragmentation of the education's agency in recent years has resulted in the fractured view of education particularly school education. Today, there are several authorities that are concerned about school education. There are about five agencies that deal with school education on a vertical basis and the same number is involved at the horizontal line. For instance, control starts from panchayat, zillaparishad, State, Government of India and CBSE for school education. At the level of the Ministry, it is CBSE, NCERT,

NCTE and several others who handle school education. As a result of the multiplicity of agencies, the focus is lost. Each agency feels that they are expected to work within the mandate given to them. For instance, preparation of curriculum is the duty of one agency, Text Books another, teacher education and infrastructure and soon are the concern of others.

Education should not be considered as a process like any other manufacturing sector that produces a commodity or product. Division of labour cannot be applied here to reap the benefits of productivity. It is to be viewed as a complex process that needs to be supervised by a single agency so that there can be an overall control over the end product, the behavioral modification of the child. Unfortunately, this ideal has been given a back seat and the real pivot of the system, the teacher is totally neglected.

In the recent debate on the curriculum framework we found that neither the protagonist nor the antagonist has considered the role of the teacher in the transaction of the curriculum. Those who are familiar with our class room transactions at the school level know how the teacher is important. Scholars have produced voluminous literature on student centered, teacher centered, curriculum centered, etc, education and the pros and cons of such curriculum. But one must realise here that the teacher is the ultimate in taking the curriculum to the school institute and to the child. Unfortunately, most of our experts in school education come from elite universities and have very little understanding of the class room transactions. The teachers who are really involved in teaching at the grassroots have very little access to such debates and deliberations. As a result, the crucial point in the debates of school curriculum, the teacher is missing. There are schools in the rural areas where there are no text books and there are children who do not have any access to such resources. It is here, the teacher plays an important role. In fact, the teacher is the king in the classroom (now it is under cloud), despite the so-called frameworks. You may prescribe any framework, any syllabus it is the teacher who translates it into a class room transaction. And it is the teacher who has been maintaining the identity of the Indian school system with or without a framework.

Teacher as Gnanadata

The composition of the teacher as a guide, philosopher, friend and '*gnanadata*' has been maintained in the guru-shishya parampara till the 1970's. They could maintain the status not under the shadow of a framework, but through the tradition of 'total surrender' to the profession (unlike the present ones who have several distractions). It is this teacher who has been eulogized by Tagore, Radhakrishnan and several other thinkers as the maker of a country's destiny. This teacher used to imbibe values in the students not only through their exemplary character but also through their inspiring talk in the classroom despite the given syllabus. The world of knowledge and the vision of the teacher should be high so that he could talk anything in the classroom once he is in. This autonomous power of the teacher was productively/professionally utilised by the teacher in their lessons and through their empathy for the learner. These great teachers have produced excellent leaders in politics, science and engineering and in all walks of life. They did not follow any frameworks except their conscience. Now, this teacher is shattered. As in the US, he is going to be censored.

The teacher is in crisis today. He is alienated from his classroom because of the invasion of the technology. The student is not interested in him as a 'gnanadata' as there are several alternative sources of knowledge available in the market. The village is not enthusiastic about him as the influential and powerful are sending their children to the elite convent. The politicians are curious about them only during elections as they are the sources of influence at grassroots. The Governments' commitment to education is dubious in terms of the service conditions and the piling up of thousands of vacant teachers posts in the public sector. There are teachers who are deficient in their knowledge and skills. There are teachers who are working at Rs. 395/- per month at the school stage and less than Rs. 2000/- per month in the rural colleges. Now, the classroom has become a complex place of teaching and learning as it is attended by students from different social, cultural, language and age groups.

The teacher has no training in dealing with a heterogeneous and culturally diverse classroom. Increasingly, the classrooms of government schools are becoming dumping grounds for socially and educationally deprived groups. It is for these disadvantaged schools the framework is made. Therefore, it is no more exciting either to the teacher or to the policy maker. Many scholars and thinkers are interested in the class room of the elite school that doesn't care for our frameworks. They have their own frameworks and hidden agendas. It is these schools that are producing the future leaders for various walks of life in the 21st Century. They are well equipped and the teachers in such schools work under the threat of security of tenure. They are not teachers. They are just employees of the organization. Therefore, it is necessary to recognize that the teacher is an inalienable part of the system of education and is to be empowered not only with technological inputs but also with socio-economic status.

Teaching in Higher Education

The system of higher education that is evolved in the post liberalization period is not very sure of its learning outcomes. We know that the British were sure of the learning outcomes of the education as enunciated by Macaulay. It was relevant to the times and the purpose for which the colonial education was imparted. Is there any change in the objectives and purposes of education today particularly at the higher education level? Can we declare that our effort to educate our children through quality institutes like IIT's and IIMs and our universities will be ultimately utilized to exploit our natural and human resources for national development? It is very difficult now to say this after internationalization of education and cross border education permitted through GATS. Then, how can we tell the teachers to mend their business of teaching. As some management experts emphasise that teaching is not so much important today as compared to learning; the problem here is how to make the student learn. Is it not the responsibility of the teacher to make the learner learning how to learn? Do we have the infrastructure and superstructure of education to leave the business of teaching learning process to the learner and make the teacher to concentrate on his research?

In fact, the 'Learning Report' of the club of Rome in the 1980s has brought out the concepts of Anticipatory learning and participatory learning. Both the concepts along with the level of learning at different phases of the individual, group, society and civilizational stages need the involvement of a good and enlightened teacher. Can we deny this?

The quality of higher education teaching was considered till now, consisted of obtaining a research degree and few publications. No one was bothered to look at the diversity that has taken place in the enrollment in higher education and the need to train the teachers to deal with a diversified student intake in the classrooms. Teaching in colleges and universities was never considered important. Many of the good teachers have also neglected their teaching careers to obtain research degrees and after some time left the universities and the country. The brain drain through research at the cost of public is much higher than the normal route of students going abroad. However, neither the government nor the academics have reflected on what is good teaching. Every one who is undergone university training knows that all those who have good degrees and publications are not good teachers. Some of them are worst communicators and even failed to live as good fellow human beings in terms of their interpersonal relations. Majority of the young Post graduates who enter in to teaching profession do not know how to write on the chalk board if not a white board. In fact, majority of our colleges in the rural areas do not have black boards. It is not the school that is considered as an institution without walls, but in the private sector several colleges were established in such an environment. Therefore, the academic staff orientation scheme based on experiments of K.S. Chalam in 1985 became UGC programme in 1987. Though some teachers have opposed the scheme in the beginning, it was considered by the teachers in rural areas and in affiliated colleges as an important scheme and a boon to non traditional groups who have entered teaching profession for the first time.

Measuring Good Teaching

The basic function of a college teacher for that matter even in the university is to teach the students and see how the young people are learning and acquiring cognitive skills. The subject matter is as important as the method of teaching. In fact, teachers in the colleges and universities are paid to teach. Research and extension activities are complementary to teaching. It is very easy to asses research in terms of the number of publications or patents or similar qualifications. But, teaching is hardly measured. The quality of teaching is seen in terms of the publications in majority of the government or UGC regulations. This in fact has caused more damage to our higher education than other weaknesses of the system. Then, how is it possible to measure teaching. Chalam K.S. has developed several instruments to measure good teaching in colleges and universities. The 18 competencies that are expected of a teacher in higher education are given in the Annexure 4.1. Those who participated in the orientation courses at Andhra University know that every participant has to under go Micro teaching exercise that will be self evaluated to quantify good teaching[(2)]. It is necessary that the teacher has to spend more time for preparing for the class than doing experiments in a lab or doing field work for research paper. Most of the young teachers don't know how to prepare for the class and some of them also do not know how to identify a research topic. Teaching is an art. It can be learnt through constant practice and observation. There are several studies attempted to measure good teaching in the West in terms of student evaluation of teacher. This is one of the ways of measuring good teaching. Academic scholars have developed Teacher Quality Index (TQI) consisting of 5 important components. It relates to the teacher first as a human person and then he should be accepted by the students as an academic leader. Second, he should know how to manage the classroom. There are several problems in the class rooms today with divergent social, academic and economic background students attending the class rooms and the teachers are expected to know the adult psychology. Three, the instruction or classroom transactions are to be planned in advance. It is not just playing a video or connecting to an internet. He should also know the technology of using the web material when and where. It is to be planned before hand and every time to be revised before going to the class room. Otherwise, students get the same material from the web or from notes and don't find it interesting to attend the class. Most of the class rooms are empty today because of the failure of the teachers in making the class room impressive and provocative. The teacher must inspire the students and it comes through lot of experience and training. Four, preparing for the classroom is one thing and implementing it in the class is another. The teacher should know where to stop and review the lesson and ask questions to know whether the students are following or not. Five, Monitoring the student learning and the need to understand the potential through various methods of evaluation is important. There are several such issues which can be quantified to provide incentives to good teachers rather than relying solely on research output which is not useful most of the time for the classroom.

The white paper on higher education for the 21st century in the UK has brought out the importance of good teaching [3]. It is indicated that the departments that show good practice teaching will get an additional grant of 500000 pounds a year for five years. A National Teaching Quality Enhancement fund with 180 million pounds was established in 2005. In fact, teachers and scholars have clearly identified in the UK that, 'the output of teaching is learning and the output of research is contribution to knowledge". The outcomes of learning and the common methods of teaching in higher education were differentiated by the centers of staff Development in the UK including the Oxford Center for Staff Development. We have given in Table-1 the different teaching methods that are found appropriate to different learning aims at Brighton UK [4]. The white paper on higher education was very clear in its vision to strengthen the system to emerge as a leader in the world. In India, the National policy of Education 1986 had exhibited similar farsighted vision for the country. But, the events that took shape in the 1990s and thereafter made it a fragmented dream that never came true. There were several attempts made by government to appoint committees to recommend measures to improve the quality and quantity of education. Yet, the perspective given by these committees for them an enlightened vision. Most of the recommendations reflect the technocratic or bureaucratic mind set of creating new structures and tinkering with the existing ones without substantially looking at the content, methods and process of higher education. Some of the committees and the experts including the Knowledge Commission could not reach out to the rural college or a state university where the bulk of the future generation is going to be trained. There is very little effort to define research as a component of teaching learning process and much less about the social sciences and their use in making higher education socially relevant. It is very disappointing to find that there is absolutely no mention about the improvements in the Quality of teaching except a paragraph on faculty in one of the recommendations of a national commission. The angst about the future of teaching rises with the fact that none of the experts consulted were drawn from teaching faculty of a state university or college to represent the serious problems of teaching in majority of higher educational institutions. Added to this, it is reported that 50 to 60 percent of the positions in the faculty are lying vacant even in our IITs and IIMs. This shows the apathy of our experts towards teaching and teachers. Teaching and research in higher education are inseparable. The professor in the university department is supposed to guide and train the scholar in the lab or in the field how to analyse various parameters to obtain the expected results. Here, teaching and guidance are closely connected with one to one interaction. Except one or two institutes, all universities in the country are teaching cum research oriented and we do not have a tradition of teaching only universities. Therefore, there is a need to give equal emphasis and paid time to both the functions; teaching and research.

Can Teacher be Replaced

It is in this context of indifference towards the quality of teaching; one is worried about the talk of replacing or supplementing the teacher through the use of ICT. It is strange. Are the Indians more advanced than that of UK or USA, where the governments are seriously thinking to strengthen teaching and even talking about importing teachers from abroad including India? What lessons we can learn from our Eastern neighbors like Japan, Korea etc. Never in the history of mankind was a teacher replaced by a machine! Once it is done, machines will teach machines. That is the end of human civilization!

Notes and References

1. Chalam K.S. **Performance of Academic Staff Colleges in India**, Andhra University Press, Visakhapatnam, 1994.

2. *Op. cit.*

3. UK Govt. of **The Future of Higher Education**, Report of charles Clarke, Department of Education and Skills, 2003.

4. Tom Bourner and Steve Flowers, "**Teaching and learning Methods in Higher Education: A Glimpse of the Future**" **Reflections on Higher Education**, Vol. 9, 1997 pp. 77.

Table-4.1

Learning Objectives and Teaching Methods

	Disseminate Knowledge	*Develop the capability to use ideas and information*	*Develop the student's ability to test ideas and evidence*	*Develop the student's ability to generate ideas and evidence*	*Facilitate the personal development of students*	*Develop the capacity of students to plan and manage their own learning*
Ten common teaching methods	1. Lectures 2. Up-to-date textbooks 3. Reading 4. Handouts 5. 'Guest' Lecturers	1. Case studies 2. Practicals 3. Work experience 4. Projects 5. Demonstrations	1. Seminars and tutorials 2. Supervision 3. Presentations 4. Essays 5. Feedback on written work	1. Research project 2. Workshops on techniques of creative problem solving 3. Group working 4. Action	6. Feedback 7. Experiential learning 8. Learning contracts 9. Action learning 10. Learning logs	1. Learning contracts 2. Projects 3. Action learning 4. Workshops 5. Mentors

(Contd.)

(Contd. Table 4.1)

Disseminate Knowledge	*Develop the capability to use ideas and information*	*Develop the student's ability to test ideas and evidence*	*Develop the student's ability to generate ideas and evidence*	*Facilitate the personal development of students*	*Develop the capacity of students to plan and manage their own learning*
6. Use of exercises that require student to find up-to-date knowle-dge	6. Group working	6. Literature reviewing	6. Brainstorming	6. Role play	6. Reflective logs and diaries
7. Develop skills in using library	7. Simulations (eg computer based)	7. Exam papers	7. Mind-mapping	7. Structured experience in groups	7. Independent study

(Contd.)

(Contd.Table 4.1)

Disseminate Knowledge	*Develop the capability to use ideas and information*	*Develop the student's ability to test ideas and evidence*	*Develop the student's ability to generate ideas and evidence*	*Facilitate the personal development of students*	*Develop the capacity of students to plan and manage their own learning*
8. Directed private study 9. Open learning materials. 10. Use of the Internet	8. Workshops 9. Discussion and debate 10. Essay writing	8. Open learning 9. Peer assessment 10. Self-assessment	8. Creative visualization 9. Coaching 10. Problem solving	8. Reflective documents 9. Self-assessment 10. Profiling	8. Work placement 9. Portfolio develop-ment 10. dissertation

Source: Tom Bourner and Steve Flowers.

Annexure-4.1

Ground Rules for Class Room Observation of Competencies of Teaching

1. Aims made clear to student
2. Content of the lesson appropriate to the stated aims
3. Teaching Technique appropriate to the context
4. Introduction of lesson effective – caught student attention
5. Content broken into small steps
6. Concept and principles of learning ensured through concrete examples.
7. Sequencing of lesson logical
8. Student's active participation in the class encouraged
9. Teacher questions at appropriate level to make the lesson live
10. Students were given freedom to raise doubts and ask questions
11. Positive reinforcement through student responses was evident
12. Communication effective with modulation of voice culture
13. Chalk board work and use of transparencies or power point was effective.
14. Students interest in terms of their careful listening and raising doubts was sustained.
15. Assessment of student's attainment in terms of feedback by way of questions and gestures appropriate

16. Proper link up of main points by writing on the board and repeating at the end of lesson is evident

17. Systematic lesson planning is found

18. Confidence in content evident in terms of the preparedness to answer any question appeared.

Source: Chalam K.S., Andhra University

5

Crisis in Professional Education

The concepts of professional and vocational education are being used interchangeably in our public discourse. There is hardly any attempt to look at the concepts and definitions by our policy makers. They have been used by all including government agencies ever since the British deployed them and are accepted as received wisdom. These two concepts have lot of religious orientation in the beginning. Vocation is derived from the Latin world 'vocare', meaning to call. The Christian missionaries have used 'vocation' as a calling or life purpose for those who entered the clergy. It was also used as a career. It was quite natural for the British to employ the term when they have started imparting religious education for a religious career or vocation. But, we do not have a tradition of vocation in India as priestly class used to come from a particular caste and it was not a career but a life's mission ordained by the system. However, the concept is being used to denote any technical education at the lower level or at the secondary stage before the student gets the age of 18. It has been a practice in India to use the ITI and + 2 technical courses as vocational courses. They are generally under the control of the department of labour and employment and the education department has very little functional relationship with it. Therefore, the education policy of the country has shed very little light on it except when it was referred as a provider of skills for the industry or when an external agency like the World Bank gives some aid for its improvement.

Secular Education vs. Caste Professions

Professional education was also introduced by the British to impart training to occupy secular professions like medical doctor, engineer etc. India had a typical social system where the callings of each caste were predetermined before the birth of the child. Therefore, several professions like doctor, engineer, nurse etc, are not available to others who are not born in a particular caste that is demarcated to practice that profession. This has continued for several generations till the British introduced the so called secular education and professions. There is no clear definition of professional education. Any training and education imparted to students to occupy an identified profession was called as professional education. In fact, there was a separate social group called vaidyas in our social system to practice medicine for the elite and for the lower communities and tribal people there were several sudra and even untouchable castes that were allowed to practice health care. The controversy over Quack doctors and the phenomenon called licensed doctors is a typical example still prevailing in our country. It is in the West that a profession is defined as one that has certain characteristics as an institutionalized occupation. It is elaborated that the profession will influence the work place through knowledge providing, seeking and sharing, as service orientation, invocation of field standards and participation in a knowledge community beyond the work place. Therefore, imparting of knowledge and training to fit into these characteristics in different fields of activity can be called as profession. But in India all secular occupations that were introduced by the British and the corresponding education given was called as professional education. We have been using the term uncritically ever since.

It has also been found that professional and vocational education is imparted through institutions which are affiliated to universities. They are called as professional higher education. There are several professional bodies that were originally involved to maintain standards of practice like Bar council, Medical council etc. They are all now institutionalized and recognized by the government to look after standards of education. But they were never under the control of an education department. However, majority of the educational institutions like Medical colleges, engineering colleges, Law colleges, Agriculture etc, institutes were attached to universities. The qualifications granted by these institutions allowed the people to practice secular professions. This has created an interlude between our traditional practices and modern secular orientation. Interestingly, none of our expert committees on education has ever scrutinized the system from these dimensions to work out a solution for the present complications in professional education.

Professional higher education in India appears to be in crisis today. This is not a sudden outcome. It has a long journey. Some of the professions for which academic degrees are essential have been evolved over a period of time. In fact, the occupational structure of the country was closely related with the Varna System. It was only during the British period that some of the occupations got separated from the Varna and have emerged as secular professions. The academic degrees offered to occupy these professions have also been designed by the British. In the process, these professions have lost their touch with the society with which there used to be an organic relationship. It was also reflected in the curriculum designed for some of the professional courses, particularly medical courses. That is the reason why the mainstream medical courses failed to address the tropical disease regime of the country as against indigenous systems for a long time. It has always addressed the European and Western needs. That is how majority of the medical doctors who graduated from the Medical Colleges in the 1950s and 1960s were automatically absorbed in the USA and UK without much difficulty. But now there is a lot of change and development in the curriculum of the courses in Medical Institutes and Colleges in India. This is also true in the case of other professions.

Crisis in Medical Profession

If we look at the medical profession from this background, it is perceived in recent times that there is some kind of frustration among medical doctors. This is reflected in several agitations. It is necessary to look at the real life issues behind such agitations. The years of study for medical courses vis-à-vis other professional courses and the life time earnings or market value for the courses seem to be very wide. The work schedules of the doctor vis-à-vis other professions are also quite different. The students who are undergoing training in these professional courses are now looking for jobs in lucrative sectors where opportunities in very narrow fields' of specialization are emerging. Very few are now interested in service. Therefore, there is cut-throat competition among the students to concentrate in narrow fields of specialization so as to get absorbed in jobs that provide more money and prestige. But the academic training offered in some of the Institutes is not directly related to the job market, particularly in the private sector. Therefore, there is frustration among the young minds.

The academic atmosphere in some of the Institutes is also so narrow that they focus more on the job market, rather than the needs of the people. It is observed that in one premier Medical Institute around 40 subjects are offered as specializations. But there is little space for the human sciences or discussion about the society. The subject called social and preventive medicine is not comprehensive enough to understand the dynamics of society and its implications for the profession. This is also true in the case of technology courses where there is little scope for any understanding about the society and the human relations. Except in a few IITs, there is little scope for offering courses in human sciences in majority of the Engineering, Science and Technology Colleges. The students who are coming out of these Institutes do really need to work in real life time situations in the society and have to cope up with several social and human tensions. The students are not familiar with the situations that they face in real life and are finding it very difficult to cope with the work. Therefore, there is frustration.

Elite Social Background

It is also true that majority of the students who clamour for these courses come from urban elite families. They are not familiar with the complexities of the society and therefore, when issues like caste, religion and other social issues are confronted, they are confused. They do not have any experience in comprehending the issues except the knowledge in their specialized fields of study. They are found as alienated individuals. There is also an increasing tendency of taking up the market agenda of MNCs as Research Programmes that go as inputs of the courses. But the problems encountered in real life situations on the job are found to be different from what they learn or understand from their courses. They baffle. Some of them resort to unethical practices and form into carters to prevent others to enter the Profession. There are several studies undertaken by scholars to prove this.

Social Stigma behind Some Professions

In a profession like health care, there are other complimentary services like Nursing, Pharmacy etc., which are not equitably distributed among the social groups. The majority of the Nurses in the country come from socially disadvantaged groups. Even though there is a lot of demand for this profession both in India and outside, there is no crisis of penury. Interestingly the urban elite are not interested in another emerging profession, veterinary doctors. Though veterinary graduates are also called as Doctors and there is great demand for the profession in the rural areas. There is no problem of supply and demand. Why?

The crisis in the professional education appears to be due to another important social phenomenon of our society. Most of the professions that are now made secular were traditionally held by Sudra Communities. The vaidyas were not given the same respect as they do get now in a secular mode. Therefore, there is craving for the profession. It is also true in other secular occupations which are appropriated by the educated elite who are by and large come from the Non-Sudra communities during the post colonial period. There is little space for the Sudras and others to occupy the opportunities created in modern occupations that required an academic degree. They have lost their traditional occupations and are considered as ineligible to occupy the emerging modern professions as they do not have an academic degree. No one has ever looked at professional education from this angel in our manpower planning. There is a mismatch, leading to crisis in our professional education.

Now, the Sudras in the garb of reservations wanted to enter into their traditional occupations in a secular set up as the government never formulated a policy of rehabilitation and resettlement when their occupations were appropriated by others. The crisis is imminent. The education system in the country was never bothered to examine these issues in formulating courses, policies and opportunities. There is a need to look at these issues afresh to make technical and professional higher education socially relevant to our country and times.

6

Inclusive Education and Social Empowerment

Aristotle once remarked that, "the educated differ from the uneducated as much as the living from the dead". There are similar references to education available in ancient Indian literature. These nuances clearly indicate the importance of education in human civilization. But, the kind of education that was conceptualized by the seers and philosophers of ancient civilizations was never made universal. It has remained to be a prerogative of the few. It is only with the advent of the democratic values; education became universalized in several countries. There are still areas and groups in the world who are denied access to education due to different conditions and circumstances. This phenomenon calls for a discussion on the role of education in empowering people, as it has been considered as an agency that empowers the beholder. As India is know for its inegalitarian social institutions, the development of education has several implications for the future of the country.

Concept of Empowerment

There are two important issues that are associated with the topic education and empowerment. Education has been defined by Newman as the 'art of utilization of knowledge'. Empowerment, a concept borrowed from Feminists is defined in oxford English dictionary as, "ability to do or affect something or anything to act upon a person or thing". This is considered as, 'the process of increasing personal or political power so that individuals, families and communities can take action to improve their situations'. This concept however, presupposed the concept of power. The term, power has been analyses by Social Scientists in different contexts. I have elaborated the concept of power in my recent book on 'Caste-based reservations and human development in India' (Chapter-2)[1]. I found that power is always exercised through domination and subordination. It depends upon the historical setting, social structure and nature of the state and economy. In the theory of power, social Scientists have analysed how a person's power over another person is affected in terms of the behaviour pattern. Scholars like J Pen classified seven categories of power that includes social power that depends upon the social position of the subject. The means of power is always exercised through specific actions like promises, threats, controls, commands and so on. This is always manifested in the form of inequalities. One of the important bases of power, in modern society is considered to be education. Therefore, it is necessary to understand education as a source of power and also as an agency that empowers people.

There are two approaches in understanding the role of education in empowering people; One, the radical approach of using Pedagogy as a process of conscientisation of the oppressed. The second approach of a transformation project of creating opportunities in the mainstream education to those who are hitherto denied access to education. Let us examine one after the other.

Gramsci and Paulo Freire

In this context, the work and mission of the great 20th century thinkers in education and culture need to be discussed. The analytical tool box supplied by Gramsci in his 'Prison Note Books, I believe, is relevant here[2]. Similarly one of the greatest educational thinkers of the

20th century who was influenced by Gramsci in his praxis is Paulo Freire(3). It is possible to synthesize both the thinkers in order to understand their relevance here. Gramsci while writing on culture and education critically examined the then European education as an establishment that helped to cement the existing hegemony. Therefore, Gramsci wanted that the educational and cultural formations to play the key role in evading counter-hegemonic action. He has also indicated the forms in which these actions could be built. He has promoted the spirit of equality in adult education spaces in the form of discussion circles, clubs, trade unions, political parties, cultural reviews etc. Paulo Freire in his classic, 'Pedagogy of the Oppressed' brought out a revolutionary theory of education. He wanted that education be made liberating exercise rather than a domesticating one. He has introduced several new concepts like banking system of education, dialogic etc, to elaborate his Pedagogy for the oppressed. He wanted that the educator should side with the oppressed and promote learning through dialogue on the basis of the learner's experience with praxis. He insisted that the educator should always be conscious of the cultural background of the class, gender, race etc, of the subject. Writing on the basis of their relative backgrounds, Gramsci as a political analyst and Paulo Freire as an educationalist both argued for the emancipation of the oppressed using education, particularly adult education as an agency.

Education As a Transformative Project

The dominant view of using education as a transformation project is popular among the policy makers. Realising the need for diversity in a globalised economy, World Bank and other UN agencies are now working for a democratic decentralization of education(4). In countries like USA the state is encouraging minority schools to provide meaningful experiences to the learner as a source of power to survive in a globalised economy. It is interesting to notice that these agencies which have once popularized the concept of participation have diverted their attention now to 'empowerment'. The purpose of empowerment through education here seems to provide capacity enhancement and capability provisioning.

This is seriously reflected in the Reports Published by World Bank, UNDP and others agencies.

It is instructive to find that the Human Development Report, 2004 devoted considerable space elaborating on historically rooted and socially entrenched injustices. It has recognized that one of the important factors that make the socio-economic exclusion visible is education. It is through the spread of education, the knowledge society has come of age. Therefore, redressing that exclusion requires a combination of policies. The UNDP has indicated the following :

1. Addressing unequal social investments to achieve equality of opportunity.

2. Recognizing legitimate collective claims to land and livelihoods, and

3. Taking affirmative action in favour of disadvantaged groups.

The Human Development Report 2004 has devoted a substantial part of its argument on the basis of the affirmative action policies pursued in India, Malaysia, USA and South Africa. "Educational and occupational reservations have also made lasting impact on India's political system. The entire structure of political power has changed since independence, beginning with South Indian States. A new political leadership has emerged from among the Scheduled Castes, Scheduled Tribes and other backward classes. In almost all states the beneficiaries of reservations occupy important positions in government and positions in lower levels of bureaucracy" (UNDP-2004 P. 71). This is the first time that the issue of reservations has been referred to in an international debate by a UN agency. This is recognition of the positive aspects of the affirmative action followed by the government of India for the last few decades.

However, the opportunities created through the affirmative action in education and employment in India was limited to public sector. The little progress that the reservation categories have made during the six decades of post-independence period has started dwindling during the liberalization period. There are several policy changes that have affected the educational opportunities of the dalits. The post-independent public education was almost a continuation of the colonial mode of liberal education. The government has realized the lacunae and corrective measures such as creation of institutes of excellence like IITs, IIMs, new course structures, vocationallisation of education have been initiated. But, these courses and opportunities were confined to the elite of the forward castes and may be for the creamy layer of the reservation groups. The majority of disadvantaged groups have not realized the importance of these courses and therefore remained outside the purview of vocational education except Engineering, Medical etc. Thus, the project of using education as a transformative project is seriously flawed in India due to several social rigidities. Let us now look at the educational disparity in India so that we can understand the enormity of the problem of using education for empowerment of the powerless. In India, the powerless are the ones who come from the Scheduled Castes and Tribes (dalits). A critical analysis of the status of education among the dalits will throw light on the capacity of education in empowering the disadvantaged.

Post-independent Progress in Education

A brief review of the educational progress of the dalits during the post-independent period indicates the gaps and shortcomings of the policy. The following are some dichotomies that have emerged out of the progress in school education for the scheduled castes and tribes.

1. The literacy levels of the people in general and female in particular are still very low compared to developed countries.

2. The literacy gap between males and females, between forward castes and Scheduled Castes and between male and female among these communities is very high.

3. The literacy levels of urban dwellers including Dalits in all parts of the country is around 80 per cent and therefore the problem of

illiteracy in the country is related to only rural areas and of Dalits and some OBCs.

4. The educational strategy of Madhya Pradesh (Digvijay Singh) government like the EGP educational guarantee programme, has helped to increase the literacy levels in the states of Madhya Pradesh and Chattisgarh as per 2001 census that includes the literacy levels of dalits.

5. The enrolment levels at Primary education presented in Table – 1 show that they are increasing from 1980-81 and have reached a record level of 19.8 per cent of the total enrolment in 2006-2007. This is in excess of the proportion of the population of SCs. As it is gross enrolment, there is a possibility of incorporating in it the backlog of enrolments. However, the data are to be disaggregated at the Taluk/Mandal level to find out the gaps.

6. The enrolment at the upper primary level is also nearing the proportion of the population of Scheduled Castes. However, the enrolment in higher secondary is short of the proportion of SC population. This shows the gap between primary and secondary levels, which is due to high dropout rates at upper primary. The dropout rate among SC girls at primary stage is very high.

7. The recent government of India Act on compulsory education 2009 does not contain any specific reference to Dalits. It has not proposed any strategy for enrolling more number of students from these sections and is silent about reservations in the recruitment of teachers.

8. The dropout rates presented in Table-2 clearly indicate the gap between universalisation of school education and the actual number of students who are passing out from X class. It is found that out of 100 children admitted in Class I only 27 complete X class among SC and 22 among STs.

Present Situation in Higher Education

The enrolment of SCs/STs into various courses of study in higher education is given in Table – 3. The data is for the year 2006-2007. The following are some of the in inferences that emerge out of it.

1. The enrolment ratio of higher education at different degrees provided in the table show that the ratios are still remain at single digit level except for B.A. and M.A. The lowest proportion of students from SCs is found at M.Com and Ph.D. enrolment. The proportion of enrolment in engineering and medicine is considered to be nearer to 10 per cent.

2. The recent incident in Kerala where a S.C. girl has committed suicide for not getting proper response from Bankers for an educational loan shows the lacunae in the scheme.

3. The policies pursued by different state governments are responsible for imbalances in the enrolment of scheduled castes in terms of the drawal of post-matric scholarships from government of India. The states like Bihar, Uttar Pradesh, West Bengal, Orissa are underrepresented in terms of their proportion in Scheduled Caste population in the Country.

4. There are around 20 castes among dalits which are found to be dominant in the entire country in terms of their overwhelming representation in education and literacy.

Who is Responsible for Higher Education?

In a knowledge-based economy, empowerment of a person is possible through higher education. School education is now relegated to a position of preparing the child for future life including access to higher education. Therefore, the government of India is very careful now in owning its responsibility for educating the people of India. The World Bank has been insisting since 1986, that the government should concentrate on school education and leave higher education to market. The national policy of education 1986 and the programme of Action 1992 are very clear about the educational development of Scheduled Castes and Tribes. A separate chapter is devoted to the educational development of Scheduled Castes and Tribes where in the school education of the dalits is mentioned. There is no mention about higher education and particularly quality institutions like IIT's and IIM's. The government has already brought out the compulsory primary education Act, 2009. All these initiatives indicate that the government is responsible for primary education of all the people in the country and only up to secondary education for dalits. Interestingly, the Scheduled Castes and Tribes Commission is also not aware of the fact that dalits are under-represented in professional and vocational education. The ministry of social justice and empowerment releases the post-matric scholarships to different states on the basis of the requisition for states. It seems, they do not have a mandate to question the under representation of dalits in professional and vocational courses. One can observe from the data in the tables that dalits are now fully represented in school education and in some liberal arts and sciences courses at higher education. But, their representation in the emerging courses that provide opportunities of employment and skills is seriously missing.

The progress of dalits in education is of recent origin. The first generation learners of dalits have realized the importance of education and have started encouraging their children to go for higher education. It is exactly at this juncture that the World Bank and the government of India wanted higher education to be provided through market. The government has appointed a committee under the chairmanship of Sri Atal Bihari Vajpai with Mukhesh Amabani and Aditya Birla as members in the year 2000. The committee gave a report recommending the privatization and corporatization of higher education. There was no mention about the interests of the disadvantaged groups. Perhaps the committee foresaw the implementation of GATS in education from 2005. Already several private foreign institutions and universities have established their offices in India to admit students in courses that are considered to be important in the 21st century. (See Annexure for the Bill on Private Foreign Universities) Though the idea of privatization was in nascent stage in our education system for a long period of time, it has come out openly after liberalization in 1991. Several colleges and even universities have come up under the category of self-financing institutions. Interestingly all these institutions offer vocational and job oriented courses keeping in view the emerging opportunities in the globalized economy. The dalits have not even realized the existence of such courses nor they are allowed to enter the institutions without paying fees. Once again dalits seem to have been excluded from higher education under a different context. I am not bringing here the recent debate on reservations in Central Government Quality institutes as it is under litigation.

What are the Opportunities Available?

The expansion of the educational development of the scheduled castes can be divided into two periods: One, the pre-liberalization period.Two, the post-liberalization period, (1991 and after). The educational achievements of the first generation of dalits immediately after independence were related to the opportunities created by the state. Several state governments have started welfare hostels to promote school education. Very few opportunities were however, provided for vocational courses. Therefore, majority of the dalits have joined the mainstream courses of Arts and Sciences. The expansion of the public sector during this period helped the educated dalits to get absorbed in this sector. Some of them have appeared for civil services and entered the bureaucracy.

The post-liberalization period witnessed tremendous changes in the world of higher education. There is a revolution in science and technology, consequently it has influenced the communication and information networks. They have affected the education system also. The creation of WTO and GATS has brought in new opportunities of free mobility of resources and technology. This has facilitated the expansion of educational market in response to the needs of the expanding world market. The public sector started shrinking and the opportunities of employment in secure jobs have disappeared. The dalits have not perceived the danger of dwindling opportunities in public sector and the opening up of ever expanding possibilities in the globalized private sector. The global labour market has started influencing the educational programmes, particularly courses in electronics, computer science and related courses. Practically hundreds and thousands of courses are created to meet every small skill requirement of the job market. In fact the course structures have undergone a change. There are now two categories of courses: One, the short life courses and two, the long life courses. The long life courses require long period of time, resources and knowledge to enter the market. They are very expensive and the benefits are life long and useful to the entire society. The short life courses are very short in duration. They meet the immediate requirements of any tiny skill. The cost therefore is to be borne by the individual as it directly benefits the individual. But, its durability is limited. It runs the risk of short duration and therefore state does not take the responsibility of providing it on its own. It is exactly here the private sector is expanding to meet the requirements of the growing manufacturing and service sector. This has not been realized by the disadvantaged groups, who do not have a social network at the global level. But the groups who have a historical advantage in education have transformed themselves and already entrenched very much in the global market. This has an impact on higher education. It is now clear that the elite have refrained from entering the liberal Arts and Science courses. On the other hand, all the liberal courses in government and aided colleges are filled in by the so called reserved categories and the private colleges are left out for the so called merit students. The merit can be bought here. The self financing courses are related to the emerging areas of skills in the job market. This has a bearing on the empowerment of the disadvantaged through education.

Are the Dalits Excluded from Quality Institutes?

In a knowledge based economy empowerment of individual depends upon the amount of knowledge and the quality of Knowledge possessed by a person. Though dalits and artisan castes have traditional and indigenous knowledge and are able to survive with that knowledge, it is found that it is not just sufficient to survive in a competitive global world. The history of education in India has provided enough hints to understand that those who possess knowledge and are in a position to refine it and update it will alone develop and all others either suffer or obtain natural attrition. In this context, we have seen in an earlier chapter that the modernization projects in India have paid very little attention to dalit's education and empowerment. It was only after Mahatma Phooley and Ambedkar's People's education movement some progress was achieved in Maharashtra. The so called modernist project of Ambedkar was confined to Maharashtra and to South Indian States and the gift of english did not reach the cow belt consisting of Bihar, UP, MP, Rajasthan, Orissa and even West Bengal where more than 60 percent of the Indian dalits live. Even in the state of Maharashtra and South Indian states, the spread of english education was limited to the upcoming middle classes among the dalits. It is no doubt, created an intellectual class and job holders who are emerging as organic intellectuals of the 21st century.

Globalization and privatization of education in 1990s had adversely affected the small minority of upward mobile dalits who were capable of entering into Quality institutes like IIMs, IITs and others. The implementation of GATS from 2005 and the popularization of self financing courses in the vocational stream particularly in higher education, made the dalits to confine to liberal Arts and Science courses. Realising the futility of these courses for the dalits in a modern economy Ambedkar has pointed out around 1945 that, "from the point of raising the economic condition, technical education for the Scheduled Castes is more important than literacy education. But, technical education is also very costly and it is not possible for children of the Scheduled castes to take technical education and without technical education their economic condition will not be improved."[(5)] Apart from technical education, several job oriented courses are emerging in the private sectors which have potential to get absorbed in private sector. But, the dalits and even some OBCs do not have knowledge of these courses particularly in the so called cow belt or hindi belt. Therefore, the empowering of dalits through education must concentrate on these emerging courses apart from encouraging them to occupy the void created in social sciences by the upper castes that migrated to greener pastures after liberalization in India.

Limitations of Inclusive Education

The mid term appraisal of Tenth plan process has brought out the gaps and divides in our education. Realising the impending danger of exclusion of certain social groups like dalits in education the government has proposed the strategy of inclusive growth for the 11th Plan, (2007-2012) Education is considered here as one of the important factors to achieve inclusion. The notion of inclusive growth has its roots in the European concept of social exclusion. The European Commission has recognized the problem of social exclusion of certain groups of people like the mentally and physically handicapped, single parents, asocial people etc, in 1995. The member countries of the Commission have adopted several measures including separate ministries to deal with the problem. Thus, it can be considered as a construct imported into India through international agencies. Perceiving this link, our policy makers and some researchers have popularized this concept without knowing its origin, context and relevance. The concept became a preamble to the Eleventh Plan. J.B. Tilak while evaluating the approach to Eleventh Plan in his article in Economic and Political Weekly has expressed his disappointment for its inconsistencies [(6)]. He has brought out several contradictions in our educational policy in the so called inclusive growth strategy of Eleventh Plan. He said that the approach paper is indeed found to be full of 'contradictions, lack of vision for development of education, and absence of a critical outlook of the strategies required'. He has almost captured the reason for it in his last sentence of the paragraph may be inadvertently, but could not ensign it properly when he said that these polices are 'broadly correspond to the suggestions made by the World Bank (2006)'.

Educational policy in India has always been given a tepid treatment by the ruling classes since the time of East India Company. The company has followed a policy that benefited only the upper castes. They have even justified it by saying that, 'the character which may be given to the classes possessed of leisure and natural influence ultimately determines that of the whole people'[7]. To bring this inequitable and unfair policy to the notice of the British, we have noted that Mahatma Phooley submitted a memorandum to the Hunter Commission in 1882.

The class bias in education is as old as the caste system. No where in the civilized world a system of education is deliberately promoted to categorise the people into three classes from the stage of primary education. We have in India three classes of schools, one for the wretched of the earth through the municipal-panchayat school, the aided school for the middle classes and the private public school for the rich and possessed. In other words, the future citizens are divided and prepared at the school stage to occupy their mutually exclusive functions in the economy and society. It is a caste system in a different mould. In order to do a way with the harmful effects of it, the Kothari Commission to which Tilak has referred to in his article, recommended a common school. No one has taken it very seriously and it is now almost a formality both in the rural and urban areas that the practice of 'class school' is real. The class school has moved such a long distance today that the rich and powerful in the village including the sarpanch do not send their children to the school and put them in an urban school or in the same village in the so called english medium convent. As a result of it, the panchayat or municipal school became the dumping school for weaker sections. This has an impact on the teacher's attendance and the apathy of indifference of policy makers towards Government schools. These conditions have led to the degeneration of the school system. It is a known fact that thousands of vacancies of teachers' posts are available at school stage in all the states and there are very few who raise this issue in the state legislatures or parliament? The SSA, a variant of the World Bank funded DPEP is given the charge of the schools and they are accorded according to Tilak, status equal to formal schooling, thereby making formal school not a basic necessity. Interestingly, if there is any discussion at the Zillaparishad or a public debate on education, people refer only to SSA and almost forgot about the formal system of schooling.

One significant departure from the earlier plans is found in the Eleventh Plan in the area of secondary education. The Government has recognized that universal education of eight years is not enough for a country that aims at 8-9 percent growth. In fact the literature on Economics of Indian Education is elaborate with contributions by Panchamukhi, Tilak, Chalam and several others to establish the relationship between enrolment as a flow variable or years of schooling as a stock variable and rates of growth of an economy. It is strange that the approach paper being an intellectual output of highest order paid scant attention to these contributions and repeated contradictory statements. The Eleventh Plan document need to be however commended as it has recognized the gap between elementary and higher education; the secondary education. This is the first time that the Government has seriously considered to improve the quality and quantity of secondary education, despite of questionable strategies.

Knowledge Syndrome

There are several scholarly studies on higher education in India. But, the approach paper of the XI plan seems to be obsessed with the 'knowledge syndrome' in higher education. It is not very clear from the document what do they mean by knowledge and how is it related to higher education. There are epistemological differences between knowledge and education, information and knowledge and knowledge and wisdom. It appears that the document has assumed that all information including ICT becomes knowledge and it should automatically get into the university education. Tilak J B G has concluded that the approach paper has a limited vision as 'skills are equated to knowledge, knowledge is dominated by ICT; and knowledge economy is to be created by vocations and technical education'. This logic of the approach paper appears to be that of a management consultant or HR professional and not of an educationist or planner. Educational Planning is an exercise in timing and is a deliberate and conscious choice of educational priorities by a central agency. Higher education as distinguished from that of school education creates knowledge. This knowledge needs to be disciplined so as to make it a course structure to be used in universities and institutes. It has a definite process and a time frame. It cannot be produced and supplied like a commodity in the market on the basis of short-term demand. It is heartening to cite here that the first female president of Harvard has remarked recently that, 'the essence of a university is that it is uniquely accountable to the past and to the future- not simply or even primarily to the present' [(8)]. The planners have a responsibility to estimate the value of long life of knowledge and short life of knowledge before making policy prescriptions in higher education. The approach paper seems to have plagued with short life of knowledge that reacts to market demand. It is an irony that the malnonourished higher education in India is now called as sick child.

The major hitch in the policy of the Government comes from the inadequate understanding of the Indian Society. The plan document seems to be interested in linking education with the economy and society. It is therefore, necessary that one must understand the nature of Indian society. However, the concept of social exclusion, from where the question of inclusive growth conceived is being elaborated by economists who have very limited understanding now about our society. It is alleged that the generation of economists who are trained in the medium of English and in Western concepts have turned out to be good economists, statisticians and technocrats but sadly lesser social scientists. But, the concept of inclusive growth was picked up by them and imported into India have limitations of perception of an economist. Even the concept as developed by the Indian economists has little focus on the structurally divided Indian society. Is it possible to bring inclusive growth by raising the rate of growth of the economy? How the rate of growth of the economy is related to different stages of education? Is it possible to bring equity through the process of privatization, decentralization, NGO'sation of education? How is it different from the 'trickle down' theory of education of East India Company that failed to bring universalisation of education? Why the government has failed to achieve universalisation of elementary education, 60 years after its constitutional vow? Who are the people or groups or castes that are deprived of education and what requires to be done to bring them into the mainstream (inclusive growth)? These are some of the important questions that need to be raised and answered to achieve inclusive education.

It seems that the major flaw in the approach to inclusive growth (education) comes from its limited understanding of the Indian society or may be a westernized understanding of India. India is a land of contradictions and diversities. It is perhaps possible to resolve economic contradictions by achieving a rapid rate of economic growth. But, its impact on the structurally and hierarchically divided society will be nominal as revealed in our historical experience. Thinkers like Paulo Frere explained how literate education has been used as one of the important agents to suppress the disadvantaged groups to carry on the hegemony of the ruling classes. In India, education is neither an economic problem nor purely an educational issue. It is a social enigma. Social exclusion is structurally constructed. Unless the structures that protect the inequities are broken or at least consciously manipulated, social exclusion will be recreated at every stage in society. The iron frame of caste structure is so strong that it absorbs whatever improvements are attempted and finally allow them to settle within the frame. This unique innovation that has an Indian patent, is reincarnated time and again. This cannot be tinkered with western hammers. We need to innovate methods to weaken the links that are structurally built so that the weakest links become independent and assert their strength to show that they are horizontally as strong as any one else. This is possible by providing additional inputs through a deliberate choice of priorities as advocated by thinkers like Phooley, Lohia, J P Naik and others.

How does the Present Education Affect Empowerment?

We have examined the present status of education among the disadvantaged groups in India. It is reported in some studies that there are several gaps in terms of inequalities in enrolment, course structures, access to job oriented courses etc., between the elite and the educationally dispossessed groups such as Dalits, Women, Muslims, etc.,[(9)] Therefore, it is difficult to assess the affect of education on empowerment. The effect of social empowerment can be considered only when the education offered to different categories of people in the society are equitably distributed or accessed. Further, empowerment is considered as "the Process of enhancing individual's or group's capacity to make purposive choices and to transform those choices into desired actions and outcomes". If we assume that the education dispensed to different groups is the same, it is possible to measure the outcomes to find out the affect of education on social groups. The World Bank has provided 6 indicators to measure empowerment. They are as follows:-

1. Psychological Assets - capacity to envisage change

2. Informational Assets - Frequency of radio listening or access to different media

3. Organizational Assets - membership in an organization

4. Material Assets - ownership of productive Assets such as Land

5. Financial Assets - value of household savings in last year (cash & other assets)

6. Human Assets - Literacy level.

It appears that there are very few studies to indicate how different types of education with varied content of education influence the empowerment of different social groups. For instance, how the content of a discipline at an undergraduate stage in subjects like Electronics, Fish and Fisheries, Biotechnology, Food and Nutrition etc. impact the students with different social and occupational backgrounds. How the knowledge base of the subject do enhance the capability of the student to break occupational traditions thus caste barriers in India? If a student from a fishermen community studies Fish and Fisheries, does it help him to enhance his understanding about Fish. If it does, will he remain in the same sector and gain social acceptability outside his community? Similarly if a person from a non-fishermen community studies the subject what is its impact on the society and his community? There are several such questions that need to be answered to find out the impact of education on social empowerment in India. Education in India (even if it is uniformly offered) has failed to transform the society from that of a feudal mode to a modern capitalist society where everyone is supposed to be treated as equal in the labour market. The education system and the content are supposed to provide skills and abilities to the people who in turn offer them in the market. Except in a small section of the population in the white collar occupations, education did not bring any social mobility in India. It seems that the education system has failed to provide the necessary impetus for social empowerment. There is a growing evidence to show that the system of education as practiced in the post-liberalisation period has economically transformed several groups and social categories. But, it has failed to bring in a common culture permeating all social groups. If the education system strengthens sub-culture and not a popular culture (not pop culture) which is essential according to educationists to promote fruits of excellence, there is something wrong with our education! It is, therefore, necessary to introduce new educational practices to make the future citizen experience diversity and still appreciate the unity of India. The objective of 'Inclusive growth' as enunciated by the Eleventh Five Year Plan need to be translated into practice through several educational programmes of the Government starting from school stage to University level.

End Notes

1. Chalam K.S. **Caste-based Reservations and Human Development in India**, Sage Publications, Delhi, 2007.

2. Gramsci A. **Prison Note Books**, Lawrence and Wishart International Publishers, London, 1971.

3. Paulo Freire, **Pedagogy of the Oppressed,** Penguin, 1979.

4. Ruth Astop, M.F Bertelsen and J Holland, **Empowerment in Practice: From Analysis to Implementation The World Bank**, Washington DC, 2006.

5. Chalam K.S., **Modernisatin and Dalit Education: Ambedkarvision,** Rawat Publications, Jaipur, 2008.

6. Tilak JBG, **"Knowledge Commission and Higher Education"** Economic and Political Weekly, 24 Feb, 2007.

7. Chalam K.S. op. cit.

8. Times of India, 14 October, 2007, p. 19.

9. Mamata Rajawat, **Women Education and Social Empowerment,** Reference Press, Delhi, 2005.

References

Barry Brian, **Justice as Impartially** Oxford, Clarendon Press, 1995.

Beiteille Andre, **The Backward Classes in Contemporary India** Oxford, Delhi, 1992.

Bowles S and Gintis H **Schooling in Capitalist America,** Basic Books, Newyork, 1976.

Chalam K.S **Education and Weaker Sections,** Inter India, Delhi, 1988.

Chalam K.S **Challenges of Higher Education** Anmol, Delhi, 2005.

Rawls John **A Theory of Justice** Cambridge, Harvard University Press, 1971.

Sen Amartya, **Social Exclusion: Concept Application and Scrutiny** ADB, Bangkok, 1994.

Table – 6.1

Educational Development of Scheduled Castes At School Stage 1980-81 to 2006-2007

(in '000)

Year	*Primary*	*Middle*	*Higher Secondary*
1960-61	(12.0)	(8.7)	(7.1)
1980-81	10981	2223	152
	(14.8)	(10.7)	(10.5)
1985-86	13921	3619	1810
	(15.9)	(13.3)	(10.9)
1991-92	16037	4693	2581
	(16.0)	(11.7)	(12.6)
1995-96	19176	5445	2741
	(17.9)	(14.5)	(11.9)
2000-2001	21195	6694	3812
	(18.6)	(15.6)	(13.8)
2006-2007	25000	9000	4000
	(19.08)	(17.6)	(16.6)

Note: Figures in brackets indicate percentage to total enrolment in that category.

Source: Ministry of HRD, Government of India, 2007.

Table 6.2: Stage-wise Drop-out Rates 2006

(in % age)

Classes	*Total*			*SC*			*ST*		
	Boys	*Girls*	*Total*	*Boys*	*Girls*	*Total*	*Boys*	*Girls*	*Total*
I-V	28.7	21.8	25.7	32.1	33.8	32.9	40.2	39.3	39.8
I-VIII	48.7	49.0	48.8	53.7	57.1	55.2	62.9	62.7	62.9
I-X	60.1	63.6	61.6	68.2	73.7	70.6	78.0	79.2	78.5

Drop-out Rate is the percentage of pupils who drop out from a given grade or cycle or level of education in a given school year. It does not include repeaters.

TABLE – 6.3

Enrolment Of Sc/St in Higher Education 2006-2007

(in ooo)

Class	*Scheduled Castes*		*Scheduled Tribes*	
	No.	*% to total*	*No.*	*% to total*
Ph.D.,	3.6	10.0	1.5	4.1
M.A.,	76.6	15.9	25.0	5.2
M.Com.,	13.4	8.5	8.0	5.1
M.Sc.,	23.1	10.0	4.5	1.9
B.A.,	569.3	15.2	210.6	5.6
B.Sc.,	188.0	11.9	53.3	3.3
B.Com.,	135.8	9.3	47.9	3.3
B.E.,	162.5	9.7	57.2	3.4
M.B.B.S.,	44.6	14.5	19.3	6.3

Source: Ministry of HRD, Government of India, 2008.

7

Productivity of Higher Education and Economic Reform

The chapter is addressed itself to three important issues of higher education. It examines the concepts of internal and external productivity of higher education in the context of contemporary realities of the system. It also throws light on the technological development and its impact on higher education in the coming decades. Finally, the expected changes in the employment market under this background are hinted out.

I

It is ever since the 'Campus Crises' in the late 60's in the West, that the governments and intellectuals have started giving attention to the question of future of higher education. It is only during this period that the concept of 'human capital' has come into prominence. International organizations like UNESCO, OECD, etc., have made detailed studies on the various aspects of education and brought out the 'world educational crisis' into light. Though the trend seems to be a part of the innovation phase of education, but in essence, it has deep-rooted structural imbalances within and outside the educational system. Economists have produced a good amount of literature explaining the economic context of education, of course with inadequate attention to the structural changes in the economy and society. Therefore, they have come to realize their 'jaundiced view', as one prominent expert in the field has commented. However, it has contributed a lot to the field of knowledge in general and to the education sector in particular. It has clarified a number of issues which have been so far unsettled. The most important contribution of this period was the cost-benefit analysis of education. The concepts of internal and external productivity of education are associated broadly with this concept.

It is widely accepted that higher education has a 'seed value'. Therefore, it is reasonable here to limit ourselves to higher education. We must distinguish between the 'external productivity' of education from 'internal productivity' in the educational system. There is a lot of ambiguity and ambivalence in the use and application of these two concepts. Realising the importance of this controversy, the UNESCO's European centre has conducted a seminar on this topic at Bucharest in 1975. Similarly, the Carnegie Commission on Higher Education has also expressed its opinion on this issue. Yet the ambiguity seems to prevail still in the academic circles.

The term 'productivity' refers to the input-output relationship over a period of time and it is more of an analysis of the product on process. There is also a related term known in the literature as 'efficiency'. The term explains the way in which the resources are being used in the production process. In fact there is a cause and effect relationship between efficiency and productivity, the cause being the efficient combination of input resources and the outcome is productivity. Therefore, it is perfectly possible that education is conducted inefficiently at every moment in time yet enjoys productivity improvements as time passes. Similarly, education may be conducted efficiently at every point in time yet exhibit no technical dynamism over time, simply because there are no inventions forthcoming that can be adopted to the educational process. Further, when these two concepts are used within the internal operation of the educational system they are called as internal productivity [illegible] internal efficiency while their use with reference to the economic system as a whole of which the educational system in a sub-system, are referee as external productivity and efficiency. To elaborate a little further, internal productivity is a measure of input-output ratio over a period of time, given the educational system and its characteristics with reference to specific operational targets of the educational system. In contrast, internal efficiency is a measure of cost of output at a point in time and its relation to least cost combination of inputs or least cost production of output. This can be reflected in the distribution of the unit costs of operation by several institutions comprising the educational system. In other words, the maximization of output with the given educational expenditure can be called as internal efficiency.

Following the same reasoning, external productivity measures the success of the whole educational system over a period of time by considering the broader objectives and goals of education in addition to the narrowly defined specific operational targets connected with the concept of internal productivity. The most commonly used technique in this case is the cost-benefit analysis. The term external efficiency is often used as a synonym of external productivity.

However, we must be very cautious in applying and deriving conclusion from these concepts. Because sometimes the operation of an educational system may be internally efficient yet the use of its products outside the system may turn out to be externally unproductive. Coombs and Hallak have illustrated this point in their book "Managing Educational Costs", saying that "when an educational system spends its time and resources efficiently teaching the wrong things, that is, in terms of the real needs of particular students in light of their environment and future prospects, it is like requiring all Eskimo children to learn ancient Greek or tropical agriculture".

These concepts are intensively used in Economics of Education under the assumption that the 'feudal values' of education are no more imaginable. They are also used within certain limitations like that of the impossibility of capturing all the changes in the quality of education over a period of time in productivity estimates.

Most of the research studies in this area have revealed a number of contradictions that prevail in higher education, particularly in the developing countries. It is found that the external and internal productivities move in the opposite directions in the developing countries. The reasons are not far to seek. It is a known fact that most of the developing countries, till recently, were the colonies of some of the industrialized nations of today. As a result, they have been following a system of education which is more akin to the conditions of their former colonial powers, than to the reality of the present situation. This has proved the Eskimo example of Coombs and Hallak right, as the educational systems have successfully produced outputs, with an increasing internal productivity. Yet, these output's external productivity seems to be marginal in these countries. This means that these countries are pursuing an inappropriate education to their conditions. Therefore, the contradiction of increasing internal productivity and declining trend of external productivity of education is observed there. Another important contributing factor for this trend is attributed to the growing public expenditure on higher education. In recent years, the cost of higher education, particularly in the technical component, has increased manifold due to the expensive content of the courses. While this is the situation in developing countries, the situation in socialist block is little exposed to tests like these, as the objectives of education are claimed to be different there. However, it was pointed out by some experts of these countries that there was a serious imbalance between the internal and external productivities of higher education whose social consequences were reinforced in countries like Poland in the 1980s. The slow down in the economies of these countries seem to be to a certain extent due to the non-economic criteria assigned to education (though Strumlin is the first economist to apply economic calculation to education) among many things. Therefore it is alleged that there is no relationship between the outcomes of the universities and their effective use in the economy.

There is a growing tendency of de-socialisation of education in the West particularly in USA and UK in recent years. Whatever may be the political intentions of these governments, the socioeconomic repercussions from such a change seem to be far reaching. So far, the public sector has been managing the majority of the educational institutions with decreasing rates of internal productivity in the West (for instance UK) due to the increase in the costs of education. But it seems that they would not come down immediately, even if the current science and technology continues. In fact, there may appear to be a situation where in both internal and external productivities might come down. This is due to the non-interference of the governments in standardizing the outputs of private institutions. In that case, the private sector would not last long since the individuals make their own economic calculations. A rational individual prefers the institutions to be both internally and externally effective so that he will be benefited by a large margin of profit. Who is going to send his children to school if he is not sure of his children's successful graduation and there after their productive use in the economy as inputs?

II

Higher education has been increasingly influencing science and technology. Today, science and technology have emerged as a productive force and its contribution to development has been measured by economists in many ways. Not only that, it has become a way of life with the democratization of education every where. Now, the contemporary industrialized nations demand more skilled and quickly renewable labour force for their sustenance. As a result, the higher education systems are burdened with the dispensing function of science and technology. This has also increased the learning years and reduced the active life of the worker. The so called structural and frictional unemployment in the industrialized nations are seen to be again due to the astounding changes in technology and the time gap taken to reach the people through educational systems.

In the labour surplus developing economies, technology has a complex function to perform. Technology in these countries cannot be directly taken to the people as is done in the West since it should reduce the use of labour force. At the same time, it cannot be kept away from the masses since it has a 'magic wand' in its command to cure the backwardness of the backward people. Therefore, it has a limited application with a purpose. The higher education systems in these countries must adopt the rapid changes in science and technology to act as seeds and also as agents of modernization. Therefore, the vocationalisation of education at the secondary stage is inevitable both to limit the access of higher technical education to a large public, and also, produce skilled labour force without creating the consequences of unemployment. Alternatively the industrialised nations can supply the highly specialized science and technology to these nations as aid without draining their best brains on a large scale.

The intensity of science and technology in the industrialized nations indicate that the adverse relationship between internal and external productivity will continue to exist for some more years. As long as the cost of acquiring science and technology continue to rise, the decline in internal productivity cannot be arrested. Similarly, the productive capacity of science and technology will step up the external productivity of higher education. This paradox in higher education in the industrialized nations needs to be examined and resolved. However, the most pertinent question now seems to be the one that points out the effect of this on the enrolments of higher education. The trend seems to have already effected the enrolments in some of the OECD countries. It is reported in some OECD reports that the projected enrolment in non-technical subjects is more than in the technical subjects in the 90's. One of the factor responsible for the disparity in enrolment appear to be the unit costs of higher education. This will definitely influence the demand for enrolment in higher education in the fast growing private sector, in spite of the increase in external productivity. So far, the government has been subsidising the technical higher education making the technical subjects more attractive. Now, the private institutions will become dumping grounds for no-technical subjects at least for some time on the basis of cost. Even if the private sector attracts enough enrolment in technical subjects from among the affluent, because of its higher rates of return (external productivity), can the objective of redistribution of income through education as a social welfare measure be achieved?

III

The ultimate aim of any education is to employ the outputs of the system as inputs in the process of production of the economy. The educated individuals take different roles either in the economy or in the society depending upon their educational background. In other words, the employment opportunities of the people are seriously limited by their educational background and training. The cost of such education and training and their effective employment depends upon the productivity of their skills. It is a known fact that most of the technical subjects are narrowing down to 'specific training'. The cost of such training according to Gary Becker needs to be borne by the firm which employs the workers because the increase in productivity goes to the firm. In the case of general training the individual pays from his pocket. This general training can be broadly interpreted as general higher education, as some of the science and technical subjects are transforming into general subjects with the increase in the application of science and technology. Similarly, new areas of specialization will enter into the production process creating demand for more specialized skills even in narrowly defined fields of study. The reaction of the private higher educational institutions to such a situation needs to be examined.

Another possibility is that all the private institutions will make contracts with firms for the supply of graded products or the firms themselves will enter into the higher education sector for the training of their specific needs. Then the competition among the firms for similar skills will reduce the cost of production and thus increase the internal productivity. The increase in internal productivity will effect the labour market as more number of trained people will enter the skilled labour force. The distinction between specific and general skills will fade out gradually over a period of time due to the increase in the supply of specific skills. This increase in the supply will bound to increase the mobility of labour, making the training as 'general'. Naturally, the worker himself will pay for the expenses of the training. The private institutions will thrive as long as the worker gets what he pays for his training. This influences the labour market and the salary structure because the worker demands a higher wage equivalent to the cost of production of the training plus the wage or a wage equivalent to his marginal productivity. The question of productivity of the worker does not arise once the training is offered by a large number of firms or private institutions as formal education. One more possibility from the increase in external productivity to technical education seems to arise from the side of production. The increase in productivity due to specialization will create less demand for the labour force resulting in unemployment and thus a fall in the demand for higher education. In that case, the private institutions will be forced to close down. This creates a reduction in the standards of products and quality of life or stagnation over a period of time. Government intervention is inevitable at this stage to protect the interests of the future as well as present generations. Higher education may re-emerge then in the form of full-fledged public institution. A full control over the system will be ensured by linking the education with the thoroughly surveyed manpower requirements of the economy. As India has opened up its economy in 1991, the links between higher education and technology need to be kept in mind for economic relations. The fact that OECD and advanced countries have an advantage in trade is because of their strength in higher education and research. This is crucial for our reforms.

This analysis has assumed that the public sector education will have a passive role in future. All this will happen over a period of time. However, it is very difficult to forecast as to how fast the situation is approaching. It is based on some theoretical underpinnings that exist today but not on speculative thinking. However, there is so much that needs to be probed based on sound empirical and theoretical foundations.

The educational reforms initiated in countries like India need to take into consideration the technical efficiency of their exports. The competitiveness of exports depends upon the internal and external productivity of higher education with an emphasis on the relevance of education to exploit their own resources. The Eskimo example is expected to be kept in mind while devising content and courses.

Notes and References

Chalam K.S. **Finances, costs and productivity of Higher Education**, Inter India, New Delhi, 1986.

"Concept and Measures of productivity in Education: Some observations". Economic Papers Warsaw, No.16, 1983.

Susan Gates, **Understanding productivity in Higher Education Annstone**, Rand Corporation, California, 1997.

8

Financial Strategy for Educational Reforms

Most of the policies of education that were made in the past in India could not get through due to lack of a strategy. The strategy of education is generally developed to guide and inspire the whole of education system. The development of a strategy for education, however, must survey its problems as the strategy of education in general must seek to resolve the problems by reciprocal action. A strategy for education more than any other human activity is an exercise in timing. A strategy is also an innovation and must take into consideration the specific conditions of a country. Therefore, there is no strategy which is universally applicable at every stage of education development of every country. As a matter of fact, the UNESCO has denounced such common and universal strategies of education. It has suggested that the countries, particularly the less developed, should develop their own strategies matching their situation, needs and possibilities. The successful implementation of a strategy ultimately depends upon the availability of resources. Thus, the strategy at the final stage essentially develops as a financial strategy. Adam Curle for instance has given a strategy for the development of education in the developing societies wherein he says that, "the education system must be able to make as large an impact on the economy, and as rapidly as possible without excessive investment, and at a later stage when this policy is bearing fruit, to concentrate more on the heavy long term expenditure required for formal education". The Education Commission, 1964-66, has also developed a broad strategy of education for the country and for each level of education. In the area of education finance, the commission has mentioned two lines of action. The first is that the country should strive to allocate the largest proportion of GNP possible to educational development. It follows, therefore, that in the long run education, to some extent, to be self-financing because the increased incomes generated by a relatively better educated labour force would provide resources for greater allocations of education. The second is the need to realize the simple but elementary point that it would be necessary to make every rupee be effectively used in the longest way possible by adopting measures of economies for reduction in wastages and for intensive utilization. The Commission has also provided sixteen measures to realize the above lines of action.

In 1972, J.P. Naik, the member secretary of the Education Commission, 1964-66, has suggested a strategy for the breakthrough in higher education policy in India. After a detailed survey of the problems of higher education, he has suggested some possible solutions like: (1) freezing of grant-in-aid to private colleges by the year 1973-74, (2) recruitment of students to various cadres in the public sector at the end of their secondary stage, (3) employment of unemployed graduates as teachers at the primary and secondary stages, (4) a considerable increase in the fees amount so that the colleges can maintain themselves without aid, and (5) reservation of sufficient amount of seats for weaker sections in all educational institutions. Similar solutions have also been given by various experts for the development of education in India.

The Punnayya Committee appointed by UGC to recommend on the financing of higher education has examined several options to fund higher education. The Committee has opined that collecting 25 percent of the unit cost as fees, keeping the objective of equity and justice, as one of the solutions to increase the resources for higher education. Student loans to cover the cost of education was suggested on the lines of the existing Bank schemes for study abroad based on collateral security. The Ambani and Birla committee on education suggested fee recovery of cost from the students through fees. The planning commission has also done an exercise on funding higher and Technical education. There are conflicting views on the public funding of higher education. However, there is unanimity, among experts as far as financing of school education. The government of India is going to fund the Right to Education initiative from April, 2010. The Act was delayed because of the incongruous estimates made by experts about the cost of public delivery of primary education. In fact, the funding of primary education does not appear to be a problem in view of the increasing revenue received by government through education cess. The centre and states combined together have already been spending Rs.105459 crores on education in 2005 as it comes under concurrent list now. Adding Rs.35,000 crores per year is not a big issue for the governments for the implementation of the Act as per the estimates of the Ministry of Human Resources Development.

The Problems of Educational Finance

There has been an explosion in the social demand for education in almost all the countries of the world. The demand is now for more and better education as people are increasingly convinced that persons with more education obtain higher levels of income. Further, accepting the concept of equality of opportunity and democratisation of education have increased the social pressure for the Government activity in education. It is observed by a World Bank Report that the proportion of GNP devoted to education in the developed countries has increased from 4.0 per cent in 1960 to 7.4 per cent by 2007 and in the developing countries, it has been raised from 2.3 per cent to 4.2 per cent during the same period. (See Table 1.1) Most of the countries are not diverting their sources from other priority sectors to education to meet the social demand for education. As far as India is concerned, the problems can be enumerated as follows:

1. The formal system of education is increasingly turning out to be counter productive.

2. The resource allocations among the three levels of education are found to be more favorable to higher education, though the constitutional obligation of free and compulsory primary education is not yet achieved in the country.

3. Indirect expenditure of higher education such as the expenditure on buildings, equipment, etc., which are responsible for the improvements in the quality of education has grown much slower than the direct expenditure.

4. There is virtually drying up of resources from the private sources and the fees income does not cover even 10 per cent of the institutional cost.

5. The responsiveness of government aid to the private institutions is found to be more than unity.

6. There is an indiscriminate subsidization at the institution level as equal amount of fees are charged from all in come group students (particularly in the highly remunerative professional education).

7. Lower income and occupation background students are under represented in higher education particularly at the professional courses.

8. The private costs of education at different courses are not of the same value and the scholarship amounts given by the social welfare and education departments to the weaker sections and meritorious students respectively, are insufficient to meet their private costs. The subsidy amounts meet only 50 per cent of the costs incurred by the parents of the weaker sections, making the subsidies available to those who are able to provide the remaining 50 per cent of the cost.

9. The educational institutions are not 'cost conscious' in their financial management and as a result most of the institutes are run as non-viable institutes.

The brief survey of the financial problems of education suggests that a systematic strategy is essential for its development. A suggested strategy is outlined below.

Restructuring the Educational System

The cost effectiveness of a course depends upon the educational structure. The present educational structure seems to be sound on paper but in practice its achievements are far from satisfactory. However, some modifications can be made keeping the 10+2+3 system unaltered. At present some of the institutions particularly in the rural areas are maintained as non-viable institutions while others are over-burdened. A systematic school location planning seems to be necessary before granting a school or a college. In some of the states, the +2 stage is attached to the secondary schools where the enrolment starts with 6th class. Instead of keeping the 6th, 7th and 8th classes in the junior colleges, they can be transferred to upper primary schools leaving much scope for more resources at the disposal of the junior colleges for improvements in the quality of instruction. Even post-graduate teachers can be appointed to teach 9th and 10th classes making the +2 stage sufficiently vocational biased. For instance, the curriculum and the programme schedule of the Russian secondary – general and polytechnic – schools with vocational training can be introduced at the secondary stage. In fact this was the intention of the Education Commission, 1964-66, in restructuring the education into 10+2+3.

The unbridled expansion of general higher education was responsible for graduate unemployment. Therefore, enrolment into these courses (taking into account their position in the employment exchanges) must be put under strict control. The non-format education through correspondence courses or distance education can be made an alternative to the formal system of general education. The cost of education through the non-formal system, both to the student and to the public exchequer, is ten times less than the formal system. Along with the formal education colleges, some of the colleges of excellence can be identified to share the burden of post-graduate education. The unit cost estimates of the post-graduate courses revealed that they cost thousands of rupees to the government by way of subsidy to the institutional cost. If the same post-graduate courses are offered in the affiliated colleges instead at the university colleges, the cost can be reduced to ten times as compared to the cost in the university centre. However, the post-graduate courses should be offered only in those colleges where the facilities are available and are marked as institutions of excellence. These institutions can be identified by expert committees constituted either by the university or University Grants Commission. In fact the UGC has already started schemes for such colleges named as 'Lead Colleges' and 'Autonomous Colleges'. Out of these identified colleges, a few of them can be selected for P.G. courses in each university area. This will reduce the financial burden on the university as well as on the government. Then it will be possible for the universities to develop research oriented post-graduate courses in priority areas to carry out both fundamental and applied research to suit the socio-economic needs of the country. The experience with such colleges in the south can be shared with North Indian states where the progress is very slow.

At present, the students' work for about six to eight months in a year, wasting the remaining period of the paid time of teachers and resources either in holidays or in some agitations. Therefore, the course work should be effectively utilized to reduce the unit costs. An attempt has already been made in reducing the length of engineering courses from 5 years 4 years from the year 1980-81. Similar attempts should also be made to reduce the length of the courses by adjusting the syllabi without lowering the standards. All the courses of study should be put to review by expert committees as is suggested by the Venkataramaiah Committee in A.P. on higher education in such a way that they should take the day to day changes in the technology and the requirements of the various sectors of the economy. The curriculum of the students should be arranged in such a way that even the holidays of the students should be productively used for the development of the students as well as the economy by technical institutions which require expensive equipment, should be attached to factories, hospitals, workshops, laboratories, etc., so that the cost of equipment and learning machinery be minimized. The whole traditional system of syllabi and the evaluation be replaced by new and creative methods to give scope for experimentation at least in some fields of study. The practical application of the courses to the situation in the industry, agriculture, services and the society will enable the students to concentrate more of their time for productive work by inculcating new set of values in education like manual labour, learning-by-doing, etc.

Research Universities

There is also a need for changing the methods of teaching in the higher learning institutions. More than half of the time should be devoted to solve practical problems by directly interacting with the problems both in the classroom and outside. This should be introduced not only in the field of sciences and technology but also in social sciences. As the pace of development in science and technology is fast growing making each field contracted to a narrow specialization, the humanization of the subjects are very essential. This needs an interaction of all the courses of study, at least at the beginning of the study of each course.

Research and development activity in India was integrated with university teaching. Even after the establishment of CSIR, DRDO and other laboratories as structures outside the university, the largest producers of Ph.Ds and other research products still come from universities. Therefore, there is a need to review and examine the dual functions of teachers in the universities so that senior faculty can be devoted to research and public service with sufficient incentives for junior faculty to concentrate on teaching so that the university can achieve maximum return from investment on teachers. There is also a need to establish separate universities for academic scientific research functions. The contribution of Private industry to higher education teaching and research seems to be very small. Therefore the university industry link should be strengthened first before they are given a pivoted position in higher eduction.

Linking Education with Manpower Requirements

The problem of graduate unemployment is more pronounced in the faculties of commerce and medicine as compared with other faculties and the quality of education in terms of indirect expenditure seem to be alarming. Therefore, the requirements of the industry and other sectors of the economy should be kept in view in permitting enrolments in different faculties at all stages of education. At the same time, it is to be recognized that as long as the economy is growing at a speed lower that than of the enrolments, there is bound to be a gap between these two, resulting in unemployment. However, the government funds which have been used so far for the production of unemployable graduates can be put to proper use, if a manpower requirement of the economy is considered as criteria for admission policy. There is a positive development in the economy in terms of rate of growth of GDP in recent years. But the service sector component in GDP needs to be kept in mind in devising courses. The ICT has played chaos with our education as the best brains of one generation have gone into it. This needs to be corrected keeping in view our identity and future.

Linking Salaries with the Rates of Return

The economic profitability of private investment in education is one of the factors responsible for the demand for education in India. Further, the axiom 'supply creates its won demand' is applicable to the education situation since graduates' line up for the post of matriculates. In spite of the underemployment, the graduate gets a higher rate of return on his investment. The waiting period of a graduate to get a job as compared with a matriculate is less and the graduates get more salary for the same job due to financial incentives for degrees. Therefore, the salary structure should be modified in such a way that there should be marginal differences in the salary slabs of matriculates and graduates so that the marginal rates of return between these two levels are narrowed down. Along with this, the recruitment policy as suggested by J.P. Naik and M. Blaug in the 1970s should be effectively put into practice. These changes will ultimately make the degrees less attractive.

Importance to Individual Subsidy

The present policy of institutional subsidization through the grant-in-aid system cannot discriminate the students on the basis of their ability to pay and is responsible for the creation of consumers' surplus for the well-to-do. A well administered individual subsidy like the scholarship scheme, which discriminates the beneficiary on the basis of the socio-economics background, can be introduced as an alternative. For instance, Maureen Wood hall has provided the above alternative methods of financing of education. The individual subsidies in higher education in countries like USA are effectively used by both Private and Public Universities to reduce wastage and underutilisation in education.

Alternative Methods of Financing

Along with the alternative methods of financing as suggested above, an income tax on all graduates produced in the country to cover the cost of University education has also been proposed by Howard Glennersten et al, but, the administration of a graduate tax is difficult. In place of the graduate tax, a cess on the net income of the industrial sector seem to be a more meaningful and manageable proportion.

Further, such a cess has sound economic reasoning since economists have already proved that out of the total increase in productivity in the process of production, a significant proportion of the output is contributed by education. Moreover, higher education has been used as a 'filter' to screen the candidates for employment without any burden to the employers. Taking these aspects into consideration, education can legitimately claim a share in the incomes of various sectors of the economy particularly from the industrial sectors. A special educational cess on the income of the industries both in the public and private sectors of the economy is easy to administer as most of the industries are in the organized sector and maintain accounts. In fact, an

Table 1

Alternative Methods of Finance and Subsidizing Higher Education

	Methods of Subsidy		*Methods of Financing*
1.	Direct subsidy to institutions to or reduce fees	1.	General taxation of eliminate income (at central or local level).
2.	Direct subsidy to student in the unconditional grants	2.	General taxation of form of expenditure e.g. sales tax, excise duties (at central or local level).
3.	Direct subsidy to select students form of means tested grants scholarships or business.	3.	Special taxation of in the graduates' incomes.
4.	Direct subsidy to students in the form of guaranteed loans at interest rates below maket rates.	4.	Loan repayments of past students.
5.	Direct subsidy to students in the form of specially provided part time paid employment or meals and accommodation at prices below market prices.		
6.	Direct subsidy to parents or graduates in employment in the form of tax concessions for educational expenditure.		

Source: Woodhall, M., "The Arguments for and against Loans" in Baxier (Ed.).

incentive scheme can also be introduced through this cess by exempting those industries which strictly follow the scheme of on-the-job training and devote a good amount of its resources for research and development purposes. Dr. Manmohan Singh introduced a variant of it in 1993-94 budget. The educational cess on income tax introduced in 2004 and 2007 is being used for Sarva Sisksha Abhiyan, leaving very little for higher education.

The concept of full-cost pricing is popular in the pricing policy of public enterprises in India. Since higher education is an investment good and gives the same type of benefits as that of the investments in physical capital, full-cost pricing principle can be used as a policy of pricing in higher education, keeping the socio-economic background of the students. Of course, some experts have put forward the 'neighbourhood effect of education' argument as a case for the subsidization of education. It is only on this ground that primary and secondary educations are made free in India. The argument cannot be extended to professional higher education where the private rate of return is higher than general education. Further, it is not rational to subsidise higher education to those who are capable of paying for it by keeping the rates of fees at a lower level. However, in a country like India, we have a number of problems to leave education to the over play of market forces. It is very difficult to overcome the problems of market imperfections in the educational sector and the economy may not get the desired skills from the education sector, if it is purely left to market forces. In order to overcome this problem, the alternative methods of subsidization as suggested by Woodhall, particularly items 4, 5 and 6, can be used to support the deserving students who are required to pay the full cost price of education.

An Education Grants Committee in Each State

Education in the states as well as at the centre is financed through various departments. About 21 departments are involved at the state level to finance the education at different levels for various categories of education. But, the involvement of the non-academic departments such a agriculture, medical and health, police, etc., in the administration and distribution of funds for education have been responsible for lack of coordination and thus lack of academic planning. Therefore, a committee at the state level on the lines of UGC should be established to augment funds from various sources and distribute them to various educational institutions. The state committee should be made responsible both for general and professional education for the maintenance of standards in consultation with all India bodies like UGC, AICTE, ICMR etc. Some of the studies on higher education have proved that post-graduate education and research have been neglected in the professional courses as the departments concerned with the management of this sector of higher education are non-academic departments and are more involved in other matters. Therefore, a permanent Education Commission (in place of State Councils) at the state level as a coordinating agency among different departments within the state, and with the centre and all India academic bodies is essential. The recent discussion on the creation of a regulatory authority for higher education amalgamating all the existing bodies like UGC, AICTE etc., is not based on the experiences of other countries. The UK where the UGC was first introduced in 1919 was later abolished and started a new body called Higher Education funding council. The council has 4 branches in different parts of UK. Therefore, it is better to differentiate the grant giving functions of UGC from that of quality control. There can be a separate regulatory body for quality control, but it cannot be entrusted with the functions of financing. The concept itself is not correct as the same body that gives grants to institutions cannot evaluate and regulate its own activities as a regulatory body. It is ethically and administratively found to be unjustifiable, apart from its constitutional validity in a federal setup. The recent incidents of corruption can be tackled by blinging them under vigilence commission and through continous monitoring of staff.

There are several alternatives available in the Asian region including the Japanese experiment. It is reported that the public universities in Japan were given autonomy and made to compete with private universities. They can raise the fees of students for entrance and tution upto 10 percent above the norm of unit cost determined by a Govt. agency

MEXT. It can be experimented here. The UK had a similar system where the unit costs for each course are fixed by the HEFC and the universities are given freedom to operate below that level through better practices. This gives them incentive to work efficiently and save money for the university. We need to rethinic about the autonomous Porouly given to regulatory bodies as they have failed in their mission.

Equality of Opportunity

The Principle of equality of opportunity in a democratic system, that too in a stratified society like India, needs protection for the educational development of certain disadvantaged groups. It is also pointed out by experts that public education is provided to maintain the 'protection principle' and the 'redistribution of income' through the principle of equality opportunity. A system of communal reservation is introduced to protect the legitimate claims of the weaker sections in the educational institutions. But the present system of subsidies benefits those weaker sections who can afford to pay for the receipt of the benefits. It is not possible for majority of the weaker sections among the week to bear the cost of maintenance of their children at the colleges to get the benefits of subsidy. The present system of subsidy covers only 50 per cent of the total private cost and is inherently devised to benefit those weaker sections who can afford to pay the remaining. This can be eliminated if the present scholarship amount is linked with the full cost of education which should also include the opportunity costs. Some of the students of the weaker sections might prefer to go for jobs despite the free education, as they forego the expected earnings, if they are in the college. In order to induce the weakest among the weaker sections, and discourage the strong among the weaker to get all the benefits of education, the scholarship amount should be enhanced to cover the full costs of education for those who really deserve such a help. A new criteria like that of eliminating the rich and the second or third generation of learners from the weaker sections can be evolved to implement such a scheme. A systematic review of the schemes so far implemented for the benefit of the weaker sections by an expert committee consisting of both the weaker sections and experts in the field, is needed to revamp the system of subsidies to benefit the weakest among the weaker sections.

The survey of the financial problems of education brought to light some specific issues for discussion to bring a change in policy. It is on the basis of these issues, a strategy for the development of education is outlined. However, the suggested strategy is not an end by itself. It needs above all the effective participation of parents, the public, the students and the policy maker in carrying out this strategy. A dialogue must be always kept open between the government and the public through seminars, mass media, etc., to elicit the opinions of the people and also involve them in implementing the strategy of education. The efficient implementation of the strategy is, nowadays, essentially a democratic process.

Overcoming Underinvestment through Budget Provisions

Public expenditure on education in general and school education in particular has always received half hearted support. Though the budget is an estimate of revenue and expenditure for the coming financial year, it contains some cues to indicate the direction the government intends to take. The Budget document does contain information on Plan and Non-Plan expenditure. It is increasingly realized that our budgets include very little on the development policy of the Govt. except what was already envisaged in a Plan. The Eleventh Plan approach paper and outlays were accepted in the year 2007 and the current budget is in the second year of the eleventh Plan (2007-11). However, the Finance Minister has the advantage of making use of the tax rates, subsidies and other financial parameters to direct the economy as per the strategy of the Government. He is obliged to meet the declared objectives of the Plan through the financial allocations. We are all aware that the Eleventh Plan was initiated towards a faster and inclusive growth. The Plan has identified some monitarable programmes. In this context, it is to be remembered that the Finance Minister has presented an outcome budget during the year 2007-2008 indicating the physical targets and achievements. Given the theoretical constraints and political compulsions, the Finance Minister has to balance between the expectations of the common man and the financial prudency of a growing economy. It is under this background, the budget is to be read with caution.

Education has been a neglected subject of the governing classes from the very beginning. But, policy makers have been prescribing several schemes and programme to achieve universal literacy by the end of 2015. The target year is now fixed by the UNO under its Millennium Development goals. But, the problem of illiteracy and underinvestment in education in India is a social problem due to several historical and social factors. For instance, elementary education has not been guaranteed as a fundamental right though it was indicated under directive principles of the Constitution tri a long time. The Right to education Act is still in the nascent stage. At the same time, the country has produced world class scientists, engineers and technocrats and is now in a position to reap the returns of IT boom. It clearly shows that there are contradictions in our Education Policy. We have failed to realize the democratization and universalisation of education as a policy. It has been indicated by scholars time and again that the State is under-investing in education and a certain percent of investment is inevitable in order to achieve a specific rate of growth in the economy. The policy-makers and investors who are now projecting shortage of manpower and skills have never pointed out that we have underinvested in education and created islands of excellence and squalor in education. They have also not shown any philanthropy in investing in education of the common man. But, it is suddenly realized that education is important to sustain the present rate of growth and become critical for inclusive growth. The Eleventh Plan indicated that, "development of children is at the centre of the 11th Plan. We are committed to ensure that our children do not lose their childhood because of work, disease and despair".

The enormous gap in resources for education was envisaged to augument through an educational cess in the year 2004-05. It was estimated that an amount of Rs. 5010 crores were collected in 2004-05 and the amount is increased to Rs. 8746 crores in 2006-07. It appears that the extra resources have made the government to strengthen the Sarva Shiksha Abhiyan to address the needs of the children in the age group of 6-14 years. The achievements in the area of 2.41 lakh school buildings, construction of 2.86 lakh toilets, supply of text books to 9.05 crores children and appointment of 10.11 lakh teachers by 2009 is considered to be not a mean effort. It is reported in the economic survey that the mid day meals is strengthened benefiting approximately 9.70 crores children in 9.50 lakh government schools. It is extended upto upper primary stage in 3479 educationally backward blocks during the year 2007. This would not have been possible had there been no additional resources from education cess. But the gap remains to be still larger as there are approximately 18.5 crores children in the age group of 6-14. It means that the government has only covered 50 per cent of the children under MDMS.

It is pointed out that the economy will have a competitive edge if more skilled personnel are involved in the production of goods and services. With the increase in the economic opportunities and the expansion of the global network, the small creamy layer who were benefited by the past investment in public education got exhausted. There is shortage of educated people everywhere. But there are no short cuts for the production of quality education as education requires a long gestation period. It is to be systematically planned by State. We can not leave it to the market. We are now experiencing the shortage of quality personnel in all fields of study including teachers because of the operation of market forces that have attracted all the talent into ICT Sector. Had the state taken a little care and heeded to sane advice to plan and invest wisely a decade ago, the present situation would not have taken place. There are several dichotomies in our technical and higher education. There is shortage of skills in modern sector while there are surpluses in traditional skills. China seems to have expanded its skill base with around 4000 skills while India narrowed its base to around 40 skills through its technical institutes. Now the government is experiencing the heat and would like to expand higher education to overcome the shortage. Again the government is relying on education cess for additional resources for higher education. In addition to education cess of 2% an additional 1% on the aggregate of duties of customs was imposed for secondary and higher education in the year 2007-08 budget. It appears that it has yielded around Rs. 2000 crores. It is expected that the amount will be spent on the scheme for universalisation of access to secondary education (SUCCESS). Unless secondary education is expanded and strengthened, it is not possible to expand higher education. The obsession with an American system of university education in India seems to be misplaced. One can create thousands of universities over night in India by converting some of our affiliated colleges, given the size of a college which is of the same dimension of a university in the USA. But, the problem is quality of teachers, infrastructure and the basic input, students. The plan outlay for higher education during the year 2007-08 was Rs. 2729 crores and non Plan was Rs. 6480 crores. Though the amount of plan and non plan budget is doubled from Rs. 5018 crores in 2006-07 to Rs. 9,000 crores in 2007-08, it was found inadequate given the insufficient infrastructure, ill-equipped teachers and outdated curriculum. It is reported that the UGC has not been able to spend the money allocated to it during XI plan due to several bottlenecks and inconsistencies.

The Finance Minister in his budget speech in 2008 indicated that education as a special service is recognized and the expenditure made by corporate houses on crèches, sports events will be exempt from tax. But there is a change in the budget allocation in 2010-11. This time, school education is given Rs. 33214 crores that includes non-plan allocation of Rs. 2178 crores. The allocation for higher education is Rs.16690 crores that includes Rs. 5694 crores for non plan component. It appears that higher education was given more importance where the increase is around 70 percent compared to 20 per cent increase for school education between 2007-08 and 2008-09. But the allocations in 2010-11 are reversed and school education is given importance. The Finance Minister mentioned in his speech that the right to education Act is getting additional allocation from Finance commission grants in the budget. The Government has already agreed to include inflation adjusted index for calculation of cooking cost and therefore much of the increase in the budget will go for this. The overall allocation for education as a proportion of the total budget of Rs. 658119 crores is only 5.8 percent in 2008-09. This has comedown to around 3 per cent during 2010-11. Therefore, the budget allocations clearly indicate that there is no significant developments in the policy of the government except small schemes like corpus for national merit scholarships, INSPIRE and the continuation of SSA. There is disappointment for those who expected that the recommendations of the Sachar Committee for muslims will be implemented as there is only an allocation of Rs 45.5 crores for modernization of madarasas and some allocation of money for scholarships next year. One of the most progressive steps in social sector spending in post-independence period is taking place through Mid Day Meal Scheme. The govt. has spent Rs.5189 crores and an estimated amount of 21.6 lakh tonnes of food grains consumed. This has definitely improved nutrition levels of children and school attendance.

The budget provisions appear to be disheartening as the Finance Minister in his Economic Survey recognised the shortage of skills and the need for universalisation of secondary education. But, the allocation did not match the size of the big task. There is no provision for development of infrastructure under capital account. Though SSA and UGC provide funds for the development of equipment, library etc., there is a backlog of up to date equipment, buildings etc. The major issue before the government is shortage of talented teachers at all levels. If the Indian boys are in demand in the international labour market, it is because of the unique training that they have received through the Guru-Shishya Parampara. There is no mention about the protection of past depleting talent of teachers either in the budget or in its programmes. This requires much more investment than what is allocated now in the present budget.

The financial allocations made by different state governments and the central government combined are presented in the Table-1. The data clearly show that there is no clear indication as to the inclination towards education among different items of social service expenditure. Though the expenditure on education has increased from Rs. 84111 crores in 2004-05 to Rs.1,98842 crores in 2009-10, the proportion of expenditure on education has almost remained around 10 percent of total budget expenditure. In fact the proportion has come down from 48.7 percent of total social service expenditure in 2004-05 to 44.6 percent in 2009-10. Even if we took at the trend of expenditure on different levels of education over a period of time, the picture remains the same. The so called vision of 6% of GDP for education budget envisaged in 1964-66 has remained a distant dream as it has not yet reached even 4 percent of GDP by 2010-11. It means that the state is allowing private sector to take care of socially important aspect of human development through education.

The data collected by NCERT through the All India Educational survey throw light on the role of private sector in education. The data for the 7th All India Educational survey (2002) published in 2007 can be compared with the 6th survey of 1993. There is a substantial increase in the enrolment at primary stage. But the number of teachers per school has almost remained the same between 2.85 in 1993 to 2.94 in 2002. Out of the total enrolment in primary schools, private un-aided schools constitute 8.5 percent out of total enrolment; S.C. boys constitute 16.6 percent and SC girls 15.8 percent. The enrolment in higher secondary including +2 in states like Andhra Pradesh is around 34 percent only in government schools. Out of 66 percent of enrolment in private schools, 25 percent is in pure private un-aided schools. The rates of fees in these private schools range from Rs.1000 to any where near a lakh of rupees per year. In a country where 40 percent of the population lives below poverty line, enrolment into quality oriented schools remains a distant dream for them or force the parents to entangle in debt trap for providing education to their children.

Conclusion

Recently, the Minister for Human Resources Development has declared that the response to the private investment in education in rural areas was almost zero. If we compare the philanthropic enthusiasm shown during the independence period for support to education like Nai Talim etc, it was very encouraging. Those who talk about private sector's role in education do not look at the value of endowments of universities in USA like Harvard whose value ($36.9 billion) is double the size of GDP of small countries like Srilanka ($ 23.0 billion) or three times that of Jordan ($12.7 billions). Further, the state has total control over the school education which is common for every one, though the managements may vary from one state to another in countries like USA. In Japan, universal literacy was achieved by 1912 through state support during Meiji regime. In other words, the advanced countries of the 20th century have achieved economic and social development by sufficiently investing in their people's education in the past. There is no short cut to achieve universal literacy and minimum levels of learning. The state has to invest in elementary education. There is already a beginning is made here through budget provision to implement Right to education Act. It must continue. If we need to achieve universal elementary education and to produce a universal man as per the Indian Constitution, it is time that we should shift to the idea of 'common school' of D.S. Kothari, Under- investment in elementary education can be surmounted through a simple policy decision of cross subsidy by charging the rich in common school and by imposing an education cess on the private school. As the enrolments in private schools and colleges are growing at a rapid pace, it will generate sufficient funds to support quality elementary education to all. This will have a cascading effect on higher education in India.

References

Ambani M and Birla A, **Report on a Policy Framework for Reforms in Education Govt. of India**, New Delhi, 2001.

Belfield, Clive R and Henry M Levin (Ed.) **The Economics of Higher Education,** Edward Elgar Publishing Ltd. Chettenham, UK, 2003.

Planning Commission, **Report of the CABE Committee on Financing of Higher and Technical Education**, NIEPA, Delhi, 2005.

Punnayya K., **Funding of Institutions of Higher Education :Report of Justice Punnaya Committee**, UGC, New Delhi, 1993.

UNESCO, **Financing Education – Investments and Returns**, Analysis of the World Education Indicators, UNESO & OECD, Paris, 2002.

Table- 8.1

Trends in social services expenditure by Central Government

(Central and State Governments combined)

Items	*2004-05 Actual*	*2005-06 Actual*	*2006-07 Actual*	*2007-08 Actual*	*2008-09 (RE)*	*2009-10 (BE)*
Total Expenditure	8,69,757	9,59,855	11,09,174	12,95,903	16,59,109	18,70,955
Expenditure on Social Services of which	1,72,812	2,02,672	2,39,340	2,88,500	3,98,828	4,45,751
i) Education	84,111	96,365	1,14,744	1,27,547	1,67,981	1,98,842
ii) Health	37,535	45,428	52,126	60,869	76,489	89,314
iii) Others	51,166	60,879	72,470	1,00.084	1,54,358	1,57,595
As per cent of GDP						
Total Expenditure	26.85	25.90	25.89	26.19	29.76	30.35
Expenditure on Social Services Of which	5.33	[illegible]	5.59	5.83	7.15	7.23
i) Education	2.60	2.60	2.68	2.58	3.01	3.23
ii) Health	1.16	1.23	1.22	1.23	1.37	1.45
iii) Others	1.58	1.64	1.69	2.02	2.77	2.56

(Contd.)

(Contd. Table 8.1)

Items		*2004-05 Actual*	*2005-06 Actual*	*2006-07 Actual*	*2007-08 Actual*	*2008-09 (RE)*	*2009-10 (BE)*
		As per cent of total expenditure					
Expenditure on Social Service		19.9	21.1	21.6	22.3	24.0	23.8
of which							
i)	Education	9.7	10.0	10.3	9.8	10.1	10.6
ii)	Health	4.3	4.7	4.7	4.7	4.6	4.8
iii)	Others	5.9	6.3	6.5	7.7	9.3	8.4
		As per cent of social services expenditure					
i)	Education	48.7	47.5	47.9	44.2	42.1	44.6
ii)	Health	21.7	22.4	21.8	21.1	19.2	20.0
iii)	Others	29.6	30.0	30.3	34.7	38.7	35.4

Source: RBI as obtained from Budget Documents of Union and State Governments.

B.E. budget estimates; RE: revised estimates.

9

Addressing Inequity in Human Capital under Foreign Universities Regime

The development of education in India is broadly linked with the socio-economic structure of the society. It was during the East India company rule; the foundation for the modern higher education was laid. But, the system according to some scholars has remained elitist and therefore, did not bring far reaching changes in the country. Further, higher education policy formulation in India from the very beginning was fraught with dichotomies and discord. The imbalances in terms of regional, social and linguistic divides have not been addressed by the colonial rulers that became a serious weakness in our system after independence. The inequalities in the provision of education are also reflected in the formation of the human capital which is considered in modern economies as crucial for development. The benefits of liberalisation according to some researchers have been largely confined to those areas and sections that had the benefit of English medium education particularly in the area of ICT. Now ICT plays a very important role in the formation of human capital.

The concept of human capital is as old as the discipline of political economy. It is common knowledge of every parent that children with more education earn higher incomes than those who have less education. But, it was Adam Smith, the father of political economy who discussed about the economic behavior of educated man in his 'Wealth of Nations'[1] He has said that 'a man educated at the expense of much labour and time to any of those employments which require extraordinary dexterity and skill, may be compared to one of those expensive machines. The work which he learns to perform, it must be expected over and above the usual wages of common labours will replace to him the whole expenses of his education with at least the ordinary profit of an equally valuable capital" (Smith 1776, bk1 chapter 10pt1)[2] Though scholars in economics discipline dates the concept implicitly to Sir William Petty [3] it was however Adam Smith who had explicitly explained the economic value of education. Alfred Marshall[4] who was familiar with the definition of capital of Irving Fisher[5] , 'as simply any stock at any given point of time that yields a stream of services whose value is calculated by capitalizing the income flow', did mention about economic value of education in the first edition of his 'Principles'. But he later dropped the idea, thinking that the individual is his own inalienable property in a non-slave society and therefore cannot be compared with a machine. It is however realized that human beings cannot be treated as produced means of production in the full sense that capital goods are. Because a non-slave society prohibits people from contracting to deliver their future services; 'free' people must keep their human wealth tied up in the form of labour services and cannot hedge against unforeseen changes in the future demand for their services (Blaug. M)[6]. But, the situation has undergone a change in the hands of neo-classical economists such as T.W. Schultz, the noble laureate. The concept is further strengthened with the indulgence of modern economists and management experts who consider 'human beings' as experts and skilled personnel and can be traded in the market in the name of body shopping, franchise players and so on.

It is necessary to understand the unique character of education here. Education is considered as an important item of investment that gives both consumption as well as investment benefits simultaneously. The investor gets consumption benefit in the form of getting psychic income. It is at the same time provides investment return through a stream of life long earnings. It is to be noted that the consumption and investment effects of education are inseparable and investors are invariably conditioned by social, cultural and other factors. However, T.W. Schultz has observed that the consumption element in education in modern times seems to be of minor importance and the future consumption element is consistent with an investment view of education. It was T.W. Schultz again who made an attempt to link the concepts of physical capital and human capital in his study on 'Investment in human capital'(7). He is regarded as the pioneer of the theoretical study with his estimate of stock of human capital in USA for 1900 and 1957 and its overall contribution to growth. There are several such studies on every country today linking education, as one of the important investments in human capital, to economic growth, measured in GDP.

Human Capital and Human Development

The concept of human development evolved in 1990 by UNDP is different from human capital. It is defined as, "the process of enlarging the range of people's choices, increasing their opportunities for education, health care and income and employment and covering the full range of human choices from sound physical environment to economic and political freedom"(8) Human development is now used as an alternative measure of GDP to measure development. It is the end of human capital while human capital is a means to achieve human development. There are concepts like social capital, finance capital, cultural capital etc. that are being used by social scientists to convey the stream of benefits that one gets once these are acquired. It seems, the concept of social capital is being used to explain the caste net works of social relations which are characterized by norms of trust and reciprocity that lead to outcomes of mutual benefit in India.

Human Capital Formation

T.W. Schultz in his presidential address to the American Economic Association in 1961 identified five major categories as investments in human capital. They are: (1) health facilities and services broadly conceived to include all expenditures that affect life expectancy, strength and stamina and the vigour and vanity of a people, (2) on-the-Job training including old style apprenticeship organized by firms, (3) formally organized education at elementary, secondary and higher levels, (4) study programmes for adults that are organized by firms, including extension programmes, notably in agriculture, and (5) migration of individuals and families to adjust to changing job opportunities. Gary Becker [(9)], who has produced a monograph on 'Economics of Discrimination' in 1957 has developed a general theory of investment in human capital based on conventional neo-classical capital theory. He has provided the methods to calculate costs of education and training and the total returns as the present value of the income differentials occurring in each period during the active life of workers in the relevant occupation. He has concluded in his study that the increased supply of skills in the USA during the past century was induced by higher returns to education. He has developed the theory under the neo-classical assumptions of perfect competition, marginal 'product equals wage 'at equilibrium', technical progress as neutral etc. The empirical studies carried by scholars have so far provided four important measures of human capital. They are all related to education.

The measures of human capital are;

(1) the number of school years adjusted for length of year. It is also necessary to adjust the content, structure and types of education, (2) the productivity of earnings of appropriate members of the labour force with weights for years of schooling, (3) the present value of the expected lifetime income yield of education, and (4) the costs of education measured with base year prices including the earnings forgone or opportunity cost. The stock of human capital can be estimated by using any one of the four measurements. Therefore, human capital is broadly

equated with education, though expenditures on health and migration would equally contribute to the flow or stock of human capital. Education is broadly defined as formal or informal schooling including time spent on research, extension and other activities of higher education.

The Stock of Human Capital in India

There are various studies available on the measurement of stock of human capital in India. The recent study conducted by an young European Scholar on the Stock of human capital and Economic growth in Japan, Indonesia and India for the period 1890-2000 is fascinating [(10)]. It is found that the value of stock of human capital in India was $81.64 billion US dollars in 1890 compared to $2.4 billion in Indonesia. In 1895 Japan had a stock of human capital of $ 120.8 billion compared to India with $84.1 billion, a difference of around $ 40 billion. By the time India attained its independence in 1947, Japan had a value of $ 2090.8 billions while India had only $ 224.5 billions. It is found that the increase in the stock of human capital between 1895 and 1947 was 166.9 percent in India while it was 1630.7 percent in Japan. The value of the stock was doubled in Japan with $4805 billion between 1947 and 1980 while it was a five times increase in India ($1037 billion) during the same period. The stock of human capital was found to be $8641 billions in 2000 in Japan while it was $2064 billions in India.

The average years of schooling or education obtained by the population in the age group of 15 years and above is found to be nearly 2 years in Japan in the year 1900 while it was a dismal 0.30 years in India.The years of education have increased substantially in Japan due to Meiji restoration while it was just 1.6 years in India in 1947. The gap between Japan and India continued to remain about 5 years in 1991 the year in which we have started liberalisation akin to advanced countries like Japan and the West.The gap has come down to 3 years as the years of education in india have increased to 7.3 years. But, the average years of education remain more than 10.5 years and still continuing to grow in Japan.The enrolment ratios in higher education in Japan and other advanced countries are several times higher than India as per UNESCO report 2010.

Economists have established that the rate of growth of an economy is related to the availability of human capital in a country. Therefore, the rate of economic growth of India and Japan are found to be very diverse as were their stock of human capital. It is very interesting to see that India had invested heavily on education, during the post-independence period upto 1980 when education including higher education, research and training in the quality institutions was subsidized by the state. This is the period in which the elite of the country were educated at the cost of the ignorant masses particularly those who have not seen the doors of higher education. The policy of education in India seems to be lopsided and prejudiced against some groups and heavily inclined towards few. It is here that we can reflect whether education was universal from the beginning of the East India company rule in India or parochial from the beginning? What is the modernist project of the British? Whether the criticism that Lord Macaulay system of education had replaced indigenous education is misplaced or genuine? What has happened to the policy of education that made only 16 percent of the population literate by the time we attained independence? What is the social base of the underdevelopment of education of certain social groups who have remained poor, ignorant and disadvantaged? Whether the foreign universities that are supposed to provide quality education would address this problem?

Disparities and Divides

The formation of human capital over the years in India has not considered the issue of inequity in the beginning. The inequitable instinct is manifested even in the formation of human capital. India was literate to the extent of 10 percent in 1931, of which the literacy rates for scheduled castes and tribes were only 1.9 percent and 0.7 percent respectively. The disparity between scheduled castes, tribes, service castes and others has remained the same in terms of literacy rates. The gap is much wider if the enrolment rates in quality institutes are considered [11]. The disparity has increased during the last one decade due to the emergence of private sector where the so called reserved categories do not have access. However, the social reform agenda and the state support for education of the educationally backward classes as per the constitution mandate have created a nucleus to press for opportunities. The policy makers have been emphasizing on the creation of equality of opportunity in education, a term seems to have been derived from the American experience to bridge the gap. In this context, some scholars have pointed out that the concept of equality of opportunity is possible within a stratification that has high degree of inequality with a tall and narrow pyramid of society. But India has a graded social inequality and it is structurally built into the caste system. Further, the term opportunity according to some contains a grain of colonial arrogance as if some one is providing a chance to some other to gain entry into education even though they don't deserve it. The American experience is related to settlers and natives. Therefore, the educational opportunities were created there to reduce the racial inequalities between African Americans and whites. Thus, their entry into education is not a right, may be a charity?

Though, the educational differences have slowly declined due to the opportunities created, the class inequalities have continued to exist and have in fact raised the so called status anxiety. It is pointed out by scholars like Murray Milner Jr [12], that it is through redistribution of wealth and income rather than through equality of opportunity in education that inequalities can be reduced. It is an illusion to reduce inequalities through education. On the other hand, the distribution of income would sufficiently create equality of opportunity in education and eliminate inequalities both in education and income. It is established by research studies both in USA and in India that the educational performance of students are broadly influenced by the prestige of the college and the socio-economic status of the students. Therefore, the so called merit is not just based on the numerical marks obtained in an examination, but due to a host of other contributing factors that need to be taken into consideration in judging the worth of a candidate.

The concepts of merit and efficiency have an historical context. I think they are not timeless concepts. Some of the present day business houses were considered inferior to the English or European corporations before independence. They were provided with state support and protection in the initial period to achieve the present commanding heights in their own fields. In fact, the strategy of planning adopted in India has transformed several feudal lords into capitalists. This has facilitated the abolition of Varna category at least among the dvijas to transform them as, upper classes. It is made possible by providing opportunities to utilize their capital both physical and human. The state support for education and subsidies for industry helped them to emerge as great economic players over a period of five decades. But, this did not percolate down to lower castes and they have remained as castes both in rural and urban areas. This is recognized by the planning commission through the identification of the social divides in the eleventh five year plan. In fact, the divides are so flagrant that it is the creamy layer in each caste (including upper castes) that is stinkingly benefitted by the state policies. The recent media reports about the Wealth of the top 100 or 500 billionaires or the occasional out- bursts of scams in the parliament show the inequality of distribution of opportunities. This has once again shown that equality of opportunity is an illusion. The concept may be useful to employ it as an ideological smoke screen but, may not help reduce inequalities, particularly in relation to education.

Foreign Universities and the Future of Higher Education in India

It is under these circumstances, the ministry of HRD is formulating a policy for foreign providers to enter into our higher education system (See Annexure). Let us look at the so called foreign providers and the conditions that are prevailing in some of these countries. The economic slow down together with the demographic conditions in the age group of 18-24 are so desolate in these countries that the future is uncertain? The present unemployment on the one hand and the decreasing opportunities on the other seem to have created a situation of empty class rooms there? The university system in the West particularly the private operators have invested heavily in building the infrastructure. This will go waste if there are no students or few intakes. The universities should either entice third world countries that have demographic dividend to fill up the vacant positions or develop strategies like foreign campuses or twinning programmes to provide prospects to use their infrastructure and superstructure. The situation in India is quite different. We have social divides and disparities across social groups, regions and languages in higher education. The whole of North Indian university structures (except some) are not in a position to compete with some of the southern universities where the medium of instruction is English. How can they get benefited by the foreign university campuses that offer management or soft skills courses in India? Already, a majority of the products of the IITs and IIMs are going into the Finance and ICT sectors irrespective of their specialized knowledge provided by state through subsidy. It is alleged that the intake into these institutes are conditioned by the kind of entrance tests designed in such a way that only few sectors are benefitted compared to many sectors that need these inputs. Why is it happening? Who are the experts involved in the process of admission and their interests? The ministry of HRD needs to look into these aspects before inviting foreign universities as they might also resort to similar techniques and deprive the nation with the essential human resources and manpower for the development of the country .One must realize that the qualified human resources are scarce and they should be productively utilized for the overall development of the country and not to cripple the best brains cramming in to sectors that have commercial interests and deprive other emerging sectors of their utility.

India is not Delhi or Mumbai or Chennai. It is a great country with several diversities. Therefore the policy makers are required to look at the present disparities in the creation of equality of opportunities not in the traditional sense of caste reservations, but in terms of the emerging divides across regions, languages, incomes etc; that will be accentuated by the limited opportunities created by the so called quality institutes of the west. What are the costs (including social and opportunity costs) and benefits of such a policy in a country which is still struggling to implement the Right to Education in 2010? The quality of higher education is to be assessed in terms of our own needs, resources and requirements and not in terms of opportunities to work elsewhere as managers and software workers etc. We need higher education in advanced areas of science and technology to break the inertia of development and not in short-life courses to serve or mimic the West.

The policy makers, it is hoped will look into some of the issues that are raised here and anticipate more such problems in future in view of complex nature of our society. If these concerns are addressed in the formulation of rules for the foreign providers, the entry on an experimental basis may not distress us. Our system of higher education despite of its structural imbalances is well entrenched in some of the most advanced areas of human knowledge. We hope and expect that it can combat and withstand the onslaught in a healthy competition?

End Notes and References

1. Adam Smith, **An enquiry into the nature and Causes of Wealth of Nations**, Ed. Edward Cannan, Methuen and Co.London 1904.

2. Op. cit.

3. Petty William, **Essay concerning the multiplication of Mankind 2nd Ed.** 1668.

4. Marshall. A., **Principles of Economics,** Vol. I, Ed. Sh. Guillebaud, London, 1902.

5. Fisher I, **The Nature of capital and Income**, 1906, Macmillan London.

6. Blaug M. **An Introduction to Economics of Education**, Penguin, Harmendes Worth, 1976.

7. Schultz T.W., "**Investment in Human Capital**" American Economic Review, Vol. 21, 1961 No. 4.

8. UNDP, **Human Development Report**,1990, Oxford University Press,1991.

9. Becker Gary, **The Economics of Discrimination**, The university of Chicago Press, 1957.

10. Bas Leevwen Van, **"The Role of Human capital in endogenous growth in India, Indonesia and Japan,1890-2000"** International Economic History Conference, Helsinki, August, 2006.

11. Chalam.K.S. **Introduction to Educational Planning and Management**, Anmol, New Delhi, 2004.

12. Murray Milner Jr, **Equality of Opportunity as illusion**, Jossey Bass, 1972.

10

Emerging Dichotomies During Economic Crisis

Education became a part of our socio-economic development debate after the Kothari Commission Report was made available in 1966. Though majority of the recommendations were not implemented, the structure of education suggested by the Commission has emerged as a pattern by 1986, the year in which the national policy of education was introduced by the new (Rajiv Gandhi) government. This reminds us about the release of popular document on "financing of higher education in developing countries" by the World Bank in 1986 that recommended the developing countries to concentrate their scarce resources on school education where marginal returns to education are higher compared to other streams of education. This has initiated a debate on the private and social returns to higher education and provided data to show that private returns to higher education are more than social or public returns. This debate was the beginning of the end of public funding for higher education in the Third world countries. This became a dominant policy prescription in some of the developing countries thereafter. The recommendations of the World Bank have been accepted in principle and some scholars and policy makers in our country have initiated a argument on the "concept of higher education as public good or merit want versus private good". It was tentatively agreed by the policy makers that since higher education provides life long earnings and benefits to the individual, there is no economic reason in providing subsidy or state support to such an activity which is purely private. Remember the late 80s the period when a debate on the Dunkel draft of GATT was introduced in different parts of the world for discussion that ultimately led to the formation of the WTO. We are reminded of the WTO in the context of educational policy, because the WTO proposal for GATS came into operation in 2004. It was clearly mentioned in GATS that higher education markets must be opened for international competition that should include courses, the establishment of academic programmes and institutions, the open market for teachers and market facilities for all kinds of academic products without any restrictions. This is relevant in the context of making educational policies of the developing countries including India. The whole argument of making a distinction between higher education and school education and to consider higher education as a commodity or private good was initiated to make way for private markets in education for the developed countries. But some of the academics and scholars have accepted the GATS proposals with some reservations without looking at higher education as a distinct category in education.

Half Life of Knowledge

There are broadly two different streams of higher education, categorized on the basis of the speed of acquisition and deterioration of knowledge. One, the vocational and practical streams of higher education that provide skills and competencies to individuals which can be used in the labour market in the short run, two; the academic and basic knowledge of higher education that provide theoretical and abstract concepts of wisdom to the whole society at large to transform and bring development in the long run. Therefore, we must make a distinction between short life of knowledge and the long life of knowledge. The skills and abilities that are given to the individuals in the former category is of short duration in nature such as a fashion technology, industrial processes, BPO Skills, etc. There are courses like Physics, Mathematics, Economics, Political Science, Art and Culture etc., that provide benefits to the society at large on a permanent basis and will have a long life. Therefore, higher education that provides long life knowledge to the society must be supported and strengthened to make the society competitive and sustainable. The skills and knowledge that have a character of withering content at a short period of time need to be left to the individuals to bear that cost (those who got such skills will be individually benefited) and they need not be supported by the state unless the state feels that certain social groups are not adequately represented in such skills. Thus, the educational policies that are being followed in developing countries particularly in countries like India need to be looked at from a long run perspective given the recent developments in the international labour market, particularly in the area of ICT.

Subsidies in America

The experiences of higher education in the US seem to have not been reflected systematically by scholars to learn lessons in India. The political economy of higher education was studied by several scholars there and found that the largest category of federal financial support is 'student aid' that constitutes around 50 per cent of federal expenditure on higher education. Unlike in India, government subsidy to higher education is given to students and therefore, it is difficult to know to what extent the state supports an institution in the U.S. That does not mean the private and public institutes do not receive grants. It was however, found that, 'though enrolment into private colleges and universities was around 25 per cent, they receive 44 per cent of federal dollars spent on higher education'. It means that more number of students who receive federal aid join the private institutes and bring State funding to sustain the institutes. Hence the federal subsidy per student is greater at private than public institutions [(1)]. It is also found that 50 per cent of research grants in universities come from the government. But the Indian scholars policy makers etc., who were trained in the US speak differently when it comes to subsidies to higher education. There is something wrong with the policy formulations of our American trained Indian experts.

Educational policy as an action plan of state is broadly related to the discipline of political economy. We are not discussing here the political economy of higher education so as to understand the class nature of an educational policy. However, we must remember here that the educational policy in India was initiated by the British with an objective to bring modernization(2). I have discussed about the three streams of modernization project of the British elsewhere in a book and therefore, I am not going to discuss it in detail here. The educational policy of the British was launched after the 'Woods ispatch' and it was also responsible for the development of higher education including the establishment of modern Universities in India. However, when the progress of the education initiated by the East India Company was evaluated by the Hunter Commission in 1882, Mahatma Jyoti Rao Phooley contested the policy of the British saying that it had benefited only the upper castes and therefore wanted protection for the disadvantaged. It appears that was the beginning for the policy of caste based reservations implemented first in the educational institutions to satisfy Joti Rao Phuley in Bombay presidency and to Muslims of Ganjam district in Madras Presidency.

Anglo-Saxon Model of University

As far as higher education policy is concerned, Lord Curzon took interest in the expansion of it saying that university is a place for scholarly activity. After independence, the Govt. of India has appointed Dr. Radha Krishnanan Commission in 1948 to review the system of higher education and to suggest measures for its improvement. If we wanted to understand the educational policy of higher education in India, it is necessary to look at the various attempts made by the Government to evolve a policy of education. Similarly, we need to look at Kothari Commission of 1964-66, 1986 National Policy of Education, the Ambani- Birla Report on education in 2000 and the National Knowledge Commission of Sri Sam Pitroda that have made recommendations to change the contours of higher education in India from time to time. It is also necessary to look at the way in which higher education in India was influenced by various international policies pursued by different countries. It is very strange to find that Indians do not know much about their Eastern neighbours who were once influenced by India. The higher education policy of India including the content, programmes, methods and process are all influenced by the western countries, particularly Anglo-Saxon and the modern universities in India were not based on its traditional structures of Nalanda or Vikramasila or Amaravati. It was pointed out by scholars like Philip Altbach that there are three university systems now prevailing in the world. One is the Anglo-Saxon, the second is German and the 3rd category is an indigenous system developed by Japan, Thailand, China etc. It was Philip Altbach who has also coined the concept of 'pseudo universities' as those who offer a narrow and specialized curriculum for meeting vocational qualifications without providing general education or serving the broader public purposes of traditional universities[(3)]. They are seldom concerned with research and other activities except that they might increase in the programmes which bring revenue. It is in this context, that we need to examine the educational policies and reforms pursued in India and other developing countries during the last two decades which are basically providing the qualified manpower to the requirements of the western or Anglo-Saxon countries.

The demand for education in India during the last two decades, when there was explosion of higher educational institutions was only a derived demand from the manpower requirements of the West and not necessarily to meet the needs and requirements of the Indian economy and society. Therefore, it was found that all the higher educational institutions in the country were at one time competing with each other to provide the eligibles or the inputs to the management institutes and to the IT sector without realizing that they were all created on the basis of a particular policy adopted in the West particularly in the U.S. As a result of this trend, the best brains of the country and the scarce resources of the nation were utilized to supply the necessary manpower required by the West. There is no doubt, they have brought remittances and this has further helped the economy to grow to some extent. But, it was only for a short period. No one has studied the impact of the short-term benefits on the long run interests of the country as the best brains were already crippled due to short life courses. It is now found that the demand for specific manpower has come down due to the economic crises in USA and Western Europe. It is in this context, we need to look at our structure of higher education which has responded to Western demand. Higher education has a gestation period of around 20 years and the short cut that we have used to benefit from the western demand is going to create problems now. Several engineering colleges in some of the southern states are about to be closed due to lack of sufficient in take. There is no indication yet, that the educational policies of the Government are going to be redrawn given the present international economic scenario. The reforms package initiated by the government need to look at this emerging trend.

Impact of Economic Crisis on Education

There is a strong relationship between the economic development and the demand for higher education. OECD has commissioned some studies in the 1970s and 80s to establish the link between educated employment and economic growth. Therefore, it is demonstrated that the countries that wanted to pursue an independent policy should first relate their education with the manpower requirement of the economy. If a country wants to make money looking at the short run demand for manpower in the West or elsewhere, it will have problems sooner or later as it is a short-sighted policy. In this context, using such short term policies in a large and diverse country like India is questionable, where equality of opportunity in education is still a distant dream. Accordingly, there are several implications for education from the recent developments in the world economy. We have not prepared any institutional structures to retrain the repatriates from abroad and from different sectors of the economy who are going to be laid off due to economic meltdown. The latest report of the Knowledge Commission seems to have not addressed this problem.

It seems, the government was not properly advised on the implications of short life courses. There was some kind of a crowding affect in higher education during the last one decade without a proper analysis of the employment potential of the service sector. It is not the finance capital, but the human capital that comes to the rescue of a nation when it is in crisis. There are some research studies conducted by scholars like Prof. T.S. Papola who in one of his recent papers found that "services sector which has been the main contributor to GDP growth in recent years, raising its share from 36 per cent in 1972-73 to 54 per cent in 2004-05, has not made commensurate contribution to employment growth; and its employment intensity has experienced a steep decline over these years"[(4)]. In fact, he is of the opinion that the growth of employment in manufacturing sector particularly in the unorganized sector has been consistently higher than overall economy over the long period. It is also supported by the recent NSS Survey that estimated around 42 Million artisans and small business holders survive and contribute to the economy without any knowledge support. In fact, Indian Society and the academic world have never recognized the knowledge base of these groups. The skills of the artisans were never given an academic status either in the formal or informal streams of learning. This has come out clearly in the recent XI Plan document wherein it is stated that in India we are offering technical skills through the ITI and vocational schools in only 40 skills or trades whereas in China 400 skills were promoted and offered as courses. The vocational schools of the Chinese seem to have not been interested only in providing sophisticated management and IT skills as we do in India. China has been promoting the traditional skills of the artisans and it has further improved the skills of the people through educational programmes to enhance its competitive edge in the market.

Emerging Dichotomies in Education

In other words, there are several dichotomies that need to be recognized and resolved to strengthen the higher education in our country. The recent recommendations of the National Knowledge Commission has highlighted the demographic strength of the nation saying that 550 million people in the age group of less than 25 years of age in India will be one fourth of the world by 2025 and it is to be capitalized through the process of providing skills and knowledge by creating more universities and institutional structures[5]. Though the National Knowledge Commission has made some interesting recommendations like the national skills development with a national skill inventory, providing legal support to intellectual property rights and ideas like creation of Independent Regulatory Authority for higher education in place of UGC, AICTE etc., it seems the Commission did not shed light on our own strengths and weaknesses. In fact, the Commission did not mention how knowledge is to be disciplined to offer it as a course in a college or university as we know that all information is not knowledge and all knowledge is not wisdom to be offered as an academic programme. The institutional mechanism that was recommended by the Commission may not help to strengthen higher education if the content, method and process of higher education duplicate the existing Anglo- Saxon model of higher education. We have lived with these models for 200 years, but we need to develop our own system of higher education based on our own resources. In this context, I have listed out some dichotomies in our education that might help us to understand the realities. A dichotomy is a method of looking at a phenomenon which is mutually exclusive. The future of our higher education depends on how we resolve these dichotomies.

(a) We have a situation in our school education where thousands of teachers' posts are lying vacant and the Parliament has just taken a decision on the Right to Education Bill. But we wanted to have 1500 universities by 2015 mostly based on the single campus model of the American University where the college age population is declining by 15 per cent in a decade since 1977. Therefore, the universities in the US survive on the export of education. The fact is that the enrolment in higher education has not yet reached 15% of the corresponding age group in India.

(b) There are teachers in some of our unaided affiliated colleges who are paid less than Rs.2000/- per month as salaries. But we wanted to create research hubs to compete in the international market. The fact remains that the researchers per a million population is 119 persons in India while it is 708 in China and 4605 in USA. (see Table 1.1)

(c) We do not have sufficient colleges that have laboratories and black boards but wanted to introduce credit transfers to make the higher education system resilient and modern. There are 17500 colleges and 350 universities in the country and some of these colleges are as big as a university in USA. But as per NAAC only 30 per cent of the universities are considered as 'A' grade and the rest are mediocre.

(d) We have students whose MLL is very poor and cannot do simple arithmetic but wanted to invest heavily to develop subjects like Mathematics and Sciences. The enrolments data show that the socially disadvantaged has not yet reached 50 per cent of the corresponding age group in secondary and higher secondary education in India.

(e) We have private universities and pseudo universities that have a network of their own to draw quasi-rent due to excess demand in certain disciplines. But we wanted to create an inclusive education where students of reservation communities do not have access. The teachers' quality in some of the universities is so poor that the disadvantaged groups will be double marginalized if admitted in these institutes while some institutes manipulate merit.

(f) There are colleges in the government sector where students from the reservation communities study traditional subjects like B.A, B.Com and B Sc without sufficient infrastructure in the colleges. They have emerged as exclusive institutes of the weaker sections and certain communities stopped sending their children to these institutes and courses. But, we wanted to provide equality of opportunity by creating more number of seats in the IITs and IIMs as a part of inclusive education. It is reported that the rich and the powerful who were benefited by higher education in the past in India are now cross subsidizing education in the US (Indian Students) by paying fees and other charges to the extent of Rs.18, 400 crores per year.

There are several such dichotomies that can be enumerated to comprehend the weaknesses of our reforms and to provide reasonable solutions based on our strengths. Already, the USA, UK and other governments in the West have started providing additional grants to disadvantaged groups by bringing a legislation like 'No child left behind', teacher incentive fund, increasing federal grants by 30% to historically black colleges and universities, concept of adjunct teachers etc, based on their own situation and in comparison to the international test scores of students of Netherlands, Denmark, Sweden and other countries. Let us hope that the government will seriously consider the experiences of these countries in devising our own policies that relate to our own conditions and future.

Notes and References

1. John W. Sommer (Ed.) **The Political Economy of Higher Education**, Rutgers- The State University, New Brunswick, 1995.

2. Chalam K.S. **Modernisation and Dalit Education** Rawat Publications, Jaipur, 2008.

3. Philip Altbach, **"The Political Economy of Internationalisation of Higher Education cooperation: Structural Realities and Global Inequalities"**, Nuffic Conference, The Hague 23-25, May, 2005.

4. Papola T.S. **"Industry and Employment: Dissecting Recent Indian Experience"**, in Seminar on Industrial Development and Economic Policy Issues, ISID New Delhi, 27-28 June, 2008.

5. Govt. of India, **Towards a Knowledge Society** www. knowledge commission.gov.in

11

Deconstructing Dichotomies through Public Accountability

While the development of higher education in India reaches international standards and attracts clients from outside the system, it encounters new ways of dichotomies. In a developing country with a history of social tensions, the contradictions in education will be increasingly pronounced. One possible way of identifying the dichotomies and resolving them appear to be possible through the introduction of public accountability. The resolution of the dichotomies depends upon first on how we are able to deconstruct the dichotomies and contradictions. We have identified several dichotomies in the education policy and reforms in the previous chapters. An attempt is made here to look at the possible solution through accountability. However, we are not deconstructing the dichotomies on the lines of critical theory in social sciences. We have used the concept of deconstruction to understand the contradictions inherently present in polices that are manifested as dichotomies. They were discussed in the main text.

Evaluation and accountability are interrelated terms in education. The evaluation of the programme outputs in education provides the necessary ground to account for its activities to society or its users. The concept of accountability, it seems, is derived from business management and democratic practice wherein it is generally insisted that the business organization should be accountable to the shareholders of the concern through the Board of Directors. The system in its turn employs number of evaluation methods to find out the efficiency of the system. These management concepts have been employed in the education sector when education had taken the turn of a mixed enterprise in the capitalist market economies in the 1970s. However, a lot of controversy as to the application of these concepts to higher education appears to have been continuing even today. It is necessary that we should develop a mechanism through which the private operators of higher education (Indian or foreign) are make to accountable to the people in general and stake holders in particular.

Concept of Accountability

The concept of accountability has been made popular in India after the National Policy on Education, 1986. The concept has been used along with the concept of autonomy. The enthusiasm in introducing these ideas into the education system appears to be due to the intention of the government to open up the system for private philanthropy in the 1990s. The question of the utility of privatization in higher education in a Third World country like ours is a different problem and it need not startle us here. However, the concept of accountability gets much significance only in the light of the involvement of the private interests. It does not mean that higher education is not publicly accountable. But, we have taken it seriously as long as the finances for higher education have been derived from the public exchequer.

Now the higher education system in the country is taking the shape of a mixed enterprise. The private shareholders of higher education system can be identified here as the students or their parents who are either paying huge capitation fees and or nominal tuition fees. Naturally, they are all concerned about the systems' output and its external productivity. In this context, accountability, particularly public accountability, in higher education assumes a greater significance. Further, the country's human resources are being diverted on the basis of the market demand elsewhere, depriving the country to make use of them for our own needs and requirements. The remittances that they send may not be sufficient to address our immediate needs as the gestation period of higher education is 20 years. Today the opportunity costs of the dissipated manpower need to be estimated and used to resolve the dichotomies.

Objectives of Higher Education

In order to ensure private or public accountability of a system, it is foremost important to note that the system should make itself clear as to what it is aimed at or simply what are the objectives of higher education. But, the Indian system of higher education or its units, colleges or universities, have never defined the objectives for which they are offering courses. One may repeat here Bloom's Taxonomy of educational objectives. But, it has very little relevance or place in higher education as the Bloom's three categories are not mutually exclusive when applied to higher education. Even the National Policy of reform package has not come out clearly with the objectives of higher education of India. Therefore, we have to rely on unwritten and tradition-based objectives of higher education. Assuming for the moment that the objectives of higher education of the West are equally applicable to our situation in an era of globalization, we can enumerate the objectives of higher education as follows:

1. University and colleges are first and foremost expected to provide general, post-secondary education of a kind that will challenge and develop the capacities of the ablest groups of school leavers,

2. The higher education system is to assist in fulfilling the manpower needs of the expert society in various categories of professions,

3. The provisions of high level specialized education and training for future members of the academic profession and for members of occupations,

4. Act as screening mechanism through frequent testing for those who will subsequently seek high level employment in the public service, industry, commerce and other professions,

5. Provide avenues of social mobility for the able sons and daughters of working class families through a provision of scholarships etc., and make the education socially relevant,

6. Offer varieties of services and expert advice to the immediate community,

7. As exemplars of national policies such as the provision of equal opportunities for women and other socially disadvantaged groups and nurture the transmission of a common culture and common standards of citizenship,

8. Prepare men and women for the subsequent performance of leadership roles in society and economy, and

9. Come out with solutions to tackle economic, social and technological problems of a growing economy.

The above list of objectives of higher education is only illustrative. But as one American Educationist two decades ago put it: "Almost any educated person could deliver a lecture, entitled, 'the goal of the university'. Almost no one will listen to the lecture voluntarily. For the most part, such lectures and their companion essays are well-intentioned exercises in social rhetoric, with little operational content. Efforts to generate normative statements of the goals of the university tend to produce goals that are meaningless or dubious". Therefore, it is necessary to quantify and develop certain performance indicators based on the objectives so as to ensure a systematic accountability.

Efforts have been made to quantify the performance indicators of higher education system in the country. Some experts in India have indicated quantitative and qualitative indicators of accountability for autonomous colleges in the country. The present author has also done an exercise to measure the internal and external productivity of higher education in Andhra Pradesh. (See previous chapter on productivity) These studies can be used as the basis to develop advanced methods of performance indices in future. These indicators are essential because of the fact that without these indicates, accountability cannot be ensured. In some of the advanced countries, the following ratios and rates have been used as performance indicators.

1. Student success and graduation rates.

2. The average length of study for a given diploma or degree.

3. Student work load and student-teacher ratio.

4. Unit costs of the educational programme.

5. Accessibility to which graduates go and their reputations as judged by external observers.

6. The destinations to which graduates go and their reputations as judged by external observers.

7. The number of publications of the staff.

8. The volume of activity of staff in undertaking consultancies and producing inventions.

9. The frequency with which the faculty are invited to participate in the high level scientific conferences.

10. Award of major prizes, patents and distinctions to the staff.

The above indicators constitute the index of performance of the institute as a whole. But, if one desires to expect accountability from each participant of the process of higher education, it is possible to divide the indicators as institutional indicators system indicators etc. But, the individual unit-based accountability should not be insisted upon for public accountability. It can be used only as an internal audit. In a situation of public accountability which can be done through annual reports, parliamentary questioning, participation of public in the meetings of the institutions etc., accountability should be based on a composite index of all the above indicators combined. This will protect the institutions from external attack and damage. As a matter of fact, all the participating units in the internal process of the system are responsible for the performance of the system and accordingly they should be projected as a collective unit in public.

The Planning Commission has identified several disparities and divides in our society. The system of higher education that has evolved in the country through various reform programmes, needs to address these issues through its content, methods, process and governance. India had a written constitution. The founding fathers had a vision and have anticipated this predicament and then resolved the preamble and the structure. The system of education in the country cannot isolate itself from the overall objectives of the constitution and shall never contradict it. Thus, any reform or policy of the government should correspond is the will of the constitution so as to resolve the emerging dichotomies through public accountability and other democratic methods.

The Emerging Issues

1. How is it possible to account for the misuse or abuse of education? For example, if a B.Com. graduate uses his skills in accountancy to conceal income in the tax returns, dubious accounting etc., how is the system responsible?

2. How is it that the Principal or the management of an institution is accountable for the curriculum that has been imposed by a university or by government?

3. Is it possible to measure traits like the ability to think critically, self-esteem, independence, self-reliance, increased tolerance, empathy, etc., which are also the major objectives for which liberal education has been offered in this country?

4. After all higher education is a part of government and accountability has been maintained by the government and why should the institution again be made accountable?

5. Is there any compatibility between intellectual freedom and accountability?

End Notes

(1) The objectives of education are to be derived from the overall objectives of the society based on tradition and history. We have a written constitution and the objectives of education are to be derived from it. We can not have objectives from others traditions or constitution. But, we are assuming here that even if the dominent culture of the elite today is (Western and Anglo-Saxon) adopted for the systems of higher education, public accountability is to be ensured.

Annexures

Higher Education Reforms -Draft Bills

THE NATIONAL ACCREDITATION REGULATORY AUTHORITY FOR HIGHER EDUCATIONAL INSTITUTIONS BILL, 2010

A BILL *to make provisions for assessment of academic quality of higher educational institutions, programmes conducted therein and their infrastructure through mandatory accreditation by independent accreditation agencies and to establish a statutory Authority for the said purpose and to provide for matters connected therewith or incidental thereto.*

BE it enacted by Parliament in the Sixty-first Year of the Republic of India as follows:-

CHAPTER I

PRELIMINARY

1. (*1*) This Act may be called the National Accreditation Regulatory Authority for Higher Educational Institutions Act, 2010.

(*2*) It extends to the whole of India except the State of Jammu and Kashmir.

Source : www. ParliamentofIndia.gov.in

(*3*) It shall come into force on such date as the Central Government may, by notification in the Official Gazette, appoint.

2. This Act shall apply to all higher educational institutions other than the higher educational institutions engaged mainly in agricultural education and research and the programmes of study conducted therein.

3. (*1*) In this Act, unless the context otherwise requires,—

(*a*) "academic quality" means the quality of teaching, learning and research and consequently their contribution to enhancement of knowledge and includes physical infrastructure, human resources (including faculty), administration, course curricula, admission and assessment procedures, governance structures, of the higher educational institution;

(*b*) "accreditation" with its grammatical variations means the process of quality control in higher education, whereby, as a result of evaluation or assessment or by any other scientific method followed by accreditation agencies, a higher educational institution or any programme conducted therein is recognised by it as conforming to parameters of academic quality and benchmarking of such academic quality determined by the appropriate statutory regulatory authority;

(*c*) "accreditation agency" means an agency registered under section 23;

(*d*) "appropriate statutory regulatory authority" means any regulatory authority established under any law for the time being in force, for co-ordinating or determining or maintaining the standards of higher education;

(*e*) "Authority" means the National Accreditation Regulatory Authority for Higher Educational Institutions established under section 5;

(*f*) "certificate of registration" means the certificate of registration of an accreditation agency granted under section 23;

(*g*) "Chairperson" means the Chairperson of the Authority appointed under section 6 of this Act;

(*h*) "code of ethics" includes integrity, objectivity, professional competence, professional conduct, avoidance of conflict of interest, transparency and information disclosure and such other ethical principles as may be specified by regulations;

(*i*) "college" means any institution, whether known as such or by any other name which provides for a course of study for obtaining any qualification from a university and which, in accordance with the rules and regulations of such university, is recognised as competent to provide for such course of study and present students undergoing such course of study for the examination for the award of such qualification;

(*j*) "degree" means any such degree, as may, with the previous approval of the Central Government, be specified in this behalf by the University Grants Commission, by notification in the Official Gazette, under section 22 of the University Grants Commission Act, 1956;

(*k*) "diploma" means such award, not being a degree, granted by a higher educational institution certifying that the recipient has successfully completed a course of study of not less than nine months duration;

(*l*) "distance education system" means the distance education system as defined in clause (*e*) of section (*2*) of the Indira Gandhi National Open University Act, 1985;

(*m*) "higher educational institution" means an institution of learning including a university, an institution deemed to be university, a college, an institute, an institution of national importance declared as such by an Act of Parliament, or a constituent unit of such institution, which is imparting (whether through conduct of regular classes or distance education system) higher education beyond twelve years of schooling leading to the award of a degree or diploma;

(*n*) "institution deemed to be University" means an institution declared by the Central Government as deemed to be a university under section 3 of the University Grants Commission Act, 1956;

(*o*) "Member" means Member of the Authority appointed under of section 6 and includes the Chairperson;

(*p*) "memorandum of association" means, in case of a company, such memorandum as defined under sub-section (*28*) of section 2 of the Companies Act, 1956, or in case of a society, such memorandum as specified under section 2 of the Societies Registration Act, 1860;

(*q*) "National Educational Tribunal" means the National Educational Tribunal established under the Educational Tribunals Act, 2010;

(*r*) "non profit organisation" means an organisation being a company registered under section 25 of the Companies Act, 1956 or a society formed and registered under the Societies Registration Act, 1860 or a trust formed under the Indian Trusts Act, 1882 or any other law for the time being in force, which —

(*i*) undertakes any venture, profession, vocation or business without profit motive or gainful objective;

(*ii*) applies its surplus or other income in promoting its objects;

(*iii*) prohibits payment of any of its surplus or other income to its members, except by way of salaries or allowances payable for services rendered for carrying out such venture, profession, vocation or business;

(*s*) "notification" means a notification published in the Official Gazette and the expression "notify" with its cognate meanings and grammatical variation shall be construed accordingly;

(*t*) "programme" means a course or programme of study leading to the award of a degree or a diploma in a higher educational institution;

(*u*) "prescribed" means prescribed by rules made by the Central Government under this Act;

(*v*) "regulations" means regulations made by the Authority under this Act;

(*w*) "State Educational Tribunal" means a State Educational Tribunal established under the Educational Tribunals Act, 2010;

(*x*) "university" means a university established or incorporated by or under a Central Act, a Provincial Act or a State Act, and includes an institution deemed to be university;

(*y*) "Vice Chancellor" means the chief executive of a university, by whatever name called, and includes a Head of an institutions of national importance declared as such by an Act of Parliament.

(*2*) Words and expressions used and not defined in this Act but defined in the University Grants Commission Act, 1956 and not inconsistent with this Act shall have the meanings respectively assigned to them in that Act.

CHAPTER II

OBLIGATION FOR ACCREDITATION OF HIGHER EDUCATIONAL INSTITUTIONS AND PROGRAMMES CONDUCTED THEREIN

4. Every higher educational institution and every programme conducted therein shall be accredited in accordance with the provisions of this Act and the rules and regulations made thereunder and assessment of such accreditation shall be made before such institution starts the

process of admission to such programme: Provided that a higher educational institution, (other than a higher educational institution engaged mainly in medical education) existing before the commencement of this Act, shall, within a period of three years from the date of such commencement, make an application to an accreditation agency for accreditation of such institution or programme conducted therein under this Act:

Provided further that a higher educational institution engaged mainly in medical education and existing before the commencement of this Act, shall, within a period of five years from the date of such commencement, make an application to an accreditation agency for accreditation of such institution or programme conducted therein under this Act:

Provided also that the accreditation agency, to whom such application for accreditation has been made by such higher educational institution, shall, within a period of one hundred and eighty days from the date of such application, undertake and complete accreditation under this Act:

Provided also that the higher educational institution which has been accredited before the commencement of this Act by an agency setup by or under any law for the time being in force, shall be deemed to be accredited under this Act for the period of accreditation by such agency: Provided also that in case the higher educational institutions referred to in the first or second proviso fails, to, make an application for accreditation or obtain accreditation of such institution or programme conducted therein, within the specified period, such institution shall, without prejudice to any action that may be initiated by the appropriate statutory regulatory authority or proceedings under any law for the time being in force be liable for penalty under section 41 of this Act.

CHAPTER III

NATIONAL ACCREDITATION REGULATORY AUTHORITY FOR HIGHER EDUCATIONAL INSTITUTIONS

5. (*1*) The Central Government shall, by notification, establish, for the purposes of this Act, an Authority to be known as "the National

Accreditation Regulatory Authority for Higher Educational Institutions".

(*2*) The Authority shall be a body corporate by the name aforesaid, having perpetual succession and a common seal, with power, subject to the provisions of this Act, to acquire, hold and dispose of property, both movable and immovable, and to contract, and shall, by the said name, sue or be sued.

(*3*) The head office of the Authority shall be at New Delhi.

6. The Authority shall consist of a Chairperson and four other Members, of whom at least one shall be woman, to be appointed by the Central Government.

7. (*1*) A person shall be qualified to be appointed as the Chairperson, if such person—

(*a*) is not less than fifty-five years of age;

(*b*) is of ability, integrity and standing, and has adequate knowledge and experience of at least twenty-five years in dealing with matters relating to higher education and research;

(*c*) is, or has been, a Vice Chancellor of any University, or a Head of an institution of national importance.

(*2*) A person shall be qualified to be appointed as a Member, if such person—

(*a*) is not less than fifty-five years of age;

(*b*) is of ability, integrity and standing, and has adequate knowledge and experience of at least twenty-five years in higher education and research or legal matters.

(*3*) Out of the four members referred to in section 6, one each shall be chosen from amongst—

(*a*) Professors in the field of medical education in any University or an institution of national importance;

(*b*) Professors in the field of science or technology in any University or an institution of national importance;

(*c*) Professors in the field of social sciences or humanities in any University or an institution of national importance;

(*d*) persons having knowledge and experience in legal matters.

8. *(1)* The Chairperson and other Members of the Authority shall be appointed by the Central Government from a panel of names recommended by a Selection Committee consisting of—

(*a*) Cabinet Secretary ....Chairperson;

(*b*) Secretary in charge of higher education in the Ministry of Human Resource Development of the Government of India..........Member;

(*c*) an expert in the field of medical education ....Member;

(*d*) an expert in the field of agricultural education and research ....Member;

(*e*) an expert in the field of legal education ....Member;

(*f*) Chairman, University Grants Commission...... Member.

(*2*) The Secretary to the Government of India dealing with the higher education shall be the convenor of the meetings of the Selection Committee.

(*3*) The experts in the fields specified in clauses (*c*) to (*e*) of sub-section (*1*) shall be nominated, in such manner as may be prescribed, by the Central Government.

(*4*) The term of the Selection Committee and the manner of selection of panel of names shall be such as may be prescribed.

(*5*) No appointment of the Chairperson or Member of the Authority shall be invalid merely by reason of any vacancy in the Selection Committee.

(*6*) Subject to the provisions of sub-sections (*1*) to (*5*), the Selection Committee may regulate its own procedure.

9. (*1*) The Chairperson and the other Members of the Authority shall hold office as such for a term of five years from the date on which he enters upon his office and shall not be eligible for re-appointment:

Provided that the Chairperson or the Member shall not hold office as such after he has attained the age of seventy years.

(*2*) The salaries and allowances payable to, and the other terms and conditions of service of, the Chairperson and other Members shall be such as may be prescribed.

10.(*1*) The Central Government may remove from office the Chairperson or any Member, who—

(*a*) has been adjudged an insolvent; or

(*b*) has engaged at any time, during his term of office, in any paid employment; or

(*c*) has been convicted of an offence which, in the opinion of the Central Government, involves moral turpitude; or

(*d*) has become physically or mentally incapable of acting as such Chairperson or other Member; or

(*e*) is of unsound mind and stands so declared by a competent court; or

(*f*) has acquired such financial or other interest as is likely to affect prejudicially the exercise of his functions as such Chairperson or other Member; or (*g*) has so abused his position as to render his continuance in office prejudicial to the public interest; or

(*h*) has been guilty of proved misbehaviour; or

(*i*) has such other disqualifications as may be prescribed.

(*2*) Notwithstanding anything in sub-section (*1*), the Chairperson or a Member shall not be removed from his office on the grounds specified in clause (*f*) or clause (*g*) or clause (*h*) of sub-section (*1*), except by an order made by the Central Government after an inquiry made in this behalf in which such Chairperson or such Member has been informed of the charges against him and given a reasonable opportunity of being heard in respect of those charges.

(*3*) In the event of inquiry instituted under sub-section (*2*), the Central Government may suspend such Chairperson or other Member against whom inquiry has been instituted for a period not exceeding six months if it consider necessary in public interest.

(*4*) The Central Government may, by rules, regulate the procedure for the inquiry referred to in sub-section (*2*).

11. On ceasing to hold office, the Chairperson or other Member, as the case may be, subject to the provisions of this Act, shall be ineligible, for a period of five years from the date on which they cease to hold office, for further employment (including as consultant or expert or otherwise) in any higher educational institution under the Central Government or a State Government or any private higher educational institution or in any institution whose matters had been before such Chairperson or Member.

12. Any Member having any direct or indirect interest, whether pecuniary or otherwise, in any matter coming up for consideration at a meeting of the Authority, shall, as soon as possible after the relevant circumstances have come to his knowledge, disclose the nature of his interest at such meeting and such disclosure shall be recorded in the proceedings of the Authority. and the Member

shall not take any part in any deliberation or decision of the Authority with respect to that matter.

13. No act or proceeding of the Authority shall be invalid merely by reason of—

(*a*) any vacancy in, or any defect in the constitution of, the Authority; or

(*b*) any defect in the appointment of a person acting as a Member of the Authority; or

(*c*) any irregularity in the procedure of the Authority not affecting the merits of the case.

14. The Chairperson or a Member of the Authority may, by notice in writing under his hand addressed to the Central Government, resign his office:

Provided that the Chairperson or a Member shall, unless he is permitted by the Central Government to relinquish his office sooner, continue to hold office until the expiry of three months from the date of receipt of such notice or until a person duly appointed as his successor enters upon office or until the expiry of his term of office, whichever is the earliest.

15. (*1*) The Central Government shall determine the nature and categories of the officers and other employees required to assist the Authority in the discharge of its functions and provide the Authority with such officers and other employees as it may think fit.

(*2*) The officers and other employees of the Authority shall discharge their functions under the general superintendence of the Chairperson.

(*3*) The salaries and allowances payable to, and the other terms and conditions of service of, the officers and other employees of the Authority shall be such as may be prescribed.

CHAPTER IV

POWERS AND FUNCTIONS OF AUTHORITY

16. (*1*) The Authority shall, subject to the provisions of this Act and rules and regulations made thereunder and regulations made under any law for the time being in force by the appropriate statutory regulatory authority, take measures to develop and to regulate the process of accreditation of higher educational institutions and programmes conducted therein, and to monitor the functioning of accreditation agencies.

(*2*) Without prejudice to the generality of the foregoing provisions, the measures referred to in sub-section (*1*), may, *inter alia,* provide for all or any of the following matters, namely:—

(*a*) regulate accreditation agencies (registration of the accreditation agencies);

(*b*) lay down norms and policies for assessment of academic quality in higher educational institutions or of any programme conducted therein, by accreditation agencies;

(*c*) undertake periodical review of norms and policies referred to in clause (*b*);

(*d*) undertake audit and cause to be audited the adherence to code of ethics including policies on obviating conflict of interest, disclosure of information, evolving transparency in processes and procedures of accreditation;

(*e*) lay down policies for providing information to the public in regard to all aspects of quality and performance of higher educational institutions and programmes conducted therein (including student achievement, faculty availability and qualifications and research);

(*f*) specify and monitor standards on selection and training of experts for the purposes of accreditation by any accreditation agency;

(*g*) levy of fees or other charges under this Act;

(*h*) recommend for improvement of academic quality while respecting the higher educational institution's responsibility to set its priorities;

(*i*) advise the Central Government or any State Government or the appropriate statutory regulatory authority on any policy matter concerning accreditation which may be referred to it;

(*j*) take measures for development of methodologies of accreditation in collaboration with accreditation agencies or universities;

(*k*) promote research and innovation in assessment and accreditation;

(*l*) collect, compile and disseminate information regarding accreditation of higher educational instituteons and programmes conducted therein to the public including stakeholders;

(*m*) monitor adherence to such norms, guidelines and standards of academic quality, as may be specified under any law for the time being in force by the appropriate statutory regulatory authority, in higher educational institutions;

(*n*) perform such other functions as may be prescribed.

17. The Authority may engage, on such fee and remuneration and for such period as may be prescribed, for discharging its functions under this Act, such experts having such qualifications and experience, as may be prescribed.

18. (*1*) The Authority may, at any time, by order in writing, direct any person (hereinafter referred to in this section as "Accreditation Audit Committee") specified in the order to audit or inspect or inquire into the affairs of any accreditation agency or any higher educational institution in matters of accreditation and to report to the Authority on any audit or inspection made by such Accreditation Audit Committee.

Explanation.— For the purposes of this section, "person" shall include such experts engaged in the manner provided in section 17.

(*2*) It shall be the duty of every chief executive or officer or other employee of the accreditation agency and every chief executive or teacher or officer or other employee of the higher educational institution, as the case may be, to produce before the Accreditation Audit Committee directed under sub-section (*1*), all such papers and other documents in his custody or power and to furnish him with any statement and information relating to the affairs of the accreditation agency or higher educational institution, as the case may be, as the said Accreditation Audit Committee may require of him within such time as the said Accreditation Audit Committee may specify.

(*3*) The Accreditation Audit Committee, directed to audit or inspect or inquire under sub-section (*1*), may examine on oath, any chief executive or officer or other employee of the accreditation agency in relation to accreditation of any higher educational institution or programme conducted therein, and may administer oaths accordingly.

(*4*) On receipt of any report under sub-section (*1*), the Authority may, after giving such opportunity to the accreditation agency to make a representation in connection with the report as, in the opinion of the Authority, seems reasonable, by order in writing,—

(*a*) require the accreditation agency, to take such action in respect of any matter arising out of the report as the Authority may think fit; or

(*b*) modify terms and conditions of certificate of registration as it thinks fit, and terms or conditions so modified shall be binding upon and be observed by the accreditation agency and shall be of like force and effect as if they were contained in the certificate of registration; or (*c*) revoke the certificate of registration of the accreditation agency.

(*5*) The Authority shall, place the report submitted by the Accreditation Audit Committee under sub-section (*1*) and the action taken thereon by the Authority on its website.

CHAPTER V

REGISTRATION OF ACCREDITATION AGENCIES

19. No accreditation agency shall, except under, and in accordance with the conditions of a certificate of registration obtained from the Authority under this Act, and in accordance with rules and regulations made thereunder, undertake accreditation of any higher educational institution or any programme conducted therein:

Provided that any agency set up by or under any law for the time being in force, which is carrying out the work of accreditation of higher educational institutions or programmes conducted therein, on or before the date of commencement of this Act, may continue to do so until the certificate of registration is granted to it by the Authority under this Act:

Provided further that such agency shall, within a period of one hundred and eighty days from the date of establishment of the Authority under this Act, make an application under sub-section (*1*) of section 20 for registration as an accreditation agency under this Act:

Provided also that the Authority shall, within a period of one hundred and twenty days from the date of such application, either issue the certificate of registration or reject the application under section 23.

20. (*1*) Every application for registration as an accreditation agency shall be made to the Authority in such form and manner and accompanied by such other documents and on payment of such fees as may be specified by regulations.

(*2*) Every application under sub-section (*1*) shall be accompanied by the following, namely:—

(*a*) a detailed mechanism for detecting any potential conflict of interest between the applicant or its employees or experts and a higher educational institution;

(*b*) a credible mechanism for transparency in respect of the financial status and financial dealings of the applicant;

(*c*) a reliable public information disclosure policy for accreditation of any higher educational institution or any programme conducted therein;

(*d*) complete process and procedure to be followed by the applicant in the accreditation of any higher educational institution or any programme conducted therein;

(*e*) such other documents as may be specified by regulations.

21. No application for grant of a certificate of registration under section 20 shall be considered by the Authority, unless the applicant satisfies the following conditions, namely:—

(*a*) the applicant is—

(*i*) a company registered under section 25 of the Companies Act, 1956 or a society formed and registered under the Societies Registration Act, 1860 or a trust formed under the Indian Trusts Act, 1882 or any other law for the time being in force;

(*ii*) such company, society or trust is formed or controlled by the Central Government or a State Government or any authority or board or institution established under any Central or State Act;

(*b*) the applicant is a non-profit organisation;

(*c*) the applicant has, in its memorandum of association or in the trust deed, specified accreditation of higher educational institutions as one of its main objects;

(*d*) the applicant has adequate infrastructure, to enable it to provide accreditation services in accordance with the provisions of this Act or such infrastructure as may be specified by regulations;

(*e*) the applicant and the promoters of the applicant, have professional competence, financial soundness and general reputation of fairness and integrity to the satisfaction of the Authority;

(*f*) the applicant, or its promoters, or any member of the governing body of the applicant or its promoter, is not involved in any legal proceeding connected with any higher educational institution except in course of any accreditation proceedings carried out in pursuance of the provisions of this Act and regulations made thereunder;

(*g*) the applicant, or its promoters, or any director, or member, or trustee has, at any time in the past, not been convicted of any offence involving moral turpitude or any economic offence;

(*h*) the applicant has, in its employment, persons having adequate professional and other relevant experience to the satisfaction of the Authority;

(*i*) the applicant, or any person directly or indirectly connected with the applicant, has in the past not been—

(*i*) refused by the Authority a certificate of registration under this Act; or

(*ii*) subjected to any proceedings for contravention of this Act or of rules or regulations made thereunder or any other law for the time being in force;

(*j*) the applicant, in all other respects, is a fit and proper person for the grant of a certificate;

(*k*) the applicant conforms to such other conditions as may be specified by regulations.

22. (*1*) The Authority shall, on receipt of the application under section 20 for grant of certificate of registration, issue a public notice, in such form and manner as may be specified by regulations, and place the application together with all documents received with the application, for a period of sixty days from the date of issue of such public notice, on the website of the Authority.

(*2*) Any person may, within a period of said sixty days referred to in sub-section (*1*), submit his comments or objections, if any, on the application or part thereof, to the Authority.

(*3*) The Authority may, within the period of sixty days referred to in sub-section (*1*), require the applicant to furnish such other information or clarification as it may consider necessary.

(*4*) The Authority may obtain the advice of such experts, as it deems fit, for the specific purpose of evaluating the competency of the applicant.

(*5*) The applicant shall, within a period of seven days after making the application under sub-section (*1*), forward a copy of such application with other documents to all State Governments.

(*6*) The State Governments shall, within a period of forty-five days after the receipt of the copy of the application referred to in sub-section (5), send its recommendations, if any, to the Authority.

(*7*) The applicant shall be afforded an opportunity to submit his response on the comments or objections received under sub-section (*2*) or clarifications sought under subsection (*3*) or recommendations made by the State Government, if any, under sub-section (*6*):

Provided that such response shall be submitted within a period of thirty days from the expiry of the period of sixty days referred to in sub-section (*2*).

(*8*) The Authority shall, before granting a certificate of registration under section 23, conduct a public hearing, in such manner as may be specified by regulations, to consider all comments or objections or clarifications or recommendations, if any, and the response of the applicant thereto, including any other matter as the Authority may deem fit for such consideration.

23. (*1*) The Authority shall, as far as practicable within a period of six months from the receipt of such application, after considering the comments or objections or clarifications or recommendations under sub-section (*8*) of section 22, —

(*a*) issue a certificate of registration as an accreditation agency, on such terms and conditions as may be specified in such certificate, subject to the provisions of this Act and rules and regulations made thereunder; or

(*b*) reject the application for reasons to be recorded in writing if such application does not conform to the provisions of this Act or rules or regulations made thereunder or the provisions of any other law for the time being in force:

Provided that no application shall be rejected unless the applicant has been given an opportunity of being heard.

(*2*) The Authority shall, while issuing a certificate of registration, approve the documents referred to in clauses (*a*) to (*e*) of sub-section (*2*) of section 20 as such or with such modifications, as it may deem fit, and thereupon the accreditation agency shall follow the procedures and conditions so approved in the process of accreditation.

(*3*) The documents approved under sub-section (*2*) shall be considered as an integral part of the certificate of registration which shall not be modified or altered without the approval of the Authority.

(*4*) The Authority may, if it so deems fit, in the certificate of registration granted to an accreditation agency, limit the area or programme for which such accreditation agency may exercise its duties and responsibilities of accreditation.

(*5*) A certificate of registration shall be valid for a period of ten years unless such certificate is revoked earlier in accordance with the provisions of this Act.

24. (*1*) A certificate of registration granted under section 23 may, on an application made by the accreditation agency, be renewed by the Authority for such period and on payment of such fees as may be specified by regulations.

(*2*) No application for renewal of the certificate of registration made under sub-section

(*1*) shall be rejected unless the applicant has been given a reasonable opportunity of being heard in the matter.

25. No accreditation agency shall, without the prior approval of the Authority effect any change in its ownership, or governing body or board of trustees, or the memorandum of association or articles of association or the trust deed.

26. The Authority may, in the public interest or for ensuring advancement of academic quality, on an application of the accreditation agency or otherwise, make such alterations and amendments in the terms and conditions of the certificate of registration as it thinks fit, in accordance with such procedure as may be specified by regulations.

27. (*1*) If the Authority, on a complaint or otherwise, and after making such enquiry as it deems fit, is satisfied that public interest so requires, it may revoke the certificate of registration in any of the following cases, namely:—

(*a*) where the accreditation agency, in the opinion of the Authority, makes willful or continuous default in any act of commission or omission as required by or under this Act or the rules or regulations made thereunder;

(*b*) where the accreditation agency commits breach of any of the terms or conditions of the certificate of registration which is expressly declared by such certificate of registration to render it liable to revocation;

(*c*) where the accreditation agency fails, within the period fixed in this behalf by his certificate of registration, or any longer period which the Authority may have granted therefor, to show, to the satisfaction of the Authority, that such agency is in a position fully and efficiently to discharge the duties and obligations imposed on it by its certificate of registration;

(*d*) where in the opinion of the Authority the financial position of the Accreditation Agency is such that such agency is unable fully and efficiently to discharge the duties and obligations imposed on it by its certificate of registration;

(*e*) the accreditation agency has ceased to exist.

(*2*) No certificate of registration shall be revoked under sub-section (1) unless the Authority has given to the accreditation agency not less than thirty days notice, in writing, stating the grounds on which it is proposed to revoke the certificate of registration, and has considered any cause shown by the accreditation agency within the period of that notice, against the proposed revocation.

(*3*) Where in its opinion the public interest so requires or for ensuring the advancement of academic quality, the Authority may, on conclusion of the enquiry under sub-section (1), suspend the certificate of registration granted to the accreditation agency till such time as a decision on the revocation of such certificate of registration or otherwise, is taken by the Authority.

(*4*) Where the Authority revokes a certificate of registration under this section, it shall serve an order of revocation upon the accreditation agency and fix a date on which the revocation shall take effect; and such revocation shall be without prejudice to the action which may be taken against it under any other law for the time being in force.

(*5*) The Authority may, instead of revoking a certificate of registration under subsection (1), permit it to remain in force subject to such further terms and conditions as it thinks fit to impose, and any further terms or conditions so imposed shall be binding upon and be observed by the accreditation agency and shall be of like force and effect as if they were contained in the certificate of registration.

(*6*) The Authority shall publish on its website any action initiated under this section and the final decision on the revocation of the certificate of registration or otherwise together with all documents and reasons for such decision.

(*7*) Where the certification of any accreditation agency has been revoked under subsection (4) on grounds referred to in sub-section (1), the Authority shall, within a period of sixty days from the date of such revocation, conduct an audit of all the higher educational institutions accredited by such agency within a period of one year before the date of such revocation.

(*8*) The Authority shall, while suspending or revoking a certificate of registration, take, or cause to be taken, such measures which may be necessary to protect the interests of students.

28. Any person, aggrieved by an order or decision of the Authority under this Chapter or section 31, may prefer an appeal, against such order to the National Educational Tribunal within a period of sixty days from the date of the order, in such form and manner and accompanied with such documents and such fees as may be prescribed:

Provided that the National Educational Tribunal may entertain an appeal after the expiry of the said period of sixty days, if it is satisfied that the appellant has sufficient cause for not preferring the appeal within the period of sixty days.

CHAPTER VI

DUTIES AND OBLIGATIONS OF ACCREDITATION AGENCIES

29. (*1*) While undertaking accreditation of a higher educational institution or programme conducted therein, the accreditation agency shall have regard to following principles in discharging its obligations for the advancement of knowledge, namely:—

(*a*) advancement of academic quality;

(*b*) enabling uniform reference of standards of academic quality in any class or classes of higher educational institutions or any one or more programmes conducted therein;

(*c*) informing stakeholders (including students and employers) about the quality of the higher educational institution or any programme conducted therein;

(*d*) rendering assistance to higher educational institutions in managing and enhancing their academic quality working towards the development of explicit intended learning outcomes;

(*e*) adherence to such other principles for advancement of knowledge which may evolve from time to time.

(*2*) The accreditation agency shall, while undertaking accreditation of higher educational institutions or any programme conducted therein, follow the standards in respect of academic quality specified by the appropriate statutory regulatory authority.

(*3*) Every accreditation agency shall abide by the code of ethics.

30. (*1*) Every accreditation agency shall accredit a higher educational institution or a programme conducted therein on an application

made to it by such institution in such form and manner, and on payment of such fees, as may be specified by regulations.

(*2*) The process and procedure for accreditation of a higher educational institution or a programme in such institution shall be such as may be specified by regulations.

(*3*) The accreditation of a higher educational institution or a programme in such institution shall be done at such intervals and after such periods as may be specified by the appropriate statutory regulatory authority.

(*4*) The accreditation agency shall, while undertaking accreditation of a higher educational institution or a programme in such institution, provide an opportunity to the stakeholders in the higher educational institution, including students and employees, to submit their views on matters of academic quality.

(*5*) The accreditation agency shall give a reasonable opportunity to the higher educational institution to file suggestions or objections, if any, on the draft accreditation prepared by it and shall take note of such suggestions or objections, if any, while finalizing the accreditation of such institution or any programme conducted therein.

(*6*) The accreditation agency shall publish on its website the accreditation together with all documents and reasons for such accreditation.

31.(*1*)Any person, aggrieved by the accreditation decided by any accreditation agency under this Chapter, may apply to the Authority for withdrawal of such accreditation or its modification.

(*2*) The Authority shall take a decision on an application made under sub-section (*1*) within ninety days.

CHAPTER VII

FINANCE, ACCOUNTS AND AUDIT

32. The Central Government may, after due appropriation made by Parliament by law in this behalf, make to the Authority grants of

such sums of money as the Central Government may think fit for being utilised for the purposes of this Act.

33.(*1*) There shall be constituted a Fund to be called the National Accreditation Regulatory Authority for Higher Educational Institutions Fund and there shall be credited thereto—

(*i*) any grants and loans made to the Authority by the Central Government;

(*ii*) all fees and charges received by the Authority under this Act; and

(*iii*) all sums received by the Authority from such other sources as may be decided upon by the Central Government.

(*2*) The Fund referred to in sub-section (*1*) shall be applied for meeting—

(*i*) the salary, allowances and other remuneration of the Chairperson, other Members, officers and other employees of the Authority; and

(*ii*) the expenses of the Authority incurred in the discharge of its functions and for purposes of this Act.

34. (*1*) The Authority shall maintain proper accounts and other relevant records and prepare an annual statement of accounts in such form as may be prescribed by the Central Government, in consultation with the Comptroller and Auditor-General of India.

(*2*) The accounts of the Authority shall be audited by the Comptroller and Auditor- General of India at such intervals as may be specified by him and any expenditure incurred in connection with such audit shall be payable by the Authority to the Comptroller and Auditor-General of India.

(*3*) The Comptroller and Auditor-General of India and any other person appointed by him in connection with the audit of the accounts of the Authority shall have the same rights and privileges and authority in connection with such audit as the Comptroller and Auditor-General generally has in connection with the audit of the Government accounts and, in particular, shall have the right to demand the production of books, accounts, connected vouchers and other documents and papers and to inspect any of the office of the Authority.

(*4*) The accounts of the Authority as certified by the Comptroller and Auditor-General of India or any other person appointed by him in this behalf together with the audit report thereon, shall be forwarded annually to the Central Government by the Authority and the Government shall cause the same to be laid before each House of Parliament.

35.(*1*) The Authority shall prepare in every year, in such form and at such time as may be prescribed, an annual report giving a full account of its activities during the previous year, and copies thereof along with copies of its annual accounts and auditor's report shall be forwarded to the Central Government and the Government shall cause the same to be laid before each House of Parliament.

(*2*) The Authority shall also forward a copy of the annual report so prepared under sub-section (*1*) to all appropriate statutory regulatory authorities.

CHAPTER VIII

OFFENCES AND PENALTIES

36. If an accreditation agency fails to comply with the obligations referred to in subsection (*1*) of section 29 and the adherence to the code of ethics referred to in sub-section (*3*) of that section, without prejudice to any penalty which may be imposed under this Act, it shall be liable to pay such compensation, to the higher educational institution for any loss or damages suffered by such institution, as may be determined by the State Educational Tribunal:

Provided that before determination of any compensation under this section, the accreditation agency shall be given a reasonable opportunity of being heard by the State Educational Tribunal.

37. Any accreditation agency, which contravenes—

(*a*) any provision of this Act or rules or regulations made thereunder; or

(*b*) the standards specified under any law for the time being in force by the appropriate statutory regulatory authority; or

(*c*) the terms and conditions specified in the certificate of registration, shall, without prejudice to proceeding for prosecution under the provisions of this Act or any other law for the time being in force, be liable to a penalty which may extend to five lakh rupees.

38. If a person, without reasonable excuse, resists, obstructs, or attempts to obstruct, impersonate, threaten, intimidate or assault an officer of the Authority or any person assigned to discharge any function under this Act, or in exercising his functions under this Act, he shall be punishable with imprisonment for a term which may extend to three months or with fine which may extend to five lakh rupees or with both.

39. Whoever contravenes the provisions of section 19 shall be punishable with imprisonment for a term which may extend to five years or with fine which may extend to five lakh rupees or with both.

40. If any person provides any information or produces any document under this Act or under any rule or regulation made thereunder, or delivers an account or statement which is false, and which he either knows or believes to be false, or does not believe to be true, he shall be punishable with imprisonment for a term which may extend to three months or with fine which may extend to five lakh rupees or with both.

41. If any person contravenes or attempts to contravene or abets the contravention of the provisions of this Act or of any rules or regulations made thereunder, for which no punishment is provided elsewhere in this Act, he shall be punishable with imprisonment for a term which may extend to two years or with fine which may extend to ten lakh rupees or with both.

42. (*1*) Where an offence under this Act has been committed by a company, every person who at the time the offence was committed was in charge of, and was responsible to, the company for the conduct of the business of the company, as well as the company, shall be deemed to be guilty of the offence and shall be liable to be proceeded against and punished accordingly:

Provided that nothing contained in this sub-section shall render any such person liable to any punishment provided in this Act, if he proves that the offence was committed without his knowledge or that he has exercised all due diligence to prevent the commission of such offence.

(*2*) Notwithstanding anything contained in sub-section (*1*), where an offence under this Act has been committed by a company and it is proved that the offence has been committed with the consent or connivance of, or is attributable to, any neglect on the part of any director, manager, secretary or other officer of the company, such director, manager, secretary or other officer shall also be deemed to be guilty of the offence and shall be liable to be proceeded against and punished accordingly.

Explanation.—For the purposes of this section,—

(*a*) "company" means any body corporate and includes a firm or other association of individuals; and

(*b*) "director", in relation to a firm, means a partner in the firm.

43. (*1*) Where an offence under this Act has been committed by a society or trust or agency or institution, every person who at the time the

offence was committed was in charge of, and was responsible to, the society or trust or agency or institution for the conduct of the business of the society or trust or university, as well as the society or trust or agency or institution, shall be deemed to be guilty of the offence and shall be liable to be proceeded against and punished accordingly:

Provided that nothing contained in this sub-section shall render any such person liable to any punishment provided in this Act, if he proves that the offence was committed without his knowledge or that he has exercised all due diligence to prevent the commission of such offence.

(*2*) Notwithstanding anything contained in sub-section (*1*), where an offence under this Act has been committed by a society or trust or agency or institution and it is proved that the offence has been committed with the consent or connivance of, or is attributable to, any neglect on the part of any governors, vice-chancellor, directors, committee, trustees, registrar or other officer, such governors, directors, committee, trustees, registrar or other officer shall also be deemed to be guilty of the offence and shall be liable to be proceeded against and punished accordingly.

44. (*1*) No court shall take cognizance of any offence punishable under this Act or the rules or regulations made thereunder, save on a complaint made by the Authority or any officer or person authorised by it.

(*2*) No court inferior to that of a Chief Metropolitan Magistrate or a Chief Judicial Magistrate shall try any offence punishable under this Act.

45. (*1*) Save as otherwise provided in this Act, all matters under section 36 (including determination of compensation thereunder) shall be adjudicated by the State Educational Tribunal having jurisdiction.

(*2*) Save as otherwise provided in this Act, all matters under section 37 (including the penalties leviable thereunder) shall be adjudicated by the National Educational Tribunal.

CHAPTER IX

MISCELLANEOUS

46. (*1*) The Central Government may, by a general or special order, call upon the Authority to furnish, periodically or as and when required any information concerning the activities carried on by the Authority or any accreditation agency or higher educational institution in matters concerning accreditation, in such form as may be prescribed, to enable that Government, to carry out the purposes of this Act.

(2) The Authority may, by a general or special order, call upon any accreditation agency or higher educational institution to furnish, periodically or as and when required any information concerning the activities carried on by such accreditation agency or institution, in such form as may be specified by regulations, to enable the Authority, to carry out the purposes of this Act.

47. (*1*) The accreditation agency shall furnish to the Authority at such time and in such form and manner as may be specified by regulations or as the Authority may direct, such returns and statements and such particulars in regard to accreditation of higher educational institutions by such agency, as the Authority may, from time to time, require.

(*2*) Without prejudice to the provisions of sub-section (*1*), the accreditation agency shall, within a period of ninety days after the end of each financial year, submit to the Authority a report along with audited statement of accounts in such form, as may be specified by regulations, giving a true and full account of its activities, policy and programmes in regard to accreditation of higher educational institutions by such agency during the previous financial year.

48.(*1*) Without prejudice to the foregoing provisions of this Act, the Authority shall, in exercise of its powers or the performance of its functions under this Act, be bound by such directions on questions of policy, other than those relating to technical and administrative matters, as the Central Government may give in writing to it from time to time:

Provided that the Authority shall, as far as practicable, be given an opportunity to express its views before any direction is given under this sub-section.

(*2*) The decision of the Central Government whether a question is one of policy or not shall be final.

49. If the Central Government is of the opinion that it is necessary or expedient in the interests of the general public so to do, or for advancement of knowledge, it may, by notification and subject to such conditions as may be specified in the notification, exempt any class or classes of higher educational institutions from the operation of all or any of the provisions of this Act and may, as often as may be necessary, revoke or modify such notification.

50. (*1*) If at anytime the Central Government is of the opinion—

(*a*) that on account of circumstances beyond the control of the Authority, it is unable to discharge the functions or perform the duties imposed on it by or under the provisions of this Act; or

(*b*) that the Authority has persistently made default in complying with any direction given by the Central Government under this Act or in the discharge of the functions or performance of the duties imposed on it by or under the provisions of this Act; or

(*c*) that circumstances exist which render it necessary in the public interest so to do, the Central Government may, by notification and for reasons to be specified therein, supersede the Authority for such period, not exceeding six months, as may be specified in the notification:

Provided that before issuing any such notification, the Central Government shall give a reasonable opportunity to the Authority to make representations against the proposed supersession and shall consider representations, if any, of the Authority.

(*2*) Upon the publication of a notification under sub-section (*1*) superseding the Authority,—

(*a*) the Chairperson and other Members shall, as from the date of supersession, vacate their offices as such;

(*b*) all the powers, functions and duties which may, by or under the provisions of this Act, be exercised or discharged by or on behalf of the Authority shall, until the Authority is reconstituted under sub-section (*3*), be exercised and discharged by the Central Government or such authority as the Central Government may specify in this behalf;

(*c*) all properties owned or controlled by the Authority shall, until the Authority is reconstituted under sub-section (*3*), vest in the Central Government.

(*3*) On or before the expiration of the period of supersession specified in the notification issued under sub-section (*1*), the Central Government shall reconstitute the Authority by a fresh appointment of its Chairperson and other Members and in such case any person who had vacated his office under clause (*a*) of sub-section (*2*) shall not be deemed to be disqualified for re-appointment.

(*4*) The Central Government shall cause a notification issued under sub-section (*1*) and a full report of any action taken under this section and the circumstances leading to such action to be laid before each House of Parliament at the earliest.

51. No civil court shall have jurisdiction to entertain any suit or proceeding in respect of any matter which the Authority or a State Educational Tribunal or the National Educational Tribunal is empowered by or under this Act to determine, and no injunction

shall be granted by any court or other authority in respect of any action taken or to be taken in pursuance of any power conferred by or under this Act.

52. The Chairperson and other Members and the officers and other employees of the Authority shall be deemed to be public servants within the meaning of section 21 of the Indian Penal Code.

53. No suit, prosecution or other legal proceeding shall lie against the Central Government or against the Chairperson or any other Member, as the case may be, for anything which is in good faith done or intended to be done in pursuance of this Act or any rule or regulation made thereunder in the discharge of official duties.

54. Subject to the provisions of the University Grants Commission Act, 1956, the provisions of this Act shall have overriding effect notwithstanding anything inconsistent therewith contained in any other law for the time being in force or in any instrument having effect by virtue of any law other than this Act.

55. The provisions of this Act shall be in addition to, and not in derogation of, the provisions of any other law for the time being in force.

56.(*1*) The Central Government may, by notification in the Official Gazette, make rules to carry out the purposes of this Act.

(*2*) In particular, and without prejudice to the generality of the foregoing power, such rules may provide for all or any of the following matters, namely:—

(*a*) the manner of nomination of experts in the concerned field of knowledge to the Selection Committee under sub-section (*3*) of section 8;

(*b*) the term of Selection Committee and the manner of selection of panel of names under sub-section (*4*) of section 8;

(*c*) the salaries and allowances payable to, and the other terms and conditions of service of, the Chairperson and other Members of the Authority under sub-section (*2*) of section 9;

(*d*) the other disqualifications for removal of the Chairperson or other Members under clause (*i*) of sub-section (*1*) of section 10;

(*e*) the procedure for the inquiry under sub-section (*4*) of section 10;

(*f*) the salaries and allowances payable to, and other terms and conditions of service of, the officers and other employees of the Authority under sub-section (*3*) of section 15;

(*g*) the other functions which the Authority may perform under clause (*n*) of sub-section (*2*) of section 16;

(*h*) the fees and remuneration payable to, the period, qualifications and experience of, and the manner in which the Authority may engage experts under section 17;

(*i*) the form and manner in which an appeal may be preferred and the documents to be accompanied with it and the fees payable therewith under section 28;

(*j*) the form for maintaining proper accounts and other relevant records and the annual statement of accounts of the Authority under sub-section (*1*) of section 34;

(*k*) the form in which, and the time at which, the annual report of the Authority shall be prepared under section 35;

(*l*) the information concerning the activities carried on by the Authority or any accreditation agency or higher educational institution in matters concerning accreditation to be furnished to the Central Government under sub-section (*1*) of section 46;

(*m*) any other matter which is required to be, or may be, specified by rules or in respect of which provision is to be made by rules.

57. (*1*) The Authority may, by notification in the Official Gazette, make regulations, consistent with the provision of the Act and the rules made thereunder, to carry out the purposes of this Act.

(*2*) In particular and without prejudice to the generality of the foregoing power, such regulations may provide for all or any of the following matters, namely:—

(*a*) the code of ethics and such other ethical principles to be adhered to by an accreditation agency under clause (*h*) of sub-section (*1*) of section 3;

(*b*) the form and manner in which an application may be made and the documents to be accompanied with it and the fee payable therewith under sub-section (*1*) of section 20;

(*c*) such other documents that an applicant has to submit along with his application for grant of certificate of registration as may be specified under clause (*e*) of sub-section (*2*) of section 20;

(*d*) the infrastructure that an applicant shall possess for providing accreditation services under clause (*d*) of section 21;

(*e*) the other conditions of eligibility for grant of certificate of registration under clause (*k*) of section 21;

(*f*) the form and manner in which the public notice may be issued under subsection (*1*) of section 22;

(*g*) the manner of conducting public hearing by the Authority under sub-section (*8*) of section 22;

(*h*) the fees payable and the period for which the certificate of registration granted to an accreditation agency may be renewed under sub-section (*1*) of section 24;

(*i*) the procedure for grant of approval in respect of any change in the ownership structure or the memorandum of association of an accreditation agency under section 25;

(*j*) the procedure for making amendment or alteration in the terms and conditions of the certificate of registration under section 26;

(*k*) the form and manner in which an application may be made for accreditation of any higher education institution or any programme therein and the documents to be accompanied with it and the fee payable therewith under sub-section (*1*) of section 30;

(*l*) the procedure and process to be followed by the accreditation agency for accreditation of any higher educational institution or any programme conducted therein under sub-section (*2*) of section 30;

(*m*) the information concerning the activities carried on by the accreditation agency or the higher educational institutions to be furnished to the Authority under sub-section (*2*) of section 46;

(*n*) the time at which and the form and manner in which the returns and statements and particulars in regard to accreditation of higher educational institutions by the accreditation agency under sub-section (*1*) of section 47;

(*o*) the form and manner in which the report, along with audited statement of accounts, giving a true and full account of activities, policy and programme in regard to accreditation of higher educational institutions by the accreditation agency under sub-section (*2*) of section 47;

(*p*) any other matter which is required to be, or may be, specified by regulation or in respect of which provision is to be made by regulations.

58. Every rule and every regulation made under this Act and every notification issued under section 49 shall be laid, as soon as may be after it is made or issued, before each House of Parliament while it is in session, for a total period of thirty days which may be comprised in one session or in two or more successive sessions,

and if, before the expiry of the session immediately following the session or the successive sessions aforesaid, both Houses agree in making any modification in the rule or regulation or notification, as the case may be, or both Houses agree that the rule or regulation or notification, as the case may be, should not be made or issued, the rule or regulation or notification, as the case may be, shall thereafter have effect only in such modified form or be of no effect, as the case may be; so, however, that any such modification or annulment shall be without prejudice to the validity of anything previously done under that rule or regulation or notification, as the case may be.

59. (*1*) If any difficulty arises in giving effect to the provisions of this Act, the Central Government may, by order, published in the Official Gazette, make such provisions, not inconsistent with the provisions of this Act, as may appear to be necessary or expedient for removing the difficulty:

Provided that no order shall be made under this section after the expiry of two years from the date of commencement of this Act.

(*2*) Every order made under this section shall, as soon as may be after it is made, be laid before each House of Parliament.

THE EDUCATIONAL TRIBUNALS BILL, 2010

BILL

to provide for the establishment of Educational Tribunals for effective and expeditious adjudication of disputes involving teachers and other employees of higher educational institutions and other stake holders (including students, universities, institutions and statutory regulatory authorities) and to adjudicate penalties for indulging in unfair practices in higher education and for matters connected therewith or incidental thereto.

BE it enacted by Parliament in the Sixty-first Year of the Republic of India as follows:—

CHAPTER I

PRELIMINARY

1. (*1*) This Act may be called the Educational Tribunals Act, 2010.

(*2*) It extends to the whole of India except the State of Jammu and Kashmir.

(*3*) It shall come into force on such date or dates as the Central Government may, by notification, appoint; and different dates may be appointed for different States and any reference in any provision of this Act to the commencement of this Act shall be construed in relation to any State or part thereof as a reference to the coming into force of that provision in that State or part thereof.

2. This Act shall apply to all higher educational institutions other than the higher educational institutions engaged mainly in agricultural education and research.

3. (*1*) In this Act, unless the context otherwise requires:-

(*a*) "Academic Member" means a Member appointed as such under sub-section (*2*) of section 22;

(*b*) "Administrative Member" means a Member appointed as such under subsection (*3*)of section 22;

(*c*) "affiliation" together with its grammatical variations, includes, in relation to a college or institution:-

(*i*) recognition of such college or institution by a university; or

(*ii*) association of such college or institution with a university; or

(*iii*) admission of such college or institution to the privileges of a university;

(*d*) "appropriate Government",—

(*i*) in relation to a Union territory, means the Central Government;

(*ii*) in relation to a State, means the Government of the State in which the

State Educational Tribunal is established under this Act;

(*e*) "appropriate State Legislature" means such Legislature of the State as has jurisdiction over the matter;

(*f*) "appropriate statutory regulatory authority" means any authority established under any law for the time being in force for co-ordinating or determining or maintaining the standards of higher education and research;

(*g*) "Central Educational Institution" means—

(*i*) a university established or incorporated by or under a Central Act; or

(*ii*) an institution of national importance set up by an Act of Parliament; or

(*iii*) an institution, declared as an institution deemed to be University under section 3 of the University Grants Commission Act, 1956, and maintained by or receiving aid from the Central Government; or

(*iv*) an institution maintained by, or receiving aid from,—

(*A*) the Central Government, whether directly or indirectly;

(*B*) affiliated to university referred to in sub-clause (*i*) or to an institution referred to in sub-clause (*ii*), or a constituent unit of an institution referred to in sub-clause (*iii*);

(*v*) an higher educational institution set up by the Central Government under the Societies Registration Act, 1860;

(*h*) "Chairperson" means the Chairperson of a State Educational Tribunal or the National Educational Tribunal, as the case may be;

(*i*) "college" means any institution, whether known as such or by any other name which provides for a course of study for obtaining any qualification from a university and which, in accordance with the rules and regulations of such university, is recognised as competent to provide for such course of study and present students undergoing such course of study for examination for the award of such qualification;

(*j*) "contractual provisions" in relation to a teacher or an employee engaged on Application of Act. contract by an higher educational institution means the provisions of the terms and conditions of the contract governing the service of such teacher or employee to such ;

(*k*) "degree" means any such degree, as may, with the previous approval of theCentral Government, be specified in this behalf by the University Grants Commission, by notification in the Official Gazette, under section 22 of the University Grants Commission Act, 1956;

(*l*) "diploma" means such award, not being a degree, granted by a higher educational institution certifying that the recipient has successfully completed a course of study of not less than nine months duration;

(*m*) "distance education systems" means the distance education systems as defined in clause (*e*) of section (*2*) of the Indira Gandhi National Open University Act, 1985;

(*n*) "High Court" means the High Court of the State within whose jurisdiction the State Educational Tribunal is situated;

(*o*) "higher educational institution" means an institution of learning including an university, an institution deemed to be university, a college, an institute, an institution of national importance declared as such by an Act of Parliament or a constituent unit of such institution, which is imparting (whether through conduct of regular classes or distance education system) higher education beyond twelve years of schooling leading to the award of a degree or diploma;

(*p*) "institution deemed to be University" means an institution declared by the Central Government, as deemed to be a university under section 3 of the University Grants Commission Act, 1956;

(*q*) "Judicial Member" means a Member appointed as such under sub-section (*1*) of section 22 and includes the Chairperson;

(*r*) "Member" includes the Chairperson and a Member of the National Educational Tribunal or a State Educational Tribunal, as the case may be;

(*s*) "National Educational Tribunal" means the National Educational Tribunal established under section 20;

(*t*) "notification" means a notification published in the Official Gazette; and the expression "notify" with its cognote meanings and grammetical variations shall be construed accordingly;

(*u*) "prescribed" means prescribed by rules made by the appropriate Government or the Central Government, as the case may be, under this Act;

(*v*) "service" means service with an higher educational institution;

(*w*) "service matters", in relation to a teacher or an employee of a higher educational institution means all matters relating to the conditions of their service as respects,—

(*w*) remuneration including pay, allowances, pension and other retirement benefits permissible in accordance with the terms and conditions of service of, such teacher or employee;

(*ii*) tenure including appointment, probation, confirmation, seniority, promotion, reversion, premature retirement or superannuation;

(*iii*) leave of any kind;

(*iv*) disciplinary matters; or

(*v*) any other matter whatsoever;

(*x*) "service rules" means the rules or regulations or statutes or bye-laws or ordinances or contractual provisions, as the case may be, of the higher educational institution, governing service matters, of any teacher or any employee (whether appointed on permanent or temporary or visiting or contract basis) of such institution;

(*y*) "society" means a society registered under the Societies Registration Act, 1860 or under any corresponding law for the time being in force in a State;

(*z*) "State Educational Tribunal" means a State Educational Tribuna established in a State under section 4; (*za*) "Vice Chancellor" means—

(*i*) Chief executive of a university; or

(*ii*) head of a Central Educational Institution, not leaving a college.

(*2*) Words and expressions used and not defined in this Act but defined in the University Grants Commission Act, 1956 and not inconsistent with this Act shall have the meanings respectively assigned to them in that Act.

CHAPTER II

STATE EDUCATIONAL TRIBUNALS

4. The appropriate Government shall, by notification, establish a Tribunal to be known as the "State Educational Tribunal" to exercise the powers conferred upon it under this Act:

Provided that an appropriate Government may notify any Educational Tribunal existing before the commencement of this Act as the "State Educational Tribunal" for the purposesof this Act and thereafter the provisions of this Act shall apply to such Tribunal.

5. Each State Educational Tribunal shall consist of a Chairperson and two other Members, of which not less than one shall be a woman, to be appointed by the appropriate Government.

6.(*1*) A person shall be qualified to be appointed as the Chairperson of a State Educational Tribunal, if such person is, or has been, a Judge of the High Court: Provided that no appointment under this section shall be made except after consultation with the Chief Justice of the High Court.

(*2*) A person shall be qualified to be appointed as a Member of the State Educational Tribunal, if such person,—

(*a*) is not less than fifty-five years of age;

(*b*) is of ability, integrity and standing, and has adequate knowledge and experience of at least twenty years in dealing with matters relating to higher education, public affairs or administration in educational matters;

(*c*) is, or has been, a Vice Chancellor or a person who is, or has been, of the rank and equivalence of a Chief Secretary of the State Government.

(*3*) Out of the two Members referred to in sub-section (*1*) of section 5, one Member shall be chosen from amongst persons who is, or, has been, the Vice Chancellor and the other Member shall be chosen from amongst persons who is, or has been, the Chief Secretary of the State Government or equivalent rank.

7. (*1*) The Chairperson and Members of the State Educational Tribunal shall be appointed by the appropriate Government from a panel of names recommended by a Selection Committee, consisting of—

(*a*) the Chief Justice of the High Court or his nominee.......... Chairperson;

(*b*) the Chief Secretary of the State Government.........Member;

(*c*) an officer of the State Government of the rank and equivalence of a Secretary to the Government of India with experience in dealing with educational matters..........Member.

(*2*) The Secretary in charge of higher education in the Department of Education or Department dealing with educational matters of the State Government shall be the convenor of the meetings of the Selection Committee.

(*3*) The term of the Selection Committee and the manner of selection of panel of names shall be such as may be prescribed by the appropriate Government:

Provided that in the case of the Selection Committee in respect of an Educational Tribunal to be established in a Union territory, the provisions of this section shall have the effect as if for the words "State Government", the words "Central Government" has been substituted.

(*4*) No appointment of the Chairperson or Member of the State Educational Tribunal shall be invalid merely by reason of any vacancy in the Selection Committee.

(*5*) Subject to the provisions of sub-sections (*1*) to (*4*), the Selection Committee may regulate its own procedure.

8. (*1*) The Chairperson and every Member of the State Educational Tribunal shall hold office as such for a term of five years from the date on which he enters upon his office and shall be eligible for reappointment:

Provided that the Chairperson or other Members of the State Educational Tribunal shall not hold office as such after he has attained the age of seventy years.

(*2*) The salaries and allowances payable to, and the other terms and conditions of service of, the Chairperson and other Members of a State Educational Tribunal shall be such as may be prescribed by the appropriate Government:

Provided that neither the salary and allowances nor the other terms and conditions of service of the Chairperson and other Member shall be varied to their disadvantage after their appointment.

9. The Chairperson or a Member of the State Educational Tribunal may, by notice in writing under his hand addressed to the appropriate Government, resign his office:

Provided that the Chairperson or a Member of the State Educational Tribunal shall, unless he is permitted by the appropriate Government to relinquish his office sooner, continue to hold office until the expiry of three months from the date of receipt of such notice or until a person duly appointed as his successor enters upon office or until the expiry of his term of office, whichever is the earliest.

10. (*1*) The appropriate Government may, in consultation with the Chief Justice of the High Court, remove from office the Chairperson or any other Member of the State Educational Tribunal, who—

(*a*) has been adjudged an insolvent; or

(*b*) has engaged at any time, during his term of office, in any paid employment; or

(*c*) has been convicted of an offence which, in the opinion of the Central Government, involves moral turpitude; or

(*d*) has become physically or mentally incapable of acting as such Chairperson or other Member; or

(*e*) is of unsound mind and stands so declared by a competent court; or

(*f*) has acquired such financial or other interest as is likely to affect prejudicially the exercise of his functions as such Chairperson or other Member; or

(*g*) has so abused his position as to render his continuance in office prejudicial to the public interest; or

(*h*) has been guilty of proved misbehavior; or

(*i*) has such other disqualifications as may be prescribed by the appropriate Government.

(*2*) Notwithstanding anything contained in sub-section (*1*), no Chairperson or a Member of the State Educational Tribunal shall be removed from his office on the grounds specified in clause (*f*) or clause (*g*) or clause (*h*) of sub-section (*1*), except by an order made by the appropriate Government after an inquiry made in this behalf by a Judge of the High Court in which such Chairperson or such Member has been informed of the charges against him and given a reasonable opportunity of being heard in respect of those charges.

(*3*) The appropriate Government may, by rules, regulate the procedure for the inquiry referred to in sub-section (*2*).

11. If, for any reason other than temporary absence, any vacancy occurs in the office of the Chairperson or a Member of the State Educational Tribunal, the appropriate Government shall appoint another person in accordance with the provisions of this Act to fill the vacancy and the proceedings may be continued before the State Educational Tribunal from the stage at which the vacancy is filled.

12. (*1*) In the event of the occurrence of any vacancy in the office of the Chairperson of the State Educational Tribunal by reason of his death or resignation, the senior-most Member of the State Educational Tribunal shall act as the Chairperson of the Tribunal until the date on which a new Chairperson, appointed in accordance with the provisions of this Act to fill such vacancy, enters upon his office.

(*2*) When the Chairperson of the State Educational Tribunal is unable to discharge his functions owing to absence, illness or any other cause, the senior-most Member shall discharge the functions of the Chairperson until the date on which the Chairperson resumes his duties.

13. On ceasing to hold office,—

(*a*) the Chairperson or Member of the State Educational Tribunal, as the case may be, shall, subject to the provisions of this Act, be ineligible, for a period of five years from the date on which they cease to hold office, for further employment (including as consultant or expert or otherwise) in any higher educational institution within such State, whether under the Central Government or the

Government of any State or any private educational institution or in any institution whose matters had been before such Chairperson or Member;

(*b*) the Chairperson or Member shall not appear, act or plead before the State Educational Tribunal in which he had been the Chairperson or Member.

14. (*1*) The appropriate Government shall, after consultations with the Chairperson of the State Educational Tribunal, determine the nature and categories of the officers and other employees required to assist the State Educational Tribunal in the discharge of its functions and provide such Tribunal with such officers and other employees as it may think fit.

(*2*) The officers and other employees of the State Educational Tribunal shall discharge their functions under the general superintendence of the Chairperson of such Tribunal.

(*3*) The salaries and allowances payable to, and the other terms and conditions of service of, the officers and other employees of a State Educational Tribunal shall be such as may be prescribed by the appropriate Government.

15. Save as otherwise expressly provided in this Act, the State Educational Tribunal shall exercise powers and authority in relation to,—

(*a*) service matters of any teacher or any other employee of a higher educational institution;

(*b*) matters relating to affiliation of any higher educational institution (not being University) with the affiliating University;

(*c*) matters relating to use of unfair practices, by any higher educational institution, which has been specifically prohibited under any law for the time being in force;

(*d*) matters as may be assigned to it by any other law for the time being in force.

16. Every application, for redressal of grievance or settlement of disputes relating to any of the matters specified under clauses (*a*) to (*d*) of section 15, shall be made to the State Educational Tribunal in such form and accompanied by such documents and on payment of such fee and the manner as may be prescribed by the appropriate Government.

17. (*1*) The State Educational Tribunal shall, not admit any applications in respect of a matter under clause (*a*) of section 15 unless it is satisfied that the applicant had availed of all the remedies available to him under the relevant service rules for redressal of grievances or settlement of disputes.

(*2*) For the purposes of sub-section (*1*), a person shall be deemed to have availed of all the remedies available to him under the relevant service rules or contractual provisions as to redressal of grievances or settlement of disputes,—

(*a*) if a final order has been made by the higher educational institution or other authority or officer or other person competent to pass such order under such rules, rejecting any appeal preferred or representation made by such person in connection with the grievance or disputes; or

(*b*) where no final order has been made by the higher educational institution or other authority or officer or other person competent to pass such order with regard to the application or representation made or appeal preferred by such person, if a period of three months from the date on which such application or representation was made or appeal was preferred has expired; or

(*c*) where no service rules exist on the service matter in dispute.

Explanation.—For the purposes of this section, the words "final order" means an order passed by such final appellate authority of the higher educational institution as provided in the service rules but does not include an order passed in any arbitration or any conciliation proceedings under the Arbitration and Conciliation Act, 1996.

18. (*1*) A State Educational Tribunal shall not admit an application,—

(*a*) in a case where a final order referred to in clause (*a*) of sub-section (*2*) of section 17 has been made, unless the application is made, within a period of six months from the date on which such final order has been made;

(*b*) in a case where an appeal or representation such as is mentioned in clause (*b*) of sub-section (*2*) of section 17 has been made and a period of three months had expired thereafter without such final order having been made, within a period of six months from the date of expiry of the said period of three months;

(*c*) in any other matter, within a period of six months from the date the cause of action arose.

(*2*) Notwithstanding anything contained in this section, an application may be admitted after the period of six months specified in clause (*a*) or clause (*b*) or clause (*c*) of this section, if the applicant satisfies the State Educational Tribunal that he had sufficient cause for not making the application within such period.

19. Any person aggrieved by an order made by a State Educational Tribunal in respect of any matter specified under clauses (*b*) to (*d*) of section 15, may prefer an appeal against such order to the National Educational Tribunal within a period of sixty days from the date of the order, in such form and manner and accompanied with such documents and such fees as may be prescribed by the Central Government:

Provided that the National Educational Tribunal may entertain an appeal after the expiry of the said period of sixty days, if it is satisfied that the appellant had sufficient cause for not preferring the appeal within the said period.

CHAPTER III
NATIONAL EDUCATIONAL TRIBUNAL

20. The Central Government shall, by notification, establish a Tribunal to be known as the "National Educational Tribunal" to exercise the powers conferred upon it under this Act.

21. (*1*) The National Educational Tribunal shall consist of a Chairperson and such number of Members not exceeding eight to be appointed by the Central Government.

(*2*) Out of the eight Members to be appointed under sub-section (*1*) —

(*a*) two shall be Judicial Members;

(*b*) three shall be Academic Members;

(*c*) three shall be Administrative Members.

(*3*) Not less than one-third of the total number of Members appointed under subsection

(*1*) shall be women.

(*4*) Subject to the provisions of this Act,—

(*a*) the jurisdiction of the National Educational Tribunal may be exercised by Benches thereof;

(*b*) a Bench may be constituted by the Chairperson consisting of three Members of which one Member shall be a Judicial Member, one Member shall be an Academic Member and one Member shall be an Administrative Member.

(*5*) Notwithstanding anything contained in sub-section (*4*), the Chairperson may transfer a Member from one Bench to another Bench.

(*6*) The National Educational Tribunal shall sit in New Delhi.

22. (*1*) A person shall be qualified, to be appointed as the Chairperson or Judicial Member of the National Educational Tribunal, if such person is, or has been, a Judge of the Supreme Court:

Provided that no appointment under this sub-section shall be made except after consultation with the Chief Justice of India.

(*2*) A person shall be qualified to be appointed as an Academic Member of the National Educational Tribunal if such person,—

(*a*) is not less than fifty-five years of age;

(*b*) is of ability, integrity and standing, and has adequate knowledge and experience of at least twenty-five years in dealing with matters relating to higher education or administration in educational matters;

(*c*) is, or has been, a Vice Chancellor of any University, or a Director of an institution of national importance.

(*3*) A person shall be qualified to be appointed as an Administrative Member of the National Educational Tribunal if such person,—

(*a*) is not less than fifty-five years of age;

(*b*) is of ability, integrity and standing, and has adequate knowledge and experience of at least twenty-five years in dealing with matters relating to higher education, public affairs or administration in educational matters;

(*c*) is, or has been, a Secretary to the Government of India or equivalent rank.

23. (*1*) The Chairperson and Members of the National Educational Tribunal shall be appointed by the Central Government from a panel of names recommended by a Selection Committee consisting of—

(*a*) the Chief Justice of India or his nominee..... Chairperson;

(*b*) the Secretary in charge of higher education in the Ministry of Human Resource Development of the Government of India........Member;

(*c*) the Secretary in the Ministry of Law and Justice of the Government of India ....Member;

(*d*) the Secretary in charge of medical education in the Ministry of Health and Family Welfare of the Government of India..........Member;

(*e*) the Secretary in charge of the Department of Personnel and Training of the Government of India..........Member.

(*2*) The Secretary in charge of higher education in the Ministry of Human Resource Development of the Government of India shall be the convenor of the meetings of the Selection Committee.

(*3*) The term of the Selection Committee and the manner of selection of panel of names shall be such as may be prescribed by the Central Government.

(*4*) No appointment of the Chairperson or Member of the National Educational Tribunal shall be invalid merely by reason of any vacancy in the Selection Committee.

(*5*) Subject to the provisions of sub-sections (*1*) to (*4*), the Selection Committee may regulate its own procedure.

24. (*1*) The Chairperson and every other Member of the National Educational Tribunal shall, hold office as such for a term of five years from the date on which he enters upon his office and shall be eligible for reappointment:

Provided that the Chairperson or other Member of the National Educational Tribunal shall not hold office as such after he has attained the age of seventy years.

(*2*) The salaries and allowances payable to, and the other terms and conditions of service of, the Chairperson and other Members of the National Educational Tribunal shall be such as may be prescribed by the Central Government:

Provided that neither the salary and allowances nor the other terms and conditions of service of the Chairperson and other Member shall be varied to their disadvantage after their appointment.

25. The Chairperson or a Member of the National Educational Tribunal may, by notice in writing under his hand addressed to the Central Government, resign his office:

Provided that the Chairperson or a Member of the National Educational Tribunal shall, unless he is permitted by the Central Government to relinquish his office sooner, continue to hold office until the expiry of three months from the date of receipt of such notice or until a person duly appointed as his successor enters upon office or until the expiry of his term of office, whichever is the earliest.

26. (*1*) The Central Government may, in consultation with the Chief Justice of India, remove from office, the Chairperson or any other Member of the National Educational Tribunal, who—

(*a*) has been adjudged an insolvent; or

(*b*) has engaged any time, during his term of office, in any paid employment; or (*c*) has been convicted of an offence which, in the opinion of the Central Government, involves moral turpitude; or

(*d*) has become physically or mentally incapable of acting as such Chairperson or other Member; or

(*e*) is of unsound mind and stands so declared by a competent court; or

(*f*) has acquired such financial or other interest as is likely to affect prejudicially the exercise of his functions as such Chairperson or other Member; or

(*g*) has so abused his position as to render his continuance in office prejudicial to the public interest; or

(*h*) has been guilty of proved misbehavior; or

(*i*) has such other disqualifications as may be prescribed.

(*2*) Notwithstanding anything in sub-section (*1*), no Chairperson or a Member of the National Educational Tribunal shall be removed from his office on the grounds specified in clause (*f*) or clause (*g*) or clause (*h*) of sub-section (*1*), except by an order made by the Central Government after an inquiry made in this behalf by a Judge of the Supreme Court in which such Chairperson or such Member has been informed of the charges against him and given a reasonable opportunity of being heard in respect of those charges.

(*3*) The Central Government may, by rules, regulate the procedure for the inquiry referred to in sub-section (*2*).

27. If, for any reason other than temporary absence, any vacancy occurs in the office of the Chairperson or a Member of the National Educational Tribunal, the Central Government shall appoint another person in accordance with the provisions of this Act to fill the vacancy and the proceedings may be continued before the National Educational Tribunal from the stage at which the vacancy is filled.

28. (*1*) In the event of the occurrence of any vacancy in the office of the Chairperson of the National Educational Tribunal by reason of his death or resignation, the senior-most Member of the National Educational Tribunal shall act as the Chairperson of the Tribunal until the date on which a new Chairperson, appointed in accordance with the provisions of this Act to fill such vacancy, enters upon his office.

(*2*) When the Chairperson of the National Educational Tribunal is unable to discharge his functions owing to absence, illness or any other cause, the senior-most Member of the National Educational Tribunal, shall discharge the functions of the Chairperson until the date on which the Chairperson resumes his duties.

29. On ceasing to hold office,—

(*a*) the Chairperson or Member, as the case may be, of the National Educational Tribunal shall, subject to the provisions of this Act, be ineligible, for a period of five years from the date they cease to hold office, for further employment (including as consultant or expert or otherwise) in any higher educational institution, whether under the Central Government or the Government of any State or any private educational institution or in any institution whose matters had been before such Chairperson or Member; and

(*b*) the Chairperson or Member shall not appear, act or plead before the National Educational Tribunal or the State Educational Tribunal.

30. (*1*) The Central Government shall, after consultation with the Chairperson of the National Educational Tribunal, determine the nature and categories of the officers and other employees required to assist the National Educational Tribunal in the discharge of its functions and provide such Tribunal with such officers and other employees as it may think fit.

(*2*) The officers and other employees of the National Educational Tribunal shall discharge their functions under the general superintendence of the Chairperson of such Tribunal.

(*3*) The salaries and allowances payable to, and the other terms and conditions of service of, the officers and other employees of the National Educational Tribunal shall be such as may be prescribed by the Central Government.

31. (*1*) Save as otherwise expressly provided in this Act, the National Educational Tribunal shall exercise powers and authority in relation to—

(*a*) any dispute between any higher educational institution and any appropriate statutory regulatory authority;

(*b*) any reference made to it by any appropriate statutory regulatory authority amongst statutory regulatory authorities;

(*c*) any matter of affiliation between any higher educational institution (other than a University) and the affiliating University, where such University is a Central Educational Institution having powers of affiliation in two or more States;

(*d*) any constituent unit of an institution deemed to be University or a Central Educational Institution located in a State other than the State in which such institution deemed to be university or a Central Educational Institution is located;

(*e*) on the matters as may be assigned to it by any other law for the time being in force.

(*2*) The National Educational Tribunal shall exercise appellate jurisdiction, as provided in section 19, over a matter under clauses (*b*) to (*d*) of section 15 decided by any State Educational Tribunal.

(*3*) The National Educational Tribunal shall have the power to call for the records and pass appropriate orders in any matter which is pending before or has been decided by any State Educational Tribunal, where it appears to the National Educational Tribunal that such State Educational Tribunal has exercised a jurisdiction not vested in it by law, or has failed to exercise a jurisdiction so vested or has acted in exercise of its jurisdiction illegally or with material irregularity.

(*4*) Where cases involving the same or substantially the same issues, to the satisfaction of the National Educational Tribunal, either on its own motion or on an application made by a party to any such case, are pending before the National Educational Tribunal and one or more State Educational Tribunals or before two or more State Educational Tribunals, the National Educational Tribunal may withdraw the case or cases pending before the State Educational Tribunal or the State Educational Tribunal's and dispose of all the cases itself:

Provided that the National Educational Tribunal may, after determining the said issues, return any case so withdrawn together with a copy of its order on such questions to the State Educational Tribunal from which the case has been withdrawn, and the State Educational Tribunal shall on receipt thereof, proceed to dispose of the case in conformity with such order.

32. Any person, for settlement of any dispute arising out of matters referred to in clause (*a*) or in clause (*b*) or in clause (*c*) or in clause (*d*) or clause (*e*) of sub-section (*1*) of section 31 may make an application, in such form and accompanied by such documents and on payment of such fee and the manner as may be prescribed by the Central Government, within a period of six months from the date when such dispute first arose:

Provided that the National Educational Tribunal may entertain an appeal or application after the expiry of the said period of six months, if it is satisfied that the appellant had sufficient cause for not preferring the appeal within the said period.

33. (*1*) The National Educational Tribunal shall, not admit an application in respct of a service matter of any teacher or any other employee of the Constituent Unit of any Institution deemed to be a University or Central Educational Institution referred to in clause (*d*) of section 31 unless it is satisfied that the applicant had availed of all the remedies available to him under the relevant service rules for redressal of grievances.

(*2*) For the purposes of sub-section (*1*), a person shall be deemed to have availed of all the remedies available to him under the relevant service rules as to redressal of grievances,—

(*a*) if a final order has been made by the higher educational institution or other authority or officer or other person competent to pass such order under such rules, rejecting any appeal preferred or representation made by such person in connection with the grievance; or

(*b*) where no final order has been made by the higher educational institution or other authority or officer or other person competent to pass such order with regard to the application or representation made or appeal preferred by such person, if a period of three months from the date on which such application or representation was made or appeal was preferred was made has expired; or

(*c*) where no service rules exist on the service matters raised.

Explanation.—For the purposes of this section, the words "final order" means an order passed by such final appellate authority of the higher educational institution as provided in the service rules but does not include an order passed in any arbitration or any conciliation proceedings under the Arbitration and Conciliation Act, 1996.

34. (*1*) A National Educational Tribunal shall not admit an application,—

(*a*) in a case where a final order referred to in clause (*a*) of sub-section (*2*) of section 33 has been made, unless the application is made, within a period of six months from the date on which such final order has been made;

(*b*) in a case where an appeal or representation such as is mentioned in clause (*b*) of sub-section (*2*) of section 33 has been made and a period of three months had expired thereafter without such final order having been made, within a period of six months from the date of expiry of the said period of three months;

(*c*) in any other matter within a period of six months from the date the cause of action arose.

(*2*) Notwithstanding anything contained in this section, an application may be admitted after the period of six months specified in clause (*a*) or clause (*b*) or clause (*c*) of this section, if the applicant satisfies the National Educational Tribunal that he had sufficient cause for not making the application within such period.

35. Any person aggrieved by an order made by the National Educational Tribunal may prefer an appeal against such order to the Supreme Court within a period of sixty days from the date of the order:

Provided that the Supreme Court may entertain an appeal after the expiry of the said period of sixty days, if it is satisfied that the appellant had sufficient cause for not preferring the appeal within the period of sixty days.

CHAPTER IV
PENALTIES

36. Whoever fails to comply with any order made by any State Educational Tribunal or the National Educational Tribunal, as the case may be, he shall be punishable with imprisonment for a term which may extend to three years, or with fine which may extend to ten lakh rupees, or with both.

37. (*1*) An order made by every State Educational Tribunal and the National Educational Tribunal, under this Act shall be executable as a decree of a civil court, and for this purpose, the State

Educational Tribunal and the National Educational Tribunal shall have all the powers of a civil court.

(*2*) Notwithstanding anything contained in sub-section (*1*), the Tribunal may transmit to the Collector having jurisdiction over the concerned higher educational institution or against the person against whom an order had been made, and the Collector shall execute the order.

(*3*) Where the higher educational institution or any person, against whom the order is made by the State Educational Tribunal or the National Educational Tribunal, as the case may be, fails to make the payment or deposit the amount as directed by such Tribunal within the period specified in the order, such amount shall be recoverable from such institution or person as arrears of land revenue.

38. (*1*) No court shall take cognizance of any offence punishable under this Chapter, save on a complaint made by the officer authorised by the National Educational Tribunal or a State Educational Tribunal, as the case may be.

(*2*) No court inferior to that of a Chief Metropolitan Magistrate or a Chief Judicial Magistrate of first class shall try any offence punishable under this Chapter.

CHAPTER V

MISCELLANEOUS

39. (*1*) For the purpose of inquiring into an application, every State Educational Tribunal and the National Educational Tribunal shall have the same powers as are vested in a civil court under the Code of Civil Procedure, 1908, while trying a suit in respect of the following matters, namely:—

(*a*) summoning and enforcing the attendance of any person and examining him on oath;

(*b*) requiring the discovery and production of documents;

(*c*) receiving evidence on affidavits;

(*d*) subject to the provisions of sections 123 and 124 of the Indian Evidence Act, 1872, requisitioning any public record or document or copy of such record or document from any office;

(*e*) issuing commissions for the examination of witnesses or documents;

(*f*) reviewing its decisions;

(*g*) dismissing an application for default or deciding it *ex parte*;

(*h*) setting aside any order of dismissal of any application for default or any order passed by it *ex parte*; and

(*i*) any other matter which may be prescribed by the appropriate Government or by the Central Government, as the case may be.

(*2*) A person making an application under this Act may appear either in person or authorise one or more legal practitioners to present his case before the State Educational Tribunal or the National Educational Tribunal.

(*3*) Any institution may authorise one or more legal practitioners or any of its officers to present its case before the State Educational Tribunal or the National Educational Tribunal.

(*4*) The State Educational Tribunal shall not be bound by the procedure laid down in the Code of Civil Procedure, 1908 but shall be guided by the principles of natural justice and subject to other provisions of this Act and of any rules made by the appropriate Government.

(*5*) The National Educational Tribunal shall not be bound by the procedure laid down in the Code of Civil Procedure, 1908 but shall be guided by the principles of natural justice and subject to other provisions of this Act and of any rules made by the Central Government.

(*6*) The State Educational Tribunal and the National Educational Tribunal shall conduct such proceedings as may be required for it to arrive at a conclusion provided that an opportunity of being heard and produce such evidence as may be necessary, shall be adequately offered to all the parties at issue.

(*7*) Every proceeding referred to in sub-section (*6*) shall be conducted, in the case of the State Educational Tribunal, by its Chairperson and at least one Member thereof sitting together:

Provided that where a Member of the State Educational Tribunal, for any reason, is unable to conduct a proceeding till it is completed, the Chairperson and the other Member of such Tribunal shall continue the proceeding from the stage at which it was last heard by the previous Member.

(*8*) Every proceeding referred to in sub-section (*6*) shall be conducted, in the case of the National Educational Tribunal, by a bench constituted by the Chairperson of the National Educational Tribunal under clause (*b*) of sub-section (*4*) of section 21.

(*9*) On the conclusion of proceedings, the State Educational Tribunal or the National Educational Tribunal, as the case may be, shall pass such orders as it deems fit and provide such relief as may be desirable, including the award of such punitive damages, as it deems fit, to the affected party at issue:

Provided that where the proceeding is conducted by the Chairperson and one Member of the State Educational Tribunal and they differ on any point or points, they shall state the point or points on which they differ and refer the same to the other Member of such Tribunal for hearing on such point or points and the opinion of the majority shall be the order of the State Educational Tribunal:

Provided further that the order of the State Educational Tribunal on the matters covered under clause (*a*) of section 15 shall be final.

(*10*) Every order made by the State Educational Tribunal or the National Educational Tribunal, as the case may be, under sub-section (*9*) shall be signed by the Chairperson or Member or Members who heard the case and passed the order.

40. Notwithstanding anything contained in any other provisions of this Act or in any other law for the time being in force, no interim order, whether by way of injunction or stay in any other manner, shall be made by a State Educational Tribunal or the National Educational Tribunal, as the case may be, on, or in any proceedings relating to, an application unless,—

(*a*) copies of such application and of all documents in support of the plea for such interim order are furnished to the party against whom such application is made or proposed to be made; and

(*b*) opportunity to be heard is given to such party in the matter.

41. All proceedings before any State Educational Tribunal and the National Educational Tribunal, shall be deemed to be judicial proceedings within the meaning of sections 193, 219 and 228 of the Indian Penal Code.

42. No act or proceeding of any State Educational Tribunal or the National Educational Tribunal shall be questioned or be invalid merely on the ground of existence of any vacancy or defect in the establishment of the State Educational Tribunal and the National Educational Tribunal.

43. The Chairperson and other Members of the State Educational Tribunals and the National Educational Tribunal and the officers and other employees of the State Educational Tribunals and the National Educational Tribunal shall be deemed to be public servants within the meaning of section 21 of the Indian Penal Code.

44. The National Educational Tribunal shall have administrative control over all the State Educational Tribunals in the following matters, namely:—

(*a*) calling for periodical returns regarding the institution, disposal and pendency of cases;

(*b*) issuance of instructions regarding adoption of uniform procedure in the hearing of matters, prior service of copies of documents produced by one party to the opposite parties, furnishing of English translation of orders written in any language, speedy grant of copies of documents;

(*c*) generally overseeing the functioning of the State Educational Tribunals to ensure that the objects and purposes of the Act are best served without in any way interfering with their quasi-judicial freedom.

45. Where a matter instituted before any State Educational Tribunal or the National Educational Tribunal, as the case may be, is found to be frivolous or vexatious, it shall, for reasons to be recorded in writing, dismiss the application and make an order that the applicant shall pay to the opposite party such cost, not exceeding fifty thousand rupees, as may be specified in the order.

46. Every order of a State Educational Tribunal or the National Educational Tribunal, as the case may be, shall, if no appeal has been preferred against such order under the provisions of this Act, be final.

47. No civil court shall have jurisdiction to entertain any suit or proceeding in respect of any matter which the State Educational Tribunal or the National Educational Tribunal is empowered by or under this Act to determine and no injunction shall be granted by any court or other authority in respect of any action taken or to be taken in pursuance of any power conferred by or under this Act.

48. No suit, prosecution or other legal proceeding shall lie against the Central Government or any State Government or against the Chairperson or any other Member or any other person authorised by the Chairperson of any State Educational Tribunal or the National Educational Tribunal, as the case may be, for anything which is done in good faith or intended to be done in pursuance of this Act or any rule or order made thereunder in the discharge of official duties.

49. The provisions of this Act shall have overriding effect notwithstanding anything inconsistent therewith contained, in any other law for the time being in force or in any instrument having effect by virtue of any law other than this Act.

50. The provisions of this Act shall be in addition to, and not in derogation of, the provisions of any other law for the time being in force.

51. Nothing contained in this Act or the rules made thereunder shall apply to any minority institution to the extent to which they are inconsistent with the functions and powers vested upon the National Commission for Minority Educational Institutions established under the National Commission for Minority Educational Institutions Act, 2004 or provisions contained in that Act.

52. (*1*) The Central Government may, by notification in the Official Gazette, make rules to carry out the provisions of this Act. (*2*) In particular, and without prejudice to the generality of the foregoing power, such rules may provide for all or any of the following matters, namely:—

(*a*) the form and manner in which an appeal may be preferred, the documents which shall be accompanied with it and the fee payable in respect of filing of such appeal or for the service of execution of processes under section 19;

(*b*) the term of the Selection Committee and the manner of selection of panel of names under sub-section (*3*) of section 23;

(*c*) the salaries and allowances payable to, and the other terms and conditions of service of the Chairperson and other Members of the National Educational Tribunal under sub-section (*2*) of section 24;

(*d*) the other disqualifications for removal of the Chairperson or other Member of the National Educational Tribunal under clause (*i*) of sub-section (*1*), of section 26 and, the procedure for the inquiry referred to in sub-section (*3*) of that section;

(*e*) the salaries and allowances payable to, and other terms and conditions of, service of, the officers and other employees of the National Educational Tribunal under sub-section (*3*) of section 30;

(*f*) the form in which an application may be made, the documents and other evidence by which such application shall be accompanied and the fee payable in respect of the filing of such application or for the service of execution of processes under section 32;

(*g*) the other matters under clause (*i*) of sub-section (*1*) of section 39 in respect of which the National Educational Tribunal shall have the powers under the Code of Civil Procedure, 1908 while trying a suit;

(*h*) the procedure for conduct of proceedings of the National Educational Tribunal under sub-section (*5*) of section 39;

(*i*) any other matter which is required to be, or may be, specified by rules or in respect of which provision is to be made by rules.

53. (*1*) The appropriate Government may, by notification in the Official Gazette, make rules to carry out the provisions of this Act.

(*2*) In particular, and without prejudice to the generality of the foregoing power, such rules may provide for all or any of the following matters, namely:—

(*a*) the term of the Selection Committee and the manner of selection of panel of names under sub-section (*3*) of section 7;

(*b*) the salaries and allowances payable to, and the other terms and conditions of service of, the Chairperson and other Members of the State Educational Tribunal under sub-section (*2*) of section 8;

(*c*) the other disqualifications for removal of the Chairperson or other Member of the State Educational Tribunal under clause (*i*) of sub-section (*1*) of section 10, and the procedure for the inquiry referred to in sub-section (*3*) of that section;

(*d*) the salaries and allowances payable to, and other terms and conditions of service of the officers and other employees of, the State Educational Tribunal under sub-section (*3*) of section 14;

(*e*) the form in which an application may be made, the documents and other evidence by which such application shall be accompanied and the fee payable in respect of the filing of such application or for the service of execution of processes under section 16;

(*f*) the other matters under clause (*i*) of sub-section (*1*) of section 39 in respect of which the State Educational Tribunal shall have the powers under the Code of Civil Procedure, 1908 while trying a suit;

(*g*) the procedure for conduct of proceedings of the State Educational Tribunal under sub-section (*4*) of section 39;

(*h*) any other matter which is required to be, or may be, specified by rules or in respect of which provision is to be made by rules.

54. (*1*) Every rule made by the Central Government, under this Act shall be laid, as soon as may be after it is made, before each House of

Parliament, while it is in session for a total period of thirty days which may be comprised in one session or in two or more successive sessions, and if before the expiry of the session immediately following the session or the successive sessions aforesaid, both Houses agree in making any modification in the rule or both Houses agree that the rule should not be made, the rule shall thereafter have effect only in such modified form or be of no effect, as the case may be; so, however, that any such modification or annulment shall be without prejudice to the validity of anything previously done under that rule.

(*2*) Every rule made by the State Government under this Act shall be laid, as soon as may be after it is made, before each House of the State Legislature where it consists of two Houses, or where such Legislature consists of one House, before that House.

55. (*1*) If any difficulty arises in giving effect to the provisions of this Act, the Central Government may, by order published in the Official Gazette, make such provisions, not inconsistent with the provisions of this Act, as appear to it to be necessary or expedient for removing the difficulty:

Provided that no such order shall be made after the expiry of the period of three years from the date on which this Act receives the assent of the President.

(*2*) Every order made under this section shall, as soon as may be after it is made, be laid before each House of Parliament.

THE FOREIGN EDUCATIONAL INSTITUTIONS (REGULATION OF ENTRY AND OPERATIONS) BILL, 2010

A
BILL

to regulate entry and operation of foreign educational institutions imparting or intending to impart higher education (including technical education and medical education and award of degree, diploma and equivalent qualifications by such institutions) and for matters connected therewith or incidental thereto.

BE it enacted by Parliament in the Sixty-first Year of the Republic of India as ollows:—

CHAPTER I
PRELIMINARY

1. (*1*) This Act may be called the Foreign Educational Institutions (Regulation of Entry and Operations) Act, 2010.

(*2*) It shall come into force on such date as the Central Government may, by notification in the Official Gazette, appoint; and different dates may be appointed for different provisions of this Act and any reference in any provision to the commencement of this Act shall be construed as a reference to the coming into force of that provision.

2. In this Act, unless the context otherwise requires,-

(*a*) "accrediting agency", in respect of a course of study offered in India by a foreign educational institution, means an agency or body approved, recognised or authorised by the Council for Higher Education Accreditation or University Quality Agency or the Quality Assurance Authority, by whatever name called, established or incorporated under a law in the country of origin of the foreign educational institution or any other statutory authority in that country for the purpose of assessing, accrediting or assuring quality and standards of educational institutions;

(*b*) "Advisory Board" means the Advisory Board constituted under sub-section (*2*) of section 9;

(*c*) "Commission" means the University Grants Commission established under the University Grants Commission Act, 1956 or any other body or council or commission established under any Central Act for the time being in force to regulate the entry and operation of foreign educational institution;

(*d*) "fee" means all fees including tuition fee and development charges, by whatever name called, payable by the students enrolled for pursuing courses or programmes of study;

(*e*) "foreign educational institution" means -

(*i*) an institution established or incorporated outside India which has been offering educational services for at least twenty years in the country in which it had been established or incorporated; and

(*ii*) which offers educational services in India or proposes to offer courses leading to award of degree or diploma or certificate or any other award through conventional method including classroom teaching method not including distant mode in India independently or in collaboration, partnership or in a twinning arrangement with any educational institution situated in India;

(*f*) "foreign education provider" means a foreign educational institution notified by the Central Government, as a foreign education provider, on the recommendation of the Commission as an institution competent to impart education in India and to award degree, diploma or any other equivalent qualification (other than in the distance mode) at undergraduate, post-graduate, doctoral or post-doctoral level;

(*g*) "national research professor" means a person, who is an academic of high distinction, declared as such by the Central Government;

(*h*) "National Educational Tribunal" means the National Educational Tribunal established under the Educational Tribunals Act, 2010;

(*i*) "notification" means a notification published in the Official Gazette and the expression "notify" with its cognate meanings and grammatical variations shall be construed accordingly;

(*j*) "prescribed" means prescribed by rules made under this Act;

(*k*) "profession" means the profession of law, medicine and such other profession as may be notified by the Central Government from time to time;

'(*l*) "Registrar" means the Secretary of the University Grants Commission or any other officer of the Commission notified, by the Central Government, as Registrar for the purposes of this Act;'

(*m*) "regulations" means regulations made by the Commission;

(*n*) "statutory authority"—

(*i*) in relation to higher education or technical education or practice of any profession means an authority established or incorporated under a Central Act to regulate standards of such higher education or technical education or practice of any profession;

(*ii*) in relation to medical education means the statutory authority established under -

(*A*) the Indian Medical Council Act, 1956; or

(*B*) the Homoeopathy Central Council Act, 1973; or

(*C*) the Indian Medicine Central Council Act, 1970; or

(*D*) the Dentists Act, 1948; or

(*E*) the Pharmacy Act, 1948; or

(*F*) the Indian Nursing Council Act, 1947;

(*iii*) in relation to legal education means the Bar Council of India constituted under section 4 of the Advocates Act, 1961;

(*o*) "technical education" means the technical education as defined in the All India Council of Technical Education Act, 1987;

(*p*) "twinning programme" means a programme whereby students enrolled with a foreign education provider complete their study partly in India and partly in any other educational institution situated outside India.

CHAPTER II
FOREIGN EDUCATIONAL INSTITUTIONS

3. No foreign educational institution shall admit any person as a student, or collect any fee from such person or its students in India for any course of study leading to the award of a degree or a diploma, by whatever name called, unless such institution has been notified by the Central Government as a foreign education provider under sub-section (*8*) of section 4.

4. (*1*) Any foreign educational institution which intents to impart education in India, shall submit an application, for being recognised and notified as a foreign education provider under this Act, to the Registrar and such application be duly endorsed by the concerned Embassy or High Commission in India of the country in which such institution is established or incorporated and has been offering educational services in that country:

Provided that a foreign educational institution providing educational services in India before the commencement of this Act, shall apply under this sub-section within a period of six months from the date of commencement of this Act and it shall cease to provide educational services in accordance with the provisions of this Act if its application for recognition and notifying as foreign education provider has been rejected.

(*2*) The form and manner in which an application under sub-section (*1*) shall be made and the other particulars, including payment of fee, shall be such as may be prescribed.

(*3*) Every application under sub-section (*1*) shall be accompanied by -

(*a*) the documents to the effect that such foreign educational institution -

(*i*) has been established or incorporated and has been offering educational services for at least twenty years under a law of the country in which such institution is established or incorporated and registered along with the status of its accreditation, wherever applicable, from the accrediting agency of that country; and

(*ii*) has adequate financial and other resources to conduct the course or courses of study in India;

(*b*) an undertaking to maintain a corpus fund of not less than fifty crore rupees or of such sum as may be notified, from time to time, by the Central Government in consultation with the statutory authority.

(*4*) The Registrar shall, on receipt of an application under sub-section (*1*), forward a copy thereof to the statutory authority for obtaining its recommendation as to the fitness of such institution to provide quality education in India:

Provided that the statutory authority shall make its recommendation to the Registrar within a period of three months from the date of receipt of the copy of the application under sub-section (*4*).

(*5*) The Registrar shall make such inquiries, in such manner, as may be specified by regulations, to ensure that the foreign educational institution meets the requirements to provide quality education in India, as laid down under any law for the time being in force.

(*6*) The Registrar shall, as early as possible, and preferably within a period of six months from the date of receipt of the application under sub-section (*1*) by an foreign educational institution, submit his report on the fitness of such institution to provide quality education in India, along with such recommendations as may be made by the statutory authority, to the Commission.

(*7*) The Commission shall consider the report of the Registrar and recommendations of statutory authority, and recommend to the Central Government, within a period of thirty days from the date of receipt of such report and recommendations, as to the fitness of such institution proposed to be recognised and notified as a foreign education provider in India:

Provided that if the Commission is of the opinion that it shall not be in the interest of the sovereignty and integrity of India, the security of the State, friendly relations with foreign States, public order, decency or morality or sensitivity of location of the foreign educational institution or any other such reason to permit a foreign educational institution to operate in India, either independently or in collaboration or partnership or in twinning arrangement with any educational institution situated in India, it shall submit a report to the Central Government in this regard, and the decision of the Central Government thereon shall be final.

(*8*) The Central Government may, having regard to the report of the Commission, within a period of thirty days from the date of receipt of such report, recognised and notify such foreign educational institution as a foreign education provider for the purpose of award of degree or diploma or both in India and immediately after such notification, notwithstanding anything contrary or otherwise in the University Grants Commission Act, 1956, the provisions of that Act shall apply to such institution as they apply to any university in India:

Provided that the Central Government may reject the application of a foreign educational institution for reasons to be recorded in writing and communicate the same to such institution within a period of thirty days from the date of receipt of report of the Commission.

5. (*1*) A foreign education provider shall ensure that the course or programme of study offered and imparted by it in India is, in conformity with the standards laid down by the statutory authority, and is of quality comparable, as to the curriculum, methods of imparting education and the faculty employed or engaged to impart education, to those offered by it to students enrolled in its main campus in the country in which such institution is established or incorporated.

(*2*) A foreign education provider shall, out of the income received from the corpus fund, utilise not more than seventy-five per cent. of such income for the purposes of development of its institution in India and the remaining of such unutilised income shall be deposited into the corpus fund.

(*3*) No part of the surplus in revenue generated in India by such Foreign Education Provider, after meeting all expenditure in regard to its operations in India, shall be invested for any purpose other than for the growth and development of the educational institutions established by it in India.

6. (*1*) Every foreign education provider shall publish, before expiry of sixty days prior to the date of the commencement of admission to any of its courses or programmes of study, a prospectus containing the following for the purposes of informing those persons intending to seek admission and the general public, namely: -

(*i*) each component of the fee, deposits and other charges payable by students admitted to such institution for pursuing a course or programme of study, and the other terms and conditions of such payment;

(*ii*) the percentage of tuition fee and other charges refundable to a student admitted in such institution in case such student withdraws from such institution before or after completion of course or programme of study and the time within, and the manner in, which such refund shall be made to that student;

(*iii*) the number of seats approved by the statutory authority in respect of each course or programme of study for the academic year for which admission is proposed to be made;

(*iv*) the conditions of eligibility including the minimum and maximum age limit, if any, of persons for admission as a student in a particular course or programme of study, where so specified by the institution;

(*v*) the educational qualifications specified by the relevant statutory authority, or by the institution, where no such qualifying standards have been specified by any statutory authority;

(*vi*) the process of admission and selection of eligible candidates applying for such admission, including all relevant information in regard to the details of test or examination, if any, for selecting such candidates for admission to each course or programme of study and the amount of fee to be paid for the admission test;

(*vii*) details of the teaching faculty, including therein the educational qualifications and teaching experience of every member of its teaching faculty and also indicating therein whether such members are on regular basis or as visiting member;

(*viii*) the minimum pay and other emoluments payable for each category of teachers and other employees;

(*ix*) information in regard to physical and academic infrastructure and other facilities including hostel accommodation, library and hospital or industry wherein the practical training to be imparted to the students and in particular the facilities accessible by students on being admitted to the institution;

(*x*) broad outlines of the syllabus specified by the statutory authority or by the institution, as the case may be, for every course or programme of study, including the teaching hours, practical sessions and other assignments;

(*xi*) all relevant instructions in regard to maintaining the discipline by students within or outside the campus of the institution, and, in particular such discipline relating to the prohibition of ragging of any student or students and the consequences thereof and for violating the provisions of any regulation in this behalf made under the University Grants Commission Act, 1956 or any other law for the time being in force;

(*xii*) any such other information which may be prescribed:

Provided that the foreign education provider shall publish information referred to in items (*i*) to (*xii*) of this sub-section, on its website, and the attention of prospective students and the general public shall be drawn to such publication on the website through advertisements displayed prominently in the different newspapers and through other media:

Provided further that the foreign education provider may publish prospectus in accordance with this section at any time before the period of sixty days specified under this sub-section.

(*2*) Every foreign education provider shall fix the price of each printed copy of the prospectus, being not more than the reasonable cost of its publication and distribution and no profit be made out of the publication, distribution or sale of prospectus.

7. (*1*) If the Commission is satisfied that the foreign education provider has violated any provision of this Act or the University Grants Commission Act, 1956 or any other law for the time being in force or rules, regulations or orders made or notifications issued thereunder, it may, after giving a reasonable opportunity of being heard to the foreign education provider, recommend to the Central Government for withdrawal or recognition and rescission of the notification issued under sub-section (*8*) of section 4 in respect of such foreign education provider.

(*2*) Where the Central Government is satisfied that the recognition of the foreign education provider, referred to in sub-section (*1*), is to be withdrawn and notification issued under sub-section (*8*) of section 4 in respect of such foreign education provider to be rescinded, it shall require the Commission to intimate¯

(*i*) the management of the foreign education provider;

(*ii*) the teachers employed by the foreign education provider; and

(*iii*) the student council or any other body by whatever name called, and the parents of the students enrolled by the foreign education provider, by a notice, in such manner as may be prescribed, of the grounds for withdrawal of recognition and rescission of the notification issued under sub-section (*8*) of section 4 in respect of such foreign education provider.

(*3*) The management or teachers or students council or parents of students of such foreign education provider may, within a period of thirty days from date of receipt of notice under sub-section (*2*), represent to the Central Government against the proposed rescission of the notification in respect of such foreign education provider.

(*4*) If the Central Government, after considering the representations, if any, received under sub-section (*3*), is satisfied, it may withdraw the recognition and rescind the notification issued under sub-section (*8*) of section 4 in respect of the foreign education provider referred to in sub-section (*1*).

(*5*) On withdrawal of the recognition and rescission of the notification issued under sub-section (*8*) of section 4 in respect of the foreign education provider, the foreign educational institution shall cease to be a foreign education provider on and from the last date of the academic session following the previous academic session in which the notice under subsection (*2*) was issued by the Commission.

(*6*) On withdrawal of recognition and rescission of the notification issued under subsection (*8*) of section 4 in respect of the foreign education provider, the Central Government shall, as soon as may be, take such measures as may be necessary to provide alternative and appropriate educational facilities for those students who were enrolled by such foreign education provider.

(*7*) The Central Government may, in accordance with the relevant law for the time being in force, attach the corpus fund and such other properties of the foreign education provider referred to in sub-section (*4*), as it may deem fit to make payments to any person employed in India by such foreign education provider, and for making arrangements of appropriate educational facilities for students referred to in subsection (*6*).

CHAPTER III

PENALTIES

8. (*1*) Notwithstanding anything contained in the University Grants Commission Act, 1956, any person who, being associated with an educational institution or a foreign educational institution not being a foreign education provider which has not been recognized and notified under sub-section (*8*) of section 4 or whose recognition and notification has been withdrawn -

(*a*) offers or gives admission to any person as student or collects fee or awards any degree, diploma or any other equivalent qualification in violation of the provisions of section 3; or (*b*) publishes or releases any advertisement which is misleading or gives wrongful information in the print, electronic or any other media or fails to publish disclosures as required under section 13, shall be liable to a penalty which shall not be less than ten lakh rupees but which may extend to fifty lakh rupees in addition to refund of the fee, so collected, to the persons from whom it was collected and confiscation of any gains made out of it.

(*2*) Any foreign education provider, which has been recognised and notified under sub-section (*8*) of section 4, who contravenes any provision of section 5 or section 6 or any provision of the University Grants Commission Act, 1956, shall be liable to a penalty which shall not be less than ten lakh rupees but which may extend to fifty lakh rupees and the forfeiture of the corpus fund referred to in clause (b) of sub-section (*4*) of section 4 in whole or part thereof.

(*3*) All sums realised by way of penalties or the gains confiscated under this Chapter or the amount of corpus fund forfieted shall be credited to the Consolidated Fund of India.

CHAPTER IV

MISCELLANEOUS

9. (*1*) Notwithstanding anything contained in this Act, the Central Government may, by notification, on the recommendation of the Advisory Board constituted under sub-section (*2*), having regard to the reputation and international standing of foreign educational institution and such other criteria as may be prescribed, exempt such institution from operation of any of the foregoing provisions, other than sub-section (*3*) of section 5 and section 8.

(2) For the purpose of sub-section (*1*), the Central Government shall, by notification, constitute an Advisory Board consisting of -

(*a*) three distinguished persons from the field of academics, who are, or may have been at any time, declared as a national research professor, one of whom shall be designated as the Chairperson of the Advisory Board;

(*b*) Chairman of the Commission, *ex officio*;

(*c*) Chairman of one of the statutory authorities, other than the Commission, by rotation.

(*3*) The Advisory Board shall meet at such times and places, and observe such rules of procedure in regard to the transaction of business at its meetings (including quorum at such meeting) as may be prescribed.

10. (*1*) Without prejudice to the foregoing provisions of this Act, the Commission,

shall, in exercise of its powers or performance of its functions under this Act, be bound by such directions on question of policy as the Central Government may give in writing to it, from time to time:

Provided that the Commission shall, as far as practicable, be given an opportunity to express its views before any direction is given under this sub-section.

(*2*) The decision of the Central Government whether a question is one of policy or not shall be final.

11. Save as otherwise provided in this Act, all the matters (including the penalties leviable under this Act) shall be adjudicated by the National Educational Tribunal.

12. The provisions of this Act shall be in addition to, and not in derogation of, the provisions of any other law for the time being in force.

13. (*1*) Notwithstanding anything contained in this Act, a foreign educational institution (not being a foreign education provider

notified under section 4), which is imparting education leading to award of certificate or any other qualification not being a degree or diploma or equivalent qualifications, shall furnish a report to the Commission about its activities, in such manner as may be specified by regulations.

(*2*) The foreign educational institution referred to in sub-section (*1*), shall publish information on its website and draw the attention of prospective students and the general public to such publication on the website through advertisements displayed prominently in the different newspapers and through other media, indicating, *inter alia*, the following, namely:-

(*a*) the details of course or programme of study leading to the award of certificate;

(*b*) the details of enrolment of students;

(*c*) the details of infrastructure available with it;

(*d*) details of the place wherefrom such institution is operating in India;

(*e*) whether operating on its own or through collaboration or partnership or twinning arrangement with any Indian educational institution and the details thereof;

(*f*) such other information as may be considered necessary by the Commission.

14. (*1*) The Central Government may, by notification, make rules for carrying out the provisions of this Act.

(*2*) In particular, and without prejudice to the generality of the foregoing power, such rules may provide for all or any of the following matters, namely:-

(*a*) the form and manner in which an application may be made and other particulars including payment of fee under sub-section (*2*) of section 4;

(*b*) the other information required to be published in the prospectus by a foreign education provider under clause (*xii*) of sub-section (*1*) of section 6;

(*c*) the manner in which notice shall be given under sub-section (*2*) of section 7;

(*d*) the criteria for granting exemption to foreign educational institution under sub-section (*1*) of section 9;

(*e*) the time and place at which the Advisory Board shall meet and rules of procedure in regard to the transaction of business at its meetings (including quorum at such meeting) to be observed by it under sub-section (*3*) of section 9;

(*f*) any other matter which is required to be, or may be, prescribed or in respect of which provision is to be made by rules by the Central Government.

15. (*1*) The Commission may, by notification, make regulations, consistent with this Act and the rules made thereunder to carry out the provisions of this Act.

(*2*) In particular and without prejudice to the generality of the foregoing power, such regulations may provide for all or any of the following matters, namely:—

(*a*) the inquiries and the manner of making such inquiries by the Registrar under sub-section (*5*) of section 4;

(*b*) the manner in which a foreign educational institution shall report of its activities under sub-section (*1*) of section 13;

(*c*) any other matter which is required to be, or may be, specified by regulations or in respect of which provision is to be made by regulations.

16. Every rule and every regulation made and every notification issued under this Act shall be laid, as soon as may be after it is made or issued, before each House of Parliament, while it is in session, for a total period of thirty days which may be comprised in one session or in two or more successive sessions, and if, before the expiry of the session immediately following the session or the successive sessions aforesaid, both Houses agree in making any modification in the rule or regulation or notification, or both Houses agree that the rule or regulation or notification should not be made or issued, the rule or regulation or notification shall thereafter have effect only in such modified form or be of no effect, as the case may be; so, however, that any such modification or annulment shall be without prejudice to the validity of anything previously done under that rule or regulation or notification.

17. (*1*) If any difficulty arises in giving effect to the provisions of this Act, the Central Government may, by order published in the Official Gazette, make such provisions, not inconsistent with the provisions of this Act, as may appear to be necessary, for removing the difficulty:

Provided that no order shall be made under this section after the expiry of a period of two years from the date of commencement of this Act.

(*2*) Every order made under this section shall be laid, as soon as may be after it is made, before each House of Parliament.

STATEMENT OF OBJECTS AND REASONS

A number of Foreign Educational Institutions have been operating in the country and some of them may be resorting to various malpractices to allure and attract students. There is no comprehensive and effective policy for regulation on the operations of all the foreign educational institutions in the country. Due to lack of policy or regulatory regime it has been very difficult to make meaningful assessment of the operations of the foreign educational institutions and absence of such meaningful assessment has given rise to chances of adoption of various unfair practices besides commercialisation.

2. At present, only the All India Council for Technical Education has notified regulations for entry and operation of foreign universities and institutions imparting technical education in India which apply only to such institutions which are providing technical education covered by the All India Council for Technical Education Act, 1987.

3. The enactment of a legislation regulating entry and operation of all the foreign educational institutions is necessary to maintain the standards of higher education within the country as well to protect the interest of the students and in public interest. The object of the proposed legislation is to regulate entry and operation of foreign educational institutions imparting or intending to impart higher education or technical education or practice of any profession in India (including award of degree, diploma and equivalent qualifications by such institutions) and for matters connected therewith or incidental thereto.

4. The Foreign Educational Institutions (Regulation of Entry and Operations) Bill, 2010, *inter alia,* provides—

(*a*) that the foreign educational institution shall,—

(*i*) not impart education in India unless it is recognised and notified by the Central Government as a foreign education provider under the proposed legislation;

(*ii*) offer and impart education which is in conformity with the standards laid down by the statutory authority, and is of quality comparable, as to the curriculum, methods of imparting education and the faculty employed or engaged to impart education, to those offered by it to students enrolled in its main campus in the country in which such institution is established or incorporated;

(*iii*) maintenance of the corpus fund of not less than fifty crore rupees or such sum as may be notified from time to time by the Central Government;

(*b*) that the Central Government may,—

(*i*) refuse to recognise and notify a foreign educational institution as foreign education provider if it is not in the interest of sovereignty, integrity of India, the security of the State, friendly relations with foreign States, public order, decency or morality or sensitivity of location of the foreign educational institutions;

(*ii*) withdraw the recognition and rescind the notification of a foreign education provider on the grounds of violation of the provisions of the proposed legislation or the University Grants Commission Act, 1956 or any other law for the time being in force and on such withdrawal or recession of notification, the Central Government shall make necessary alternative arrangements;

(*c*) that any person who, being associated with an educational institution or a foreign educational institution not being a foreign education provider which has not been recognized and notified under the proposed legislation, offer or gives admission to any person as student or collects fee or awards any degree, diploma or publishes or releases any advertisement which is misleading or gives wrongful information or fails to publish disclosures as required under the proposed legislation shall be liable to a penalty of not less than ten lakh rupees which may extend to fifty lakh rupees in addition to refund of the fee and confiscation of any gains made out of it;

(*d*) that any foreign education provider, which has been recognised and notified under the proposed legislation, who contravenes the provisions of clause 5 of the proposed legislation relating to quality of programmes offered in India, use of income from corpus fund, and investment of surplus in generated revenue or the provisions of the University Grants Commission Act, 1956 shall be liable to a penalty of not less than ten lakh rupees which may extend to fifty lakh rupees and the forfeiture of the corpus fund in whole or part thereof;

(*e*) for adjudication of all matters (including penalties leviable) under the proposed legislation by the National Educational Tribunal to be established under the Educational Tribunals Bill, 2010 proposed to be enacted.

5. The Notes on clauses explain in detail the various provisions contained in the Bill.

6. The Bill seeks to achieve the above objectives.

THE NATIONAL COMMISSION FOR HIGHER EDUCATION AND RESEARCH BILL, 2010

AN ACT to provide for the determination, co-ordination, maintenance of standards in, and promotion of, higher education and research, including university education, technical and professional education other than agricultural [**and medical**] education, and for that purpose, to establish the National Commission for Higher Education and Research.

AN ACT further to promote the autonomy of higher educational institutions for the free pursuit of knowledge and innovation, and for facilitating access, inclusion and opportunities to all, and providing for comprehensive and holistic growth of higher education and research in a competitive global environment through reforms and renovation; and to provide for an advisory mechanism of eminent peers in academia. **BE** it enacted by Parliament in the Sixty-first Year of the Republic of India as follows:-

CHAPTER I
PRELIMINARY

1. **Short title and commencement.** (1) This Act may be called the National Commission for Higher Education and Research Act, 2010.

(2) It extends to the whole of India.

(3) It shall come into force on such date as the Central Government may, by notification in the Official Gazette, appoint.

2. **Applicability of Act.** The Act shall apply to all higher educational institutions other than such institutions engaged mainly in agricultural education [**and medical education**].

3. **Definitions.** In this Act, unless the context otherwise requires,—

(a) "academic quality" means the quality of teaching, learning and research and consequently their contribution to enhancement of knowledge and includes physical infrastructure, human resources (including faculty), administration, course curricula, admission and assessment procedures, governance structures, of the higher educational institution;

(b) "accreditation" with its grammatical variations means the process of quality control in higher education, whereby, as a result of evaluation or assessment or by any method specified under the National Accreditation Regulatory Authority for Higher Educational Institutions Act, 2010 [___of 2010], a higher educational institution or any programme conducted therein is recognised as conforming to parameters of academic quality and benchmarking of such academic quality determined by the Commission under this Act;

(c) "Accreditation Agency" means an agency registered under the National Accreditation Regulatory Authority for Higher Educational Institutions Act, 2009 [___of 2010];

(d) "Act" means National Commission for Higher Education and Research Act, 2010 [____of 2010];

(e) "affiliation" together with its grammatical variations, includes, in relation to a college or institution,—

(i) recognition of such college or institution by a university; or

(ii) association of such college or institution with a university; or

(iii) admission of such college or institution to the privileges of a university;

(f) "Authorisation" means authorization granted by the Commission, under subsection

(1) of section 34, to a university or other higher educational institution empowered, by or under law, to award any degree or diploma to commence its first academic operations;

(g) "Central University" means a university, or constituent units thereto, promoted and maintained by the Central Government, either directly or indirectly, and established or incorporated by or under a Central Act;

(h) "Chair" means the Chair of the Collegium;

(i) "Chairperson" means Chairperson of the National Commission for Higher Education and Research;

(j) "college" means any institution, whether known as such or by any other name, which provides for a course of study for obtaining any qualification from a university and which, in accordance with the rules and regulations of such university, is recognised as competent to provide for such course of study and present students undergoing such course of study for the examination, conducted by or on behalf of the university, for the award of such qualification;

(k) "Collegium" means the Collegium established under section 17 of this Act;

(l) "Commission" means the National Commission of Higher Education and Research established under section 4 of this Act;

(m) "Co-opted Fellow" means such fellow referred to in sub-section (4) of section 17 to represent the States and Union Territories;

(n) "Core Fellow" means such fellow referred to in sub-section (3) of section 17;

(o) "degree" means an award, granted by a university or institution empowered by or under law to do so, certifying that the recipient has successfully completed a course of study;

(p) "diploma" means such award, not being a degree, granted by a higher educational institution, other than a polytechnic, certifying that the recipient has successfully completed a course of study of not less than nine months duration;

(q) "distance education systems" means the distance education systems as defined in clause (e) of section (2) of the Indira Gandhi National Open University Act, 1985 [50 of 1985];

(r) "Fellow" means a member of the Collegium and includes the Chair and Co-Chair;

(s) "first academic operations" means the start of the process of admissions (including the publication of prospectus), for the first time by a university or institution empowered, by or under law, to award any degree or diploma, after its establishment, in respect of any course or programme of study;

(t) "higher education" means such education, imparted by means of conducting regular classes or through distance education systems, beyond twelve years of schooling leading to the award of a degree or diploma; but does not include [**medical education or**] agricultural education in institutions other than universities;

(u) "higher educational institution" means an institution of learning including an university, an institution deemed to be university, a college, an institute, an institution of national importance declared as such by an Act of Parliament, or a constituent unit of such institution, which is imparting by means of conducting regular classes or through distance education systems, higher education or research therein;

(v) "Institution deemed to be University" means an institution declared as such, by notification, by the Central Government, before the commencement of this Act;

(w) "Institution of national importance" means an institution declared as such by a Central Act;

(x) "Overseas citizen of India" means such person registered as an overseas citizen of India under the Indian Citizenship Act, 1955 [Act No. 57 of 1955], as amended from time to time;

(y) "Member" means a member of the National Commission for Higher Education and Research and includes the Chairperson;

(z) "National Education Tribunal" means National Educational Tribunal established under the Educational Tribunals Act, 2009;

(ab) "National Research Professor" means such person appointed, by the Central Government, under the National Research Professorship Scheme;

(ac) "notification" means a notification published in the Official Gazette and the expression "notify" with its cognate meanings and grammatical variations shall be construed accordingly;

(ad) "prescribed" means prescribed under rules made by the Central Government;

(ae) "programme" means a course or programme of study leading to the award of a degree or a diploma in a higher educational institution;

(af) "prospectus" includes any publication, whether in print or otherwise, issued for providing fair and transparent information, relating to a higher educational institution, to the general public (including to those seeking admission in such institution) by the management of such institution or any authority or person authorised by such institution to do so;

(ag) "regulations" means regulations made by the Commission under this Act;

(ah) "State Educational Tribunal" means State Educational Tribunal established under the Educational Tribunals Act, 2009 [___ of 2010];

(ai) "State University" means a university, or constituent units thereto, promoted and maintained, either directly or indirectly, by a State Government, and established or incorporated by or under any State Act;

(aj) "University" means a University established or incorporated by or under a Central Act or a State Act and includes an institution deemed to be University;

(ak) "Vice Chancellor" means the chief executive of a university;

(al) "Whole-time Members" means the members of the National Commission for Higher Education and Research referred to in sub-section (2) of section 5, and includes the Chairperson.

(2) Words and expressions used and not defined herein but defined elsewhere in any law enacted by Parliament or in the General Clauses Act, 1897 [10 of 1897], and not inconsistent with this Act shall have the meanings respectively assigned to them in such law or in the General Clauses Act, 1897 [10 of 1897].

CHAPTER II
NATIONAL COMMISSION OF HIGHER EDUCATION AND RESEARCH

4. Establishment of National Commission of Higher Education and Research. –

(1) The Central Government shall, by notification, establish, for the purposes of this Act, a Commission to be called the "National Commission for Higher Education and Research".

(2) The Commission shall be a body corporate by the name aforesaid, having perpetual succession and a common seal, with power, subject to the provisions of this Act, to acquire, hold and dispose off property, both movable and immovable , and to contract, and shall, by the said name, sue or be sued.

(3) The head office of the Commission shall be at New Delhi.

5. **Appointment of Chairperson and Members of Commission.** – (1) The Commission shall consist of a Chairperson and six other Members.

(2) The office of the Chairperson and three other Members shall be whole-time and salaried.

(3) The Chairperson and the other whole-time Members shall be scholars being persons of eminence and standing in the field of academics and research possessing leadership abilities, proven capacity for institution building and governance of institutions of higher learning and research.

(4) The Members other than the whole-time Members shall be persons of eminence with high academic credentials with proven contribution to economic and social development and experience of engagement with institutions of higher learning and research.

(5) The Chairperson and other Members shall be appointed by the President on the recommendation of a Selection Committee consisting of:-

(i) the Prime Minister, who shall be the Chairperson of the Committee;

(ii) the Speaker of Lok Sabha; and

(iii) the Leader of Opposition in Lok Sabha; and

(iv) [the Minister in charge of Higher Education in the Government of India;

(v) the Minister in charge of Medical Education in the Government of India].

Explanation.—For the purposes of removal of doubts, it is hereby declared that where the Leader of Opposition in the Lok Sabha has not been recognised as such, the Leader of the single largest group in opposition to the Government in the Lok Sabha shall be deemed to be the Leader of Opposition.

(6) The Selection Committee shall make its recommendation from a panel of three names, submitted by the Collegium under clause (c) of sub-section (1) of section 19, for each vacancy.

(7) The Selection Committee shall devise its own procedure for assessing the suitability of the person from the panel of names referred to in sub-section (6) to be recommended to the President for appointment.

(8) Every appointment under this section shall take effect from the date on which it is notified in the Official Gazette by the Central Government.

(9) The Chairperson or other Member shall, before entering office make and subscribe before the President or some other person appointed by the President in that behalf, an oath of affirmation.

6. **Resignation and removal of Chairperson and Members.** - (1) The Chairperson or any Member may, by notice in writing under his hand addressed to the President, resign from office.

(2) The President may remove from office the Chairperson or any Member, who——

(a) has been adjudged an insolvent; or

(b) has engaged, at any time during his term of office, in any paid employment outside the duties of his office; or

(c) has become physically or mentally incapable of acting as such Chairperson or other Member; or

(d) is of unsound mind and stands so declared by a competent court; or

(e) has been convicted of an offence which, in the opinion of the President, involves moral turpitude; or

(f) has acquired such financial or other interest as is likely to affect prejudicially the exercise of his functions as such Chairperson or other Member; or

(g) has so abused his position as to render his continuance in office prejudicial to the public interest; or

(h) has been guilty of proved misbehavior; or

(i) has such other disqualifications as may be prescribed:

Provided that the disqualification under clause (b) shall not apply to the Members referred to in sub-section (4) of section 5.

(3) Notwithstanding anything in sub-section (2), the Chairperson or a Member shall not be removed from his office on the grounds specified in clause (g) or clause (h) or clause (i) of sub-section (2), except by an order made by the President after an inquiry made in this behalf by the Chairperson of the National Educational Tribunal, in which such Chairperson or such Member has been informed of the charges against him and given a reasonable opportunity of being heard in respect of those charges. (4) In the event of inquiry instituted under sub-section (3), the President may suspend such Chairperson or other Member against whom an inquiry has been instituted for a period not exceeding six months if it consider necessary in public interest.

(5) The Central Government may, by rules, regulate the procedure for the inquiry referred to in sub-section (3).

7. **Term of office of Chairperson and Members.** - (1) A person appointed as Chairperson and other Members shall hold office for a term of five years from the date on which he enters upon his office:

Provided that whole-time Members shall cease to hold office on attaining the age of seventy years.

(2) The Central Government shall, to the extent possible, initiate the process of appointment in respect of any vacancy due to arise on the post of Chairperson or other Member before a period of six months from the date of arising of such vacancy.

(3) The Central Government shall ensure that the process of appointment in respect of any vacancy on the post of Chairperson or other Members is completed within a period of six months from the date such vacancy had arisen.

8. Prohibition as to holding of office by Chairperson or other Member on ceasing to be such Chairperson or Members. - On ceasing to hold office, the Chairperson or other Member shall be ineligible, for a period of five years from the date on which they cease to hold office, for further employment in, or, in matters related to, any higher educational institution under the Central Government or a State Government or any private higher educational institution.

9. Member to act as Chairperson or to discharge his functions in certain circumstances. - (1) In the event of the occurrence of any vacancy in the office of the Chairperson by reason of death, resignation or otherwise, the President may, by notification, authorise one of the other whole-time Members, to act as the Chairperson until the appointment of a person to fill such vacancy.

(2) When the Chairperson is unable to discharge his functions owing to absence on leave or otherwise, such one of the other whole-time Members, as the President may, by notification, authorise in this behalf, shall discharge the functions of the Chairperson until the date on which the Chairperson resumes his duties.

10. Chairperson or Member not to participate in meetings in certain cases.

– The Chairperson or any other Member having any direct or indirect interest, whether pecuniary or otherwise, in any matter coming up for consideration at a meeting of the Commission, shall, as soon as possible after the relevant circumstances have come to his knowledge, disclose the nature of his interest at such meeting and such disclosure shall be recorded in the proceedings of the Commission, and the member shall not take any part in any deliberation or decision of the Commission with respect to that matter.

11. **Declaration by Chairperson and other Member.** – (1) The Chairperson or other Member shall, immediately after entering office and every year thereafter, make a declaration on the extent of his interest, whether direct or indirect and whether pecuniary or otherwise, in any institution of research or higher educational institution or in **any other professional or financial activity.**

(2) The declaration so made under sub-section (1) shall be placed on the website of the Commission.

12. **Terms and conditions of service of Chairperson and Members.** – (1) The salaries and allowances payable to, and the status and other terms and conditions of service of, the Chairperson of the Commission shall be the same as that of the Chief Election Commissioner.

(2) The salaries and allowances payable to, and the status and other terms and conditions of service of, the whole-time Members other than the Chairperson, shall be the same as that of an Election Commissioner.

(3) The Chairperson or other whole-time Member, if at the time of his appointment is in receipt of a pension in respect of any previous service under the Government of India or the Government of a State, his salary in respect of the service as the Chairperson or such Member shall be reduced by the amount of that pension including any portion of pension which was commuted and pension equivalent of other forms of retirement benefits excluding pension equivalent of retirement gratuity:

Provided that if the Chairperson or such whole-time Member, if at the time of his appointment is in receipt of retirement benefits in respect of any previous service rendered in a Corporation established by or under any Central Act or State Act or a Government Company owned or controlled by the Central Government or the State Government, his salary in respect of the service as the Chairperson or Member shall be reduced by the amount of pension equivalent to the retirement benefits:

Provided further that neither the salary and allowances nor the status or other terms and conditions of service of the Chairperson or such whole-time Member shall be varied to his disadvantage after his appointment.

(4) The status and privileges accorded to Members, other than whole-time Members, shall be the same as that of an Election Commissioner; and only such sitting fees and other allowances, as the Commission may decide from time to time, shall be payable to such Members.

Explanation: The words "Chief Election Commissioner" and "Election Commissioner" refers to the Chief Election Commissioner and the Election Commissioner respectively of the Election Commission of India established by Article 324 of the Constitution of India.

13. Vacancies, etc., not to invalidate the proceedings of the Commission. –

No act or proceeding of the Commission shall be invalid merely by reason of—

(a) any vacancy in, or any defect in the constitution of, the Commission; or

(b) any defect in the appointment of a person acting as a Member of the Commission; or

(c) any irregularity in the procedure of the Commission not affecting the merits of the case.

14. Officers and other staff of the Commission. – (1) The Commission may, for the efficient performance of its functions under this Act, appoint, in such manner and with such qualifications, [**Executive Directors**] and such other officers and employees, as may be specified by regulations.

(2) The number of, the salaries and allowances payable to, and the other terms and conditions of service of, the [**Executive Directors**] and other officers and employees of the Commission, shall be such as may be specified by regulations.

(3) The Commission may appoint, in such manner for such temporary period and on such terms and conditions as may be specified by regulations, such other academic, management, accounting, technical and scientific experts as it may consider necessary for the efficient performance of its functions.

(4) Every appointment under sub-section (3), including the qualifications of the person so appointed and the manner, the terms and conditions and the period of such appointment, shall be disclosed on the website of the Commission.

15. Procedure to be regulated by the Commission. - (1) The Commission may delegate such of its powers, not being matters of policy or relating to exercise of its regulatory functions provided under this Act, to a Committee of Chairperson and the other whole-time Members.

(2) Subject to the provisions of this Act, the Commission shall have the power to lay down, by regulations, its own procedure for the conduct of its business and the exercise of its powers and functions.

(3) All orders and decisions of the Commission shall be authenticated by an [**Executive Director**] or any other officer of the Commission duly authorised by the Chairperson in this behalf.

16. **General superintendence, direction and management of affairs of the Commission.** – Subject to the other provisions of this Act, the general superintendence, direction and management of the day-to-day administrative affairs of the Commission shall vest in the Chairperson.

CHAPTER III
COLLEGIUM

17. **Collegium.-** (1) There shall be established, a "Collegium" consisting of core Fellows and co-opted Fellows, being persons of eminence and integrity in academia in higher education and research.

(2) No person shall be eligible for appointment as a Fellow of the Collegium unless he -

(a) is a citizen or an Overseas citizen of India; and

(b) has made substantial contribution to the advancement of knowledge demonstrated through publications which are internationally acknowledged and peer-reviewed.

(3) A core Fellow of the Collegium shall be a person

(a) who is, or has been, a National Research Professor; or

(b) who is a recipient of the Nobel Prize or Field Medal; or

(c) who is a recipient of the Jnanpith award; or

(d) who is a Member of an Academy of international standing.

(4) The co-opted Fellows shall be chosen by the core Fellows, to represent each State and each Union Territory, in the manner provided in sub-section (5), from a panel of five persons of comparable eminence and integrity in academia in higher education and research recommended by the Government of each such State or Union Territory, as the case may be.

(5) Every co-opted Fellow shall be appointed in the manner provided hereinafter; namely, (a) The qualifications of and the contribution made to the advancement of knowledge demonstrated through publications or other scholarly activities, of every person in the panel of names recommended by each State Government or Union Territory, as the case may be, shall be made available on the website of the Collegium, for scrutiny of the core Fellows until the day of co-option.

(c) On the date and time so specified, the core Fellows shall proceed to coopt to the Collegium, one person, from amongst the panel of five persons recommended by each State and Union Territory, to represent each such State or Union Territory, in the same manner as provided for election of a person to the Council of States :

Provided that the number of first preference votes cast in favour of a candidate shall not be less than two-thirds of the core Fellows present and voting:

Provided further that the total number of votes cast shall not be less than one-half of the number of core fellows of the Collegium on the date of such cooption:

Provided also that in the process of co-option, the core Fellows may, to the extent possible, ensure representation to persons with expertise in such field of knowledge which, in their opinion, is not adequately represented in the Collegium.

(d) The person co-opted under clause (c) shall be notified by the Commission as a Fellow, and on such notification, such Fellow shall be eligible to participate in the deliberations of the Collegium.

(6) Every Fellow of the Collegium shall, as soon as may be after notification of his appointment, and every year thereafter, make a

declaration on the extent of his Interest, whether direct or indirect and whether pecuniary or otherwise, in any institution of research or higher educational institution:

(7) The declaration so made under sub-section (6) shall be placed on the website of the Commission.

(8) Every core Fellow shall, except on account of death, resignation or otherwise, continue as such.

(9) Every co-opted Fellow shall, except on account of death, resignation or otherwise, continue as such for a period of five years from the date of his notification as Fellow.

(10) No Fellow shall receive any remuneration except such sitting fees or allowances, as may be prescribed, for attending the meetings of the Collegium.

18. Resignation of Fellow.- A Fellow may, by notice in writing under his hand addressed to the Chair of the Collegium, resign his membership.

19. Functions of Collegium.- (1) The Collegium shall -

(a) aid, advise and make recommendations to the Commission for the determination, co-ordination, maintenance of standards in, and101 promotion of, higher education and research therein;

(b) recommend to the Commission a vision on the emerging trends in different fields of knowledge;

(c) when called upon to do so and in respect of appointments of Members and Chairperson of the Commission, recommend a panel of three persons for each post to the Selection Committee constituted under sub-section (4) of section 5;

(d) recommend for inclusion in the National Registry, referred :o in section 20, of persons eligible and qualified to be appointed as Vice Chancellor of a university or the head of an institution of national importance;

(e) make observations and suggestions (including an assessment of the performance of the Commission and recommendations to be taken on measures to enhance such performance) and advise on the adequacy of funding for higher education and research regarding the report prepared by the Commission under sub-section (1) of section 27 on the state of higher education and research in India and its relation to global trends;

(f) make observations and suggestions (including an assessment of the performance of the Commission and recommendations to be taken on measures to enhance such performance) on the report prepared by the Commission under sub-section (5) of section 27 on the vision for higher education and research.

(2) The Collegium shall act collectively in the performance of its functions, and decisions in such meetings shall be taken, by resolution, by majority arrived at in the manner provided in section 21.

(3) The meeting of the Collegium shall be convened annually and at such other times as may be required by the Chair:

Provided that a meeting of the Collegium shall also be convened if at least one third of the total strength of the Collegium express to the Chair, the desire to convene such meeting to deliberate on such matter as may be expressed.

(4) The Fellows of the Collegium shall constitute themselves into Advisory Committees on matters referred for advise to the Collegium by the Commission.

20. Preparation of National Registry of persons eligible and qualified for appointment as Vice Chancellor or head of institution of national importance.

(1) The Collegium shall recommend, from time to time and in such manner as may be prescribed in concurrence with the Commission, for inclusion in the National Registry, names of persons eligible and qualified for appointment as Vice Chancellor of a university or the head of an institution of national importance.

(2) The Central Government, State Governments, universities and higher educational institutions may refer, from time to time, names of suitable persons, to the Commission, for inclusion in the National Registry of persons eligible and qualified for appointment as Vice Chancellor of a university or the head of an institution of national importance:

Provided that the Commission shall forward the names of such person referred by the Central Government, State Governments and universities and higher educational institutions, along with the credentials of such person referred, to the Collegium for assessing the suitability and competence of such person in the manner provided under sub-section (1). (3) A person shall be eligible for inclusion in the National Registry of persons eligible and qualified for appointment as Vice Chancellor of a university or the head of an institution of national importance only if he satisfies the minimum eligibility conditions specified under regulations for such appointment.

21. Procedure for taking decisions by Collegium.-

(1) Subject to the provisions of this Act, the Collegium shall take decisions, by resolution, on matters for consideration before it.

(2) Each Fellow of the Collegium shall have the right to cast one vote.

(3) No resolution of the Collegium shall be considered as adopted unless supported by at least one half of the number of Fellows, present and voting:

Provided that, no resolution of the Collegium shall be considered as passed unless at least one half of the number of core Fellows and one half of the number of coopted Fellows, present and voting, have respectively supported such resolution.

(4) Subject to the provisions of this Act, the Collegium shall have the power to lay down its own procedure for the conduct of its business and the exercise of its functions.

Explanation: For the purposes of this section, the word "present" shall not be interpreted to be limited to physical presence of the Fellow but shall be construed in a broader sense in being available to cast a vote by such means, including electronic methods, as the Collegium may deem fit.

22. Executive Council of Collegium.-

(1) The Collegium shall have an Executive Council consisting of the Chair and four other Councillors, elected by majority from amongst Fellows of the Collegium, for a tenure of one year.

(2) The election for the membership of the Executive Council shall be held in the Annual Meeting of the Collegium.

(3) The Chair shall preside over all meetings of the Collegium.

(4) Where a vacancy has arisen, on account of death, resignation, removal or otherwise, on the post of Chair or in his absence, the senior-most Fellow of the Executive Council, shall perform the duties of the Chair.

(5) The Executive Council shall perform such functions for carrying out the purposes of this Act, as the Collegium may, by resolution, deem fit.

23. Funds and Administrative support to Collegium.-

(1) The Commission shall provide funds and administrative support and assistance to the Collegium in the discharge of its functions under this Act.

(2) The Collegium may obtain the services of such number of experts in management of, or in, organizations, with such qualifications and on such terms and conditions, as may be prescribed.

CHAPTER IV
POWERS AND FUNCTIONS OF THE COMMISSION

24. Powers and functions of the Commission. –

(1) The Commission shall, subject to the provisions of this Act and regulations made thereunder, take measures to promote the autonomy of higher educational institutions for the free pursuit of knowledge and innovation, and for facilitating access, inclusion and opportunities to all, and providing for comprehensive and holistic growth of higher education and research in a competitive global environment, through reforms and renovation.

(2) Without prejudice to the generality of the foregoing provisions, the measures referred to in sub-section (1), may, inter alia, provide for all or any of the following matters, namely;

(a) specify norms and standards for grant of authorization, to a university or an higher educational institution empowered, by or under law, to award any degree or diploma, to commence its first academic operations;

(b) develop, from time to time, a national curriculum framework with specific reference to new or emerging or inter-disciplinary fields of knowledge and to provide a vision and guide universities in recognizing and revising course curricula;

(c) specify requirements of academic quality for the award of any degree or diploma in any field of higher education and research;

(d) specify norms of academic quality for accreditation and benchmarking of higher educational institutions;

(e) specify norms and processes for establishment and winding up of a university;

(f) specify norms of academic quality for a university to affiliate colleges;

(g) specify norms and mechanisms to measure the productivity of research programmes funded by the Commission;

(h) encourage joint and cross-disciplinary programmes between and amongst Universities and other higher educational institutions;

(i) promote synergy of research in universities and higher educational institutions with research in other agencies or laboratories;

(j) develop measures required to lighten the work load of universities in regard to their routine functions and to enhance the quality of time available to universities for research and teaching, and take such measures including schemes for gradually enabling colleges affiliated to universities to function in an autonomous manner independent of such affiliation;

(k) specify norms and mechanisms for transparent, efficient and accountable governance in universities and other higher educational institutions;

(l) specify minimum eligibility conditions for appointment of Vice Chancellor of any university or head of an institution of national importance;

(m) maintain a National Registry of persons eligible and qualified for appointment as Vice Chancellor of a university or the head of an institution of national importance, prepared by the Collegium;

(n) encourage universities to formulate a Code of Good Practices in administrative matters and to develop a framework Code to guide universities in formulating such Code of Good Practices;

(o) encourage, through the creation of an enabling environment, universities to become self-regulatory bodies for the maintenance of academic quality in higher education and research and in colleges affiliated to it;

(p) develop policies and processes that would create an enabling environment for eligible youth to take up teaching and research as occupation and career;

(q) develop policies and processes that would enable qualitative and meaningful interaction between students and teachers in higher educational institutions; (r) establish, as may be specified by regulations, institutions for providing common facilities, services and programmes for a group of universities or for the universities in general and maintain such institutions or provide for their maintenance by allocating and disbursing such grants as the Commission may deem necessary;

(s) advise, when called upon to do so, the Central Government and State Governments, as the case may be, on policies relating to higher education and research in any field of knowledge therein;

(t) specify sources, norms and mechanisms for financing higher educational institutions;

(u) specify norms and principles for allocation of grants, for the maintenance and development or for any other general or specific purpose of a Central University or an institution of national importance;

(v) specify norms and principles for allocation of grants for the development or for any other general or specific purpose of a State University or an institution deemed to be university supported by the Central Government;

(w) disburse grants to higher educational institutions in accordance with norms and principles established by regulations;

(x) specify norms and principles for allocation and disbursement of grants for research in any field of knowledge in an higher educational institution;

(y) cause to be undertaken policy research in higher education to identify future directions and processes in higher education;

(z) cause to be undertaken research to assess future knowledge manpower requirements, both in the short-term and in the long-term, in different fields of knowledge for meeting the needs of the economy;

(aa) cause to be undertaken research to develop a vision on future trends in knowledge.

(ab) monitor, through a national database, all matters concerning the development of emerging fields of knowledge, balanced growth of higher educational institutions in all spheres and academic quality in higher education and research;

(ac) develop mechanisms for social audit of the processes in the Commission and obtain public feedback on its performance and achievements;

(ad) discharge such other functions in relation to the promotion, coordination and maintenance of standards in higher education and research as the Central Government may subject to the provisions of this Act, prescribe.

25. Role of Commission to guide and advise in establishment of university.-

The Commission shall guide and advise a body or institution, seeking such guidance or advice, in regard to a proposal for the establishment of a university, in accordance with the norms and standards specified by it.

26. National Registry of persons eligible and qualified for appointment as Vice Chancellor or head of institution of national importance.-

(1) The Commission shall maintain a National Registry of persons eligible and qualified for appointment as Vice Chancellor or head of institution of national importance, prepared by the Collegium from time to time under sub-section (1) of section 20.

(2) When called upon to do so by the Central Government or a Central University or an institution of national importance, as the case may be, the Commission shall recommend a panel of five names from the National Registry maintained under subsection (1) for appointment to the post of Vice Chancellor of such Central University or head on such institution.

(3) When called upon to do so by a State Government or a State University, as the case may be, the Commission shall recommend a panel of five names from the National Registry for appointment to the post of Vice Chancellor of such State University.

(4) No person shall be eligible for appointment as Vice Chancellor of any University or head of an institution of national importance unless his name is included in the National Registry of persons eligible and qualified for appointment as Vice Chancellor or head of institution of national importance maintained by the Commission under subsection (1).

27. Reports of the Commission.- (1) The Commission shall, annually and such other times as it deems fit, prepare a report on the state of higher education and research in India and its relation to global trends and the status of adherence to standards of academic quality; and such report shall be provided to the Collegium to enable Fellows of the Collegium the opportunity to offer comments or suggestions (including an assessment of the performance the Commission and recommendations to be taken on measures to enhance such performance) on the report, or any part of it thereof:

(2) The Commission shall, after considering such comments or suggestions (including the assessment of performance of the Commission and recommendations on measures to be taken to enhance such performance) received on the report under subsection (1), and after making such modifications and amendments as it may deem fit, present to the President, the report:

Provided that the report presented to the President shall include the comments or suggestions or recommendations received under sub-section (1).

(3) The Commission shall, in respect of every State and Union Territory, before the expiration of a period of five years from the date of commencement of this Act and at an interval of every five years thereafter, and such other times as it deems fit, prepare a report on the state of higher education and research in such State or Union Territory and its relation to national trends.

(4) The Commission shall present to the Governor of such State or the administrator of an Union Territory, as the case may be, such report prepared under sub-section (3) on the state of higher education and research in a State or Union Territory and its relation to national trends.

(5) The Commission shall present to the President, before the expiration of a period of five years from the date of commencement of this Act and at an interval of every five years thereafter, a report on the vision of higher education and research in the forthcoming decade; and shall make in such report, recommendations as to the measures

that ought to be taken for renovation and rejuvenation of higher education and research, including the following; namely,

(a) vision and strategy for emerging fields of knowledge and norms for developing requirements of such fields of knowledge; and

(b) development of curricular framework to reflect the vision of higher education and research.

(c) norms and mechanisms for evaluating cost and price of higher education and research; and Provided that before the report is presented to the President, the Commission shall provide such report to the Collegium to enable Fellows of the Collegium the opportunity to offer comments or suggestions (including an assessment of the performance the Commission and recommendations to be taken on measures to enhance such performance) on the report, or any part of it thereof; and such comments or suggestions received thereon shall be appended to the report presented to the President. (6) The President shall cause to be laid before both Houses of Parliament, such reports prepared by the Commission under sub-section (2) and sub-section (5), along with an explanatory memorandum on the action taken, or proposed to be taken, thereon in respect of each recommendation made by the Commission or the Collegium. (7) The Governor of every State shall cause to be laid before the Legislative Assembly of such State, the report prepared by the Commission under sub-section (4) concerning the state of higher education and research in such State, along with an explanatory memorandum on the action taken, or proposed to be taken, thereon in respect of each recommendation made by the Commission.

28. **Review of performance of Commission.-** (1) The President shall, within five years from the commencement of this Act and thereafter at the expiration of every fifth year, constitute a Committee to evaluate and review the performance in the said period of the Commission, and consisting of persons, being citizens of India or otherwise, of international eminence and standing, to be appointed by the President on the basis of a panel of names to be submitted by the Collegium .

(2) The Committee referred to in sub-section (1) shall evaluate and review the performance of the Commission and make recommendations to the President as to –

(a) the extent of fulfillment of the goals and objectives of the Commission stated in the Preamble to this Act, as demonstrated by the state of higher education and research;

(b) the interface between the Commission and the Collegium;

(c) such other matters referred to the Committee by the President in the interests of the development and promotion of the advancement of knowledge and learning in universities and other institutions of higher education and research and the role of the Commission thereto.

(3) The President shall cause to be laid before both Houses of Parliament, the report of the Committee constituted under sub-section (1) along with an explanatory memorandum on the action taken, or proposed to be taken, thereon in respect of each recommendation of the Committee.

29. Powers of Central Government to frame National Policy.- The Central Government shall, at such times at it deems appropriate, prepare in consultation with the State Governments and the Commission, a national policy for the development of higher education and research, which shall guide the Commission in the exercise of its powers and functions under this Act.

30. Central Government to inform Commission of decisions on matters of Policy.- (1) The Central Government shall inform the Commission of all decisions taken by it on matters of policy concerning higher education and research.

(2) If any dispute arises between the Central Government and the Commission as to whether a question is or is not a question of policy, the decision of the President shall be final.

31. Procedure in making regulations. – (1) The Commission shall issue a public notice, in such manner and form as may be specified by regulations, regarding a draft of regulation and a copy of the draft of regulation shall be placed on the website of the Commission for a period of thirty days from the date of issue of the public notice to enable Universities, State Higher Education Councils, Fellows of the Collegium and the general public the opportunity to offer comments or suggestions, as the case may be, on the draft of regulation, or any part of it thereof.

(2) The Commission shall, after considering such comments received hereinabove, and after making such modifications and amendments as it may deem fit, notify the regulations in the Official Gazette.

(3.) Every regulation, along with all comments or suggestions received to the draft of regulation and an explanatory memorandum on the action taken thereon with reasons for such action, shall be laid before both Houses of Parliament.

CHAPTER V
AUTHORISATION FOR COMMENCEMENT OF FIRST ACADEMIC OPERATIONS

32. Authorisation to University or institution empowered to award degree or diploma to commence first academic operations.- No university or institution empowered, by or under law, to award any degree or diploma established after the coming into force of this Act shall commence its first academic operations unless it is so authorized, in accordance with such norms as may be specified by regulations:

Provided further than a university or institution deemed to be university existing before the commencement of this Act shall deemed to have been authorised under this Act unless revoked in accordance with the provisions of section 36.

33. **Application for grant of authorization.-** (1) Every application for grant of authorization shall be made, by an institution or a University, to the Commission in such form and manner and accompanied by such other documents and on payment of such fees as may be specified by regulations.

(2) Every application shall be accompanied with an assessment report prepared in a manner, specified under regulations, from a registered accreditation agency.

34. **Procedure for grant of authorisation.** – (1) The Commission shall examine the application and the assessment report referred to in sub-section (2) of section 33, to ensure that it complies with the norms of academic quality specified under regulations for grant of authorization.

(2) The Commission shall, within a period of thirty days from the date of application and after such examination referred to in sub-section (1), -

(a) decide to declare its intent to grant authorization if the application complies with the norms of academic quality, specified under regulations for grant of authorization; or

(b) return, for reasons to be recorded in writing, the application it such application does not comply with the norms of academic quality, specified under regulations for grant of authorization:

Provided that the return of the application along with the reasons so recorded shall be published on the website of the Commission.

(3) The Commission shall, if it has decided to declare its intent to grant authorization under clause (a) of sub-section (2), issue a public notice, in such form and manner as may be specified by

regulations, and place such application together with all documents received with the application, for a period of sixty days from the date of issue of the public notice, on the website of the Commission.

(4) Any person may, within a period of said sixty days referred to in sub-section (3), submit his comments or objections, if any, on the application or part thereof, to the Commission.

(5) The Commission may, within the period of sixty days referred to in sub-section (3), require the applicant to furnish such other information or clarification as it may consider necessary.

(6) The applicant shall be afforded an opportunity to submit his response on the comments or objections received under sub-section (4) or clarifications sought under sub-section (5):

Provided that such response shall be submitted within a period of thirty days from the expiry of the period of sixty days referred to in sub-section (4).

(7) The Commission shall consider all comments or objections or clarifications, and the response of the applicant thereto, including any other matter as the Commission may deem fit for such consideration, before the grant of authorization to such institution or university, as the case may be.

35. **Grant of Authorisation.** – (1) The Commission shall, as far as practicable within a period of four months from the receipt of such application, after considering the comments or objections or clarifications under sub-section (7) of section 34,

(a) issue, by notification, authorisation to such institution or university, as the case may be, subject to the provisions of this Act and regulations made thereunder; or

(b) reject, by notification, the application for reasons to be recorded in writing if such application does not conform to the provisions of this Act and regulations made thereunder:

(2) The Commission shall, while issuing the authorisation, validate, periodically at such times as may be specified by regulations, the standards of academic quality to be achieved over the next ten years, by the institution or university, as the case may be, so authorised.

(3) The notification of the Commission under sub-section (1), along with reasons therefor, and the standards of academic quality to be achieved by the applicant university or institution over the next ten years under sub-section (2), shall be published on the website of the Commission.

36. **Revocation of Authorisation.** - (1) If the Commission, after making such enquiry as may be specified by regulations, is satisfied that public interest so requires, it may revoke, by notification, the authorization granted to as institution or university in any of the following cases, namely: -

(a) where the institution or university, in the opinion of the Commission, makes wilful or continuous default in doing anything required of it by or under this Act or rules or regulations made thereunder;

(b) where the institution or university fails, within the period fixed in this behalf by its authorisation, or any longer period which the Commission may have granted therefor, to show, to the satisfaction of the Commission, that such institution or university is in a position fully and efficiently to discharge the duties and obligations imposed on it by its authorisation; or

(c) where the institution or university has ceased to exist.

(2) No authorisation shall be revoked under sub-section (1) unless the Commission has given to the institution or university, as the case may be, not less than sixty days notice, in writing, stating the grounds on which it is proposed to revoke the authorisation, and

has considered any cause shown by the institution or university, as the case may be, within the period of that notice, against the proposed revocation.

(3) Where the Commission revokes authorisation under this section, it shall serve an order of revocation upon the institution or university, as the case may be, as the case may be, and fix a date on which the revocation shall take effect; and such revocation shall be without prejudice to the action that may be taken against it under any other law for the time being in force:

Provided that the Commission may, instead of revoking the authorisation, permit it to remain in force subject to such further terms and conditions as they think fit to impose, and any further terms or conditions so imposed shall be binding upon and be observed by the institution or university, as the case may be, and shall be of like force and effect as if they were contained in the authorisation.

(4) The Commission shall publish on its website any action initiated under this section and the final decision on the revocation of the authorisation or otherwise together with all documents and reasons for such decision.

(5) The Commission shall, while revoking an authorisation, take, or cause to be taken, such measures which may be necessary to protect the academic interests of students in such institution or university.

37. **Powers of Civil Court vested in Commission.** - The Commission shall have the same powers as are vested in a Civil Court under the Code of Civil Procedure, 1908, (5 of 1908) while trying a suit in respect of the following matters, namely—

(a) summoning and enforcing the attendance of any person and examining him on oath;

(b) requiring the discovery and production of documents;

(c) receiving evidence on affidavits;

(d) subject to the provisions of sections 123 and 124 of the Indian Evidence Act, 1872, (1 of 1872) requisitioning any public record or document or copy of such record or document from any office;

(e) issuing commissions for the examination of witnesses or documents;

(f) reviewing its decisions;

(g) dismissing an application for default or deciding it ex-parte;

(h) setting aside any order of dismissal of any application for default or any order passed by it ex-parte; and

(i) any other matter which may be prescribed by the Central Government.

38. Appeal. —Any person aggrieved by an order of the Commission, for the grant or refusal, or revocation of authorisation under this Chapter, may prefer an appeal, in such form and manner and accompanied by such fees as may be prescribed, against such order to the National Educational Tribunal within ninety days of such order:

Provided that the National Educational Tribunal may entertain an appeal after the expiry of the said period of sixty days, if it is satisfied that the appellant has sufficient cause for not preferring the appeal within the period of ninety days.

39. Duties and obligations of University in maintenance of standards of academic quality. – (1) Each University shall maintain standards of academic quality in higher education and research, as may be specified by regulations, in such University and in colleges and institutions affiliated to it.

(2) Each affiliating University shall take measures to support and develop academic quality in such colleges and institutions with due respect to the autonomy of such colleges and institutions in its administrative and financial matters.

40. University to be public authority under Right to Information Act. – The provisions of the Right to Information Act, 2005 [22 of 2005] shall apply to each University as if it were a public authority defined in clause (h) of section 2 of Act No. 22 of 2005.

41. Rights and Prohibitions. – (1) The right to confer or award degrees or diplomas shall be exercised only by an institution or university, as the case may be, authorized, under section 38 of this Act.

(2) Save as provided in sub-section (1), no person, institution, organization or agency shall confer, or award, or hold himself or itself out as entitled to confer or award, any degree or diploma.

CHAPTER VI
FINANCE, ACCOUNTS AND AUDIT.

42. Fund of Commission. - (1) The Commission shall have its own Fund; and all sums which may, from time to time, be paid to it by the Central Government and all other receipts of the Commission shall be carried to the Fund and all payments by the Commission shall be made there from.

(2) The Commission may spend such sums as it thinks fit for performing its functions under this Act, and such sums shall be treated as expenditure payable out of the Fund of the Commission.

43. Grants by Central Government.- (1) The Central Government shall, after due appropriation made by Parliament by law in this behalf, make to the Commission grants of such sums of money as are required to pay salaries and allowances payable to the Chairperson and Members, the administrative expenses including the salaries, allowances and pension payable to or in respect of officers and other employees of the Commission and the administrative expenses of the Collegium.

(2) The Central Government shall, after due appropriation made by Parliament by law in this behalf, make to the Commission grants of such sums of money as are required for causing to be undertaken policy research to aid the Commission in the exercise of its powers and performance of its functions under this Act.

44. Annual Financial Statement on Higher Education and Research.-

(1) The Commission shall, in respect of each financial year, provide to the Central Government a statement of the estimated expenditure on development of higher education and research for that year, referred to as the "annual financial statement on higher education and research" comprising the "annual financial support plan for higher education" and the "annual financial support plan for research" for that year;

(2) The estimates of expenditure on development of higher education and research under sub-section (1), shall be based on norms, principles and criteria specified under regulations.

(3) The Commission shall provide, that part of the estimated expenditure planned to be appropriated towards research, along with an explanatory memorandum on the research programmes proposed to be funded and an assessment of the productivity of research programmes funded in the past five years.

(4) The assessment of the productivity of research programmes under sub-section (3) shall be based on norms as may be specified by regulations.

(5) The Central Government shall cause the annual financial statement on higher education and research, with such modifications as it may recommend, to be laid before Parliament.

(6) The Central Government shall, after due appropriation made by Parliament by law in this behalf, make to the Commission grants of

such sums of money as are required for supporting the promotion and development of higher education and research.

45. Annual Funding Support Plan for higher education.- (1) The Commission shall, by regulations, establish principles, norms and criteria that would govern the block grants to be provided by it to support universities and other higher educational institutions for their general development and maintenance.

(2) The Commission shall, in respect of each financial year on the basis of grants provided to it under sub-section (6) of section 44, prepare a "annual funding support plan for higher education" detailing the universities and other higher educational institutions proposed to be supported and the grants proposed in respect of each university and other higher educational institution, along with an explanatory memorandum specifying the reasons thereto.

(3) The annual financial support plan for higher education as soon as may be after it is made, be published on the website of the Commission and laid before both Houses of Parliament.

46. Annual Funding Support Plan for research.- (1) The Commission shall, by regulations, establish principles, norms and criteria that would govern the grants to be provided by it to support or supplement research in higher educational institutions.

(2) The Commission shall, in respect of each financial year on the basis of grants provided to it under sub-section (6) of section 44, prepare a "annual funding support plan for research" detailing the research programmes in universities and other higher educational institutions proposed to be supported, along with an explanatory memorandum specifying the reasons thereto and the expected outcomes.

(3) The annual financial support plan for research as soon as may be after it is made, be published on the website of the Commission and laid before both Houses of Parliament.

47. **Accounts and Audit.** - (1) The Commission shall cause to be maintained such books of account and other books in relation to its account in such form and in such manner as may, in consultation with the Comptroller and Auditor-General of India, be prescribed.

(2) The Commission shall, as soon as may be after closing its annual accounts, prepare a statement of accounts in such form, and forward the same to the Comptroller and Auditor-General by such date, as the Commission may, in consultation with the Comptroller and Auditor-General, determine.

(3) The accounts of the Commission shall be audited by the Comptroller and Auditor- General at such times and in such manner as she thinks fit.

(4) The President shall, in respect of each financial year, cause to be laid before both Houses of Parliament, the annual accounts of the Commission together with the audit report thereon.

CHAPTER VII
MISCELLANEOUS.

48. **Returns and information by Commission.** - The Commission shall furnish to the Central Government such returns or other information with respect to its regulations, policies or activities as the Central Government may, for the purpose of reporting to Parliament or for the making of policy, from time to time, as may be prescribed.

49. **Returns and information by Commission.**- Each university and each institution empowered by or under law to award any degree or diploma, shall furnish to the Commission at such time and in such form and manner as may be specified by regulations or as the Commission may seek, such returns and statements and such particulars concerning the financial position of the University or the studies in the various branches of learning undertaken in that University, and its rules and regulations concerning standards of teaching and examination in that University in respect of each such branch of learning or in such other matters, as the Commission may, from time to time, require.

50. **Act to have overriding effect :** The provisions of this Act shall have overriding effect notwithstanding anything inconsistent therewith contained in any other law for the time being in force or in any instrument having effect by virtue of any law other than this Act.

51. **Power to remove difficulties.** - (1) If any difficulty arises in giving effect to the provisions of this Act, the Central Government may, by order published in the Official Gazette, make such provisions, not inconsistent with the provisions of this Act as appear to it to be necessary or expedient for removing the difficulty.

Provided that no order shall be made under this section after the expiry of two years from the date of commencement of this Act.

(2) Every order made under this section shall, as soon as may be after it is made, be laid before each House of Parliament.

52. **Review of Act and its provisions by Parliament.**- (1) Parliament may, at the expiration of ten years from the commencement of this Act and every ten years thereafter and on the basis of the recommendations made by the Collegium from time to time and the Committee constituted under sub-section (1) of section 28, review the Act and its provisions recognizing the continuous growth in all fields of knowledge and acknowledging the need to provide a responsive framework to adapt to the changing needs.

(2) Nothing in sub-section (1) shall be construed as restricting the power of Parliament to amend the provisions of this Act from time to time.

53. **Power of Central Government to make rules.**- (1) The Central Government may, by notification in the Official Gazette, make rules to carry out the purposes of this Act.

(2) In particular, and without prejudice to the generality of the foregoing power, such rules may provide for all or any of the following, matters, namely:–

(a) the other disqualifications for removal of the Chairperson or other Members under clause (i) of sub-section (2) of section 6;

(b) the procedure for the inquiry under sub-section (4) of section 11;

(c) the sitting fees and other allowances payable to a fellow of the Collegium for attending its meeting under sub-section (8) of section 17;

(d) the manner of investigation of a charge brought against a fellow of the Collegium under sub-section (4) of section 18;

(e) the manner of preparation of a National Registry of persons eligible and qualified for appointment as Vice Chancellor or head of institution of national importance under sub-section (1) of section 20;

(f) the manner of passing of resolution by the Collegium under sub-section (1) of section 21;

(g) the number of experts in management of, or in, organizations, and their qualifications and terms and conditions on which their services shall be obtained by the Collegium under sub-section (2) of section 23;

(h) the other functions in relation to the promotion, coordination and maintenance of standards of higher education and research to be entrusted to the Commission under clause (ab) of sub-section (2) of section 24;

(i) the other matters under clause (i) of section 37 in respect of which the Commission shall have the powers under the Code of Civil Procedure, 1908 while trying a suit;

(j) the form and manner in which an appeal may be preferred and the documents to be accompanied with it and the fees payable therewith under section 38;

(k) the form and manner in which the books of accounts of the Commission shall be maintained under section 47;

(k) the returns or other information with respect to its regulations, policies or activities required to be provided to the Central Government by the Commission under section 48;

(l) any other matter which has to be, or may be, prescribed.

54. Power of the Commission to make regulations.-(1) The Commission may, by notification in the Official Gazette, make regulations to carry out the purposes of this Act.

(2) In particular, and without prejudice to the generality of the foregoing power, such regulations may provide for the following matters, namely:–

(a) the qualifications and manner of appointment of the Executive Directors and the number, qualifications, and manner of appointment of other officers and employees of the Commission under sub-section (1) of section 14;

(b) the number of, salaries and allowances payable to, and other terms and conditions of service of the Executive Directors, other officers and employees of the Commission under sub-section (2) of section 14;

(c) the terms and conditions, the qualifications and the period of appointment of other academic, administrative, accounting, technical and scientific experts as may be considered necessary by the Commission under sub-section (3) of section 1;

(d) the procedure for the conduct of its business and the exercise of its powers and functions under sub-section (2) of section 15;

(e) the norms and standards for grant of authorization, to a university or an institution empowered, by or under law, to award any degree or diploma, to commence its first academic operations under clause (a) of sub-section (2) of section 24;

(f) the development, from time to time, of a national curriculum framework with specific reference to new or emerging or inter-disciplinary fields of knowledge and to provide a vision and guide universities in recognizing and revising course curricula under clause (b) of sub-section (2) of section 24;

(g) the requirements of academic quality for the award of any degree or diploma in any field of higher education and research under clause (c) of subsection (2) of section 24;

(h) the norms of academic quality for accreditation and benchmarking of higher educational institutions clause (d) of sub-section (2) of section 24;

(i) the norms and processes for establishment and winding up of a university under clause (e) of sub-section (2) of section 24;

(j) the norms of academic quality for universities to affiliate colleges under clause (f) of sub-section (2) of section 24;

(k) the norms and mechanisms to measure the productivity of research programmes funded by the Commission under sub-section (g) of section 17;

(l) the development of measures required to lighten the work load of universities in regard to their routine functions and to enhance the quality of time available to universities for research and teaching, and take measures including schemes for gradually enabling colleges affiliated to universities to function in an autonomous manner independent of such affiliation under under clause (j) of sub-section (2) of section 24;

(m) the norms and mechanisms for transparent, efficient and accountable governance in universities and higher educational institutions under clause (k) of sub-section (2) of section 24;

(n) the minimum eligibility conditions for a person to be qualified for inclusion in the National Registry of persons eligible and qualified for appointment as Vice Chancellor or head of institution of national importance under clause (l) of subsection (2) of section 24

(o) development of a framework Code of Good Practices to guide universities in formulating their Code of Good Practices under clause (n) of sub-section (2) of section 24;

(p) the development of policies and processes that would create an enabling environment for eligible youth to take up teaching and research as occupation and career under clause (p) of sub-section (2) of section 24;

(q) the development of policies and processes that would enable qualitative and meaningful interaction between students and teachers in universities and other higher educational institutions under clause (q) of sub-section (2) of section 24;

(r) the establishment of institutions for providing common facilities, services and programmes for a group of universities or for the universities in general and maintain such institutions or provide for their maintenance by allocating and disbursing grants to such institutions under clause (r) of sub-section (2) of section 24;

(s) the sources, norms and mechanisms for financing of higher educational institutions under clause (t) of sub-section (2) of section 24;

(t) the norms and principles for allocation of grants for the maintenance and development or for any other general or specific purpose of a Central University or an institution of national importance under clause (u) of sub-section (2) of section 24;

(u) the norms and principles fo. allocation of grants for the development or for any other general or specific purpose of a State University or an institution deemed to be university supported by the Central Government under clause (v) of sub-section (2) of section 24;

(v) the norms and principles for allocation and disbursement of grants for research in any field of knowledge in an higher educational institution under clause (x) of sub-section (2) of section 24;

(w) development of mechanisms for social audit of the processes in the Commission and obtain public feedback on its performance and achievements under clause (ac) of sub-section (2) of section 24

(x) the form and manner of issue of public notice on draft of regulations under sub-section (1) of section 31;

(y) the form and manner in which an application may be made for grant of authorization and the documents to be accompanied with it and the fee payable therewith under sub-section (1) of section 33;

(z) the manner of preparation of the assessment report by a registered accreditation agency and the norms on which such report shall be based, to be submitted with the application for grant of authorisation under sub-section (2) of section 33;

(aa) the form and manner in which the public notice may be issued under subsection (3) of section 34;

(ab) the standards of academic quality to be achieved over the next ten years after the grant of authorization and the period at which achievement of such shall be validated to be specified under sub-section (2) of section 35;

(ac) the manner of conduct of enquiry under sub-section (1) of section 36;

(ad) the standards required to be maintained in affiliated colleges and the manner in which such standards are to be maintained by a university under subsection (1) of section 39;

(ae) the norms, principles and criteria for preparation of estimates of expenditure on development of higher education and research under sub-section (2) of section 44;

(af) the principles, norms and criteria that would govern the block grants to be provided to support universities and institutions of national importance for their general development and maintenance under sub-section (1) of section 45;

(ag) the principles, norms and criteria that would govern the grants to be provided on competitive basis to support and supplement research under subsection (1) of section 46;

(ah) any other matter which is required to be, or may be, specified by regulation or in respect of which provision is to be made by regulations.

(3) No regulation shall be made under clause (b) of sub-section (2) except with the prior approval of the Central Government. (4) The first regulations under sub-section (2), after the coming into force of this Act shall be notified by the Commission expeditiously and not later than one year from the date of coming into force of this Act.

55. Laying of rules, regulations and notifications.- Every rule or regulation or notification made under this Act shall be laid, as soon as may be after it is made, before each House of Parliament while it is in session, for a total period of thirty days which may be comprised in one session or in two or more successive sessions, and if, before the expiry of the session immediately following the session or the successive sessions aforesaid, both Houses agree in making any modification in the rule or regulation or notification or both Houses agree that the rule or regulation or notification should not be made, the rule shall thereafter have effect only in such modified form or be of no effect, as the case may be; so, however, that any such modification or annulment shall be without prejudice to the validity of anything previously done under that rule or regulation or notification.

56. Repeal and Savings – (1) The University Grants Commission Act, 1956 [3 of 1956], the All India Council for Technical Education Act, 1987 [52 of 1987], the National Council for Teacher Education Act, 1993 [73 of 1993] are repealed with effect from such date, not later than one year from the date of coming into force of this Act, as the Central Government may, in consultation with the Commission, notify.

Provided that in the period between the date of coming into force of this Act and the date of repeal of the enactments mentioned in this sub-section, the University Grants Commission, the All India Council of Technical Education and the National Council of Teacher Education, shall not take any decision or action, except with the prior approval of the Commission, on any matter as specified by the Commission. (2) Notwithstanding anything contained in the Architects Act, 1972 [20 of 1972] and the Advocates Act, 1961 [25 of 1961], the provisions of this Act shall apply to any matter concerning the determination, co-ordination, maintenance of standards in, and promotion of, higher education and research:

Provided that nothing contained in this section shall be construed as restricting the power of the Bar Council of India to specify standards [**of higher education**] concerning practice in courts:

Provided further that nothing contained in this section shall be construed as restricting the power of the Council of Architecture to specify standards [**of higher education**] concerning professional practice:

(3) Nothwithstanding anything contained in the Indira Gandhi National Open University Act, 1985, [50 of 1985], the provisions of this Act shall apply to the coordination, determination and promotion of standards in distance education systems.

(4) The repeal of the enactments mentioned in sub-section (1), hereinafter referred to as the said enactments, shall not affect proceedings pending in various courts immediately before the commencement of this Act, under either of the said enactments, which shall be continued and disposed of as if this Act had not been passed.

(5) Any rule or regulation made under the said enactments shall continue to remain in force after coming into force of this Act as if such rule or regulation has been made under this Act except in so far as it is inconsistent with the provisions of this Act till such time as any rule or regulation under this Act overriding such earlier rule or regulation is notified in the Official Gazette.

(6) Any act done or purported to be done under the said enactments or rules and regulations made thereunder before the coming into the force of this Act shall continue to have effect irrespective of

the fact that such act done or purported to be done is inconsistent with the provisions of this Act

(7) On and from the date of repeal of the said enactments, -

(a) any reference to the said enactments in any law for the time being in force shall be construed to be a reference to this Act;

(b) any reference to the University Grants Commission, the All India Council of Technical Education or the National Council of Teacher Education, in any law or rule or regulation for the time being in force or any contract or other instrument, shall be construed as a reference to the Commission established under this Act.

(c) all property, movable and immovable, of or belonging to the University Grants Commission, the All India Council of Technical Education and the National Council of Teacher Education shall vest in the Commission;

(d) all rights and liabilities of the University Grants Commission, the All India Council of Technical Education or the National Council of Teacher Education shall be transferred to, and be the rights and liabilities of, the Commission;

(e) any reference, by whatever form of words, to the Chairman of the University Grants Commission, the Chairman of the All India Council of Technical Education or the Chairman of the National Council of Teacher Education in any law for the time being in force, or in any instrument or other document, shall be construed as a reference respectively to the Chairman of the Commission.

(f) The Chairman and other Members of the University Grants Commission, the All India Council for Technical Education and the National Council for Teacher Education shall be considered to have demitted office from the date of such repeal.

(8) On the dissolution of the University Grants Commission, the All India Council for Technical Education and the National Council for Teacher Education on repeal of the said enactments, the Central Government, by notification, shall take consequential action in regard to officers and staff in the regular service of the University Grants Commission, the All India Council for Technical Education and the National Council for Teacher Education.

(9) Save as otherwise provided elsewhere in this section, the mention of particular matters in this section, shall not be held to prejudice or affect the general application of section 6 of the General Clauses Act, 1897, with regard to the effect of repeals.

Note : It is reported that some of the clauses in the Bill are modified after discussion with state government.

Bibliography

Aucion Peter and Mark D. Jarvis, **Modernizing Government Accountability: A Frame Work for Reform**, Canadian school of Public Service, Attawa, 2005.

Advisory Committee on Student Financial Assistance, **Empty promises : The myth of college Access in America**, Washington DC, 2002 www.ed.gov/officer/AC/emptypromises

Altbach P.G. and Selvaratnam E. (Ed), **From Decadence to Autonomy: The Development of Asian Universities**, 2002, Tamgawa Univesity Press, Tokyo, 2002.

Altbach PG and Batan J (Ed) **World class World wide: Transforming Research University in Asia and Latin America**, Johns Hopkins University, Baltimore, 2007.

Altbach, P.G., **The Giants awake: The present and future of higher education systems in China and India**. Economic and Political Weekly. 20, June 2009.

Appadurai A, **Modernity at Large: Cultural Dimensions of Globalisation**, University of Minnesota Press, Minneapolis, 1995.

Atul Kohli (Ed), **The Success of Indias' Democracy**, Cambridge University Press, Cambridge, 2001.

Atul Kohli, **The State and Poverty in India**, Cambridge University Press, Cambridge,1987.

Agrawal P, **Indian Higher Education: Envisioning the Future**, Sage, New Delhi, 2009.

Bernasconi, A., **Is there a Latin American model of the university? Comparative Education Review**. Vol. 52, No.1, pp. 27.52, 2008.

Bloom, D., Canning, D. and Chan, K. 2005. **Higher Education and Economic Development in Africa**, World Bank, Washington, D.C. Balogna Declaration. 1999. Retrieved from: http://74.125.95.132/search?q=cache:m Ptmv IBNnc) : www.bologna-berlin2003.de/pf/bologna_declaration. pdf+ bologna+ declaration+1999& cd=I&hl= en&ct=clnk &gl=us on 1 March 2009.

Brainard, J. **Race and Ethnicity of Students at 1,400 Colleges and Universities**, Washinton DC. 2008.

Basu A, **The Growth of Education and Political Development in India**, 1898-1920, Oxford University Press, Delhi,1974.

Beimen H and Waterberrey J, **"The Political Economy of Privatization in Developing Countries" World Development 17(5), 1989.**

Clifton, Rodney A and Hymie Rubenstein, **Collegial Models for Enhancing the Performance of University Professors**, The Fraser Institute, Vancouver, 2002.

Crook RC and Manor J. **Democracy and Decentralization in South Asia and West Africa**, Cambridge University Press, Cambridge,1998.

Chanda R (Ed) **Trade in Services and India: Prospects and Strategies**, Wiley India, New Delhi, 2006.

Canton, E. and Blom, A. **Can Student Loans Improve Accessibility of Higher Education and Student Performance: An Impact Study of the Case of SOFES**, Mexico, World Bank, Washington DC. 2004.

Chalam K.S. Finances,**Costs and Productivity of Higher Education**, Inter-India, New delhi, 1986.

———— **Education and Weaker Sections**, Inter-India, New Delhi, 1988.

———— **Academic Staff Development in Higher Education** K.P. Bagchi and Co, Calcutta, 1991.

————**Introduction to Educational Planning and Management**, Anmol, New Delhi, 2003.

————**Modern Techniques of Teaching and Staff Development**, Anmol, New Delhi, 2005.

————**Caste-Based Reservations and Human Development in India** Sage Publications, New Delhi, 2007.

European Commission. **Lifelong Learning Programme – A Single Umbrella for Education and Training Programmes**. Retrieved from: http://ec.eyrioa.eu/education/lifelong-learning-programme/doc78_en.htm on 6 May, 2009.

FICCI, **Private Initiative in Higher Education: A Report of Seminar on Private Initiative in India Higher Education** www.ficci.sidf.org.

Griffith, Wyn, **The British Civil Service 1854-1954 Her Majesty Stationery Officer**, London, 1954.

Gupta A .D, Levey and Powar K.B (Ed) **Private Higher Education: Global Trends and Indian perspective**, Shipra, Delhi, 2008.

Govt. of India, **India: UNESCO Country Report MHRD**, New Delhi, 2009.

Gorard, S., Smith, E., May. H. Thomas L. Adnett. N. and Slack.K. 2006 **Review of Widening Participation Research: Addressing the Barriers to Participation in Higher Education**. Retrieved From: http://www.hefce.ac.uk/pubs/RDreports/2006/rd13_6/on 1 May 2009.

Gupta. A. **Affirmative Action in Higher Education in India and the US: A Study in Contrasts**, Berkeley, **CA Center for Studies in Higher Education**, University of California, Berkeley. 2006.

Guri-Resenblit, S., Sebkova, H. and Teichler, U. **"Massification and diversity of higher education systems: Interplay of complex dimensions". Higher Education Policy**, Vol. 20, No, pp. 373-389, 2007.

Higher Education Funding Council of England (HEFCE) Higher Education Business and Community Interaction Survey 2006-07, Bristol, England, HEFCE. 2008.

Hart Research Associates, **Trends in Learning outcomes, General Education and Assessment: A survey among Members of the AACU**, Hart Research Association, Washington DC, 2009.

Immerwahr John and Tony Foleno, Great expectations. **How the Public and parents-white, African American and Hispanic view Higher Education, The National centre for public policy and Higher Education Sanjos**, 2000 www. Higher Education.org/reports.

Institute for Higher Education Policy Higher Education Cost Measurement: public policy, Issues options and strategies, Washington DC, 2000 www.ihep.com.

Jha, Sharada and Mathur Alok Kumar, **Attempting Non-formalization of Formal Education.** Sandhan Research Centre, Jaipur, 1996.

Johns Lone D.B. **The Economics and Politics of Cost Sharing in Higher Education: Comparative perspectives, Economics of Education Review**. Vol. 23, 4, pp. 403-410. 2004.

Koolman Jan, Governing as Governance, Sage Publication, 2003.

Konnur M.B, Bhalla Veera and Y.V. Singh, **Bibliography of Higher Education in India,**1991-2000 Association of Indian Universities, New Delhi, 2002.

Kerr, C. **The Uses of the University**, Cambridge, MA, Harvard University Press. 2001.

Liston, C. **Managing Quality and Standards**, Buckingham, England, Open University Press. 1999.

Mc Burnie, G and Zigurasa C, **Transnational Education Issues and Trends in off share Higher Education**, Taylor and Francis, London, 2009.

NAFSA: Association of International Educators, **The Economic Benefits of International Education to the United States for the 2007-08 Academic Year**, A statistical Analysis, NAFSA. 2008.

National Committee of Inquiry into Higher Education (Great Britain), **Higher Education in the Learning Society**. **Report of the National Committee** (Dearing Report) 1997.

Organisation for Economic Co-operation and Development (OECD), **Quality and Recognition in Higher Education**. The Cross-border Challenge, Paris, OECD Publications, 2004.

OECD, **The Curriculum Redefined: Schooling for the 21st Century**, OECD Paris, 1994.

Probe Team, **The probe Report: Public Report on Basic Education in India**, Oxford University Press, New Delhi, 1999.

Romila Thaper, **The Penguin History of India**, Penguin, New Delhi, 2005.

Raza M and Nirmal Malhotra, **Higher Education in India A Comprehensive Bibliography**, Concept Publishing Company, New Dehli, 1991.

Singh N, Education under Seige: **A Sociological Study of Private Colleges**, Concept, New Delhi, 1983.

Sadlak, J. and Liu, N.C. 2007. **The World-class University and ranking: Aiming Beyond Status**. Bucharest, UNESCO CEPES.

Schimank, U. and Winnes, M. Beyond Humboldt? The relationship between teaching and research in European university systems. **Science and Public Policy**, Vol. 27, No. 6 pp. 397-408. 2000.

Slancheva, S. and Levy D.C. **Private Higher Education in Post-communist Europe: In Search of Legitimacy**. New York, Palgrave Macmillan. 2007.

Task Force on Higher Education and Society. **Higher Education in Developing Countries: Peril and Promise**, Wishington, DC, World Bank. 2000.

Teichler, U. Changing structure of the higher education systems: The increasing complexity of underlying forces. **Higher Education Policy**, Vol. 19. No. 4, pp. 447-461. 2006.

Tim Loreman and others Inclusive Education: **A Practical Guide to Supporting Diversity in the Classroom,** Allen and Unwin Chennai, 2006.

UGC, **Higher Education in India: Issues, Concerns and New Directions UGC**, New Delhi, 2003.

UNESCO. n.d.-a Distance Education, Retrieved from: http://portal.unesco.org/education/en/ev.php-

URL_ID=6940&URL_DO_TOPIC&URL_SECTION=201.html on 12 April 2009.

_____.n.d.-b **Higher Education Open and Distance Learning Knowledge Base**.

Retrieved from:http://portal.unesco.org/education/en/ev.php-

URL_ID=42843&URL_DO=DO_TOPIC&URL_SECTION=201.html on 12 April 2009.

_____.n.d.-c UNESCO Portal on Higher Education Institution. Retrieved from: http://_ID= 49864& URL_DO= DO_TOPIC & URL_ SECTION=201.html on1 April 2009.

_____.2005a. Mega Universities. Retrieved from: http://portal.unesco.org/ education/en/ev.php-

URL_ID=42857&URL_DO=DO_TOPIC&URL_SECTION=201.HTML on 12 April 2009.

______.2005b. Open and Distance Learing (ODL). Retrieved from: http:// portal.unesco.org/education/en/ev.php-

______.2004. **Higher Education in a Globalized Society: UNESCO Education Position Paper**, Paris, UNESCO.

Washburn, J. **University, Inc: The Corporate Corruption of American Higher Education**, New York, Basic Books. 2005.

Weisskopf, T. **Affirmative Action in the United States and India: A Comparative Perspective**, New York, Routledge. 2004.

Wells, P.J. Sadlak. J. and Vlasceanu, L. **The Rising Role and Relevance of Private Higher Education in Europe**. Bucharest, UNESCO-CEPES. 2007.

William J.K. **Parties, Politics and Public Policy in America**, Hinsdale Illinois, 1980 3ed.

Weiner, **The Child and the State in India,** Oxford University Press, New Delhi, 1991.

Zhou, P. and Leydesdorff, L. 2006. **The emergence of China as a leading nation in Science Research Policy**, Vol. 35, No.1, pp. 83.

Index

A

Academic Planning, 120
Administration, 50, 120
Admission Tests, 32
Adult Psychology, 62
Affirmation Administration Policies, 80
African, American and Whites, 137
Agricultural Universities,
    Development of-, 12
AICME, 47, 120
AIU (Association of Indian Universities), 12, 31
Alternate Methods of Financing, 116, 118
Ambani, Mukesh, 84, 111
Ambani-Birla Report, 146
Ambedkar's People's Education Movement, 87
American
    And Russian Experts, 19
    Association of State Colleges/ Universities, 21
    Economic Association, 134
    Experience, 137
    System of University Education, 125
    Trained Indian Experts, 146
Andhra Pradesh, 48
    University, 12, 62
Anglican or English Education, 17
Anglo-Saxon
    Model of University, 146, 147
    Traditions of Education, 55
Aristotle, 77
Art and Science Courses, 85
Australia, 20
Autonomous
    Colleges, 114
    Power of Teacher, 59

B

Bank Services, 31
Bar Council, 73
Bihar, 87
Biotechnology, 52-53

Birla, Aditya, 84, 111
Blacks, 21
Blogs, 25
BPO Skills, 144
Brain Drain, 12, 61
British Indian Government, 18
Bureaucracy, 16
Bush, George US Pres., 55
Business Management, 20

C

Campus Crisis, 99
Carnegei Commission, 100
Caste System, 89
Castes and Women, 17
CAT Examinations, 32
CBSC (Central Board of Secondary Education), 57
Censorship, 56
Centralized Structure, 57
Chalam, KS, 52, 61, 62, 90
Charter School, 16
Childhood Education, 57
China, 124, 149
 Investment in –Education, 22
Christian Missionaries, 71
Civil Services Examination, 37
Club of Rome, Learning Report, 61
Coaching Centres, 51
Cognitive Skills, 62
Colonial
 Education, 60
 Liberal Education, 81
 Powers, 102
 Rulers, 131
Commission (s),
 Dr. Radhakrishnan, 11, 146
 Education, 1964-66, 110, 113
 Kothari, 11, 89
 Secondary Education-, 1952-1953, 19
 University Education, 1948-49, 19
Communal Reservations, 121
Competencies, 30, 55, 57, 52
 For Good Teaching, 55-64
Concept of
 Empowerment, 77
 University, 29
Correspondence or Courses, 113
Costs of Education, 103
Course in Electronics, Computer Science, 86
Cross Border Education, 49
CSIR, 115
 And DRDO Laboratories, 12
Curriculum, 51, 57, 58, 73, 115
 And Syllabus, 18
 Design, 36
Customs and Practices, 55

D

Dalits, 81, 85, 86
Dalits
 And Artisans Caste, 86
 And OBC, 82
 In Education, 88
 In India, 84
Dalits Education and Empowerment, 87
Dean, Howard, 55
Decentralization, 91

Deemed Universities, 29, 31, 52
Demand for Education in India, 147
Democratization of Education, 17
Design of Course, 35
Development of Education in India, 131
Dimensions of Personality, 36
Diploma Mills, 26
Disadvantaged
  Groups, 75, 81, 86
  Schools, 60
Discrimination Practices, 45
Dispossessed Groups, 92
Distance Education, 19, 25, 26, 49, 113
District Primary Education Program, (DPEP), 89
Diversification, 24
Diversified Education System, 24
Division of Labor, 58
Dr Radhakrishnan Commission, 146
DRDO, 115
Dropout
  Of School Children, 16
  Ratio, 82
Dworkin, Ronall, 44

E

East India Company, 20, 88, 91, 146
  Project Modernization, 21
  Rule in India, 131, 136
Economic
  Crisis on Education, 148
  Growth, 136, 148
  Growth in Japan and Indonesia and India, 135
  Reforms in India, 17
  Slowdown, 138
  Structure, 11
Economics of Education, 50, 101
  And Human Resource Development, 12
Economy, 48, 89, 90, 105, 110, 115, 116, 124, 136, 148
  And Society, 48, 91
  Of Indian Education, 90
Educated Labor Force, 110
Education
  And Empowerment, 77
  Art of Utilization of Knowledge, 78
  As a Transformative Project, 78
  Commission, 1964-66, 110, 113
  Corruption and Ethics in-, 25
  Cost Benefit Analysis of-, 100
  Decentralization, 78
Economic Value of-, 132
  For Agriculture and Industry, 19
  Globalization and Privatization, 87
  Grants Committee, 119
  Guarantee Program (EGP), 82
  History of-, 17
  In Ancient Indian Literature, 77
  In India, 94
  History, 87
  Of Minorities, 19
  Policy, 123
  Brief History, 17-20
  Policy Defined, 15
  Primary, 52, 82
  Professional and Vocational, 84
  Role in Empowering People, 78

Secular, 18
Socio-Economic Development, 143
System, (ES), 11, 12, 16, 52, 85, 94, 99, 100, 106, 109
Universal, 17
Universal Strategies of-, 109
University, 17
Educational
Development, 45, 85, 109, 110
Institutions, 20, 33, 47, 49, 51, 64, 73, 113, 121
Markets, 85
Opportunities of Dalits, 81
Policies of -, 17
Bush, 17
Margaret Thatcher, 17
NDA Government, 17
Obama, 17
Romans and Spartans, 15
Tony Blair, 17
UPA Government, 17
Policy, 146
Policy in India, 88
Policy of Ancient Period, 17
Policy of East India Company, 18
Program of Dalits, 81
Reforms, 15, 106, 109, 123
Financial Strategy for, 109-123
Skills, 47
Strategies of Madhya Pradesh, 82
Structure, 113
System, 102
Restructuring of-, 113
Educationalists, 30
In India, 17
Electronic Publications, 25
Elementary Education, 123, 128
Email, 25
Engineering, 37
Colleges, 56
English
As Medium of Instruction, 20
Education, 18, 21
Enrolment Rates, 137
Eskimo Children, 35, 106
European
Commission, 88
Education, 78
In Higher Education, 104
Evaluation, 29-41
And Accountability, 153
Methodology, 31
Techniques, 35
Examination Reforms, 19
Examination Reforms, (a Program of Action), 31
Expert Committees on Education, 73
Extension Program, 134

F

Family Background, 50
Fashion Technology, 20, 144
Faulty Policy/ Concept Practices, 16
Federal Subsidy per Student (US), 145
Finance Commission, 125
Financial
Incentives, 117
Problems, 122
Fish and Fisheries, 93
Fishermen Community, 93

Five Year Plan (11th), 19
Foreign Universities, 138, 139
  Regime, 131-141
Formal System of Education, 112, 114
Formulation of Human Capital, 131, 134
Free and Compulsory Education, 19
Freezing of Grants-in-Aid, 110
Fundamental Rights, 123

G

GATE, Test for Science and Engineering, 32
GATS, 60, 85, 87
  In Education, 87
GATT (General Agreement on Trade and Tariffs), 144
German Education Policy During Hitler Time, 15
Global
  Economy, 22
  Labor Market, 86
  Virus of Internationalization of Higher Education, 31
Globalization, 56
  Privatization Sector, 86
Globalized Economy, 78, 85
GMAT, 32
Govt. of India Act on Compulsory Education, 82
Graduate Unemployment, 116
Great Saints Poets, 18
  Kabir, 18
  Ravidas, 18
  Vemana, 18
Ground Rules for Class Room Observance, 69
Guru Shishya Parampara, 56, 58, 126

H

Harvard
  Model of Business Management, 31
  Or MIT or Oxford, 12
Health Care, 75
Hieun Tsang and I-Tsang, Travelogues, 17
Higher Education (HE), 11
  Agencies, 52
  Allocation for-, 125, 126
  And Economic Reforms, 99-107
  Challenges of-, 51
  Commercialization, 25
  Contradictions in-, 102
  Demand for-, 106
  Development of-, 11
  Educational Policy in India, 146
  Federal Expenditure on-, 145
  Funding, 120
  Future of-, 99
  Global Virus of Internationalization of-, 31
  In Budget Allocations, 12
  In India, 43, 90, 128, 138
  In Japan, Enrolment Ratio, 135
  Indicators, 23
  Indirect Expenditure, 112
  Institutions, 29, 30
  Institutions, 47
  Objectives of-, 155
  Opportunity Act, 2008, 22

Policy and Reform, 11, 12, 15-27
Policy in India, 110
Political Economy of-, 145
Privatization of-, 19
Profession, 119
Professional, 73
Quality of-, 48, 49, 53, 61
Sector, 56
Standards of-, 47, 52
Structure of-, 148
System, 21, 36, 138, 155, 159
Teacher in-, 60
Technical and Professional, 76
Westernization of-, 20
White Paper UK, 63

Higher
Learning Institutions, 115
Technical Education, 104

Hispanics, 21
Hitler, 15
Human
Capital, 131-141, 149
Concept, 132, 133
In India, 135
Development, 133
Resource Professional, 90

Hunter Commission, 1882, 18, 89

I

ICMR (Indian Council of Medical Research), 120
ICTE (Indian Council of Technical Education), 47
Ideology, 17
Inclusion
Growth, 92
Education, 77-130
Limitations of-, 88

India, 80
Status of Teachers in-, 56

Indian
Education, 21
Higher Education, 11
Institute of Management (IIM), 33, 60, 64, 81, 84, 87
Institute of Technology (IIT), 33, 60, 64, 74, 81, 84, 87

Indigenization of Education, 21
Individual Subsidy, 117
Industrial Process, 144
Industrialized Nations, 102-104
Industry, 48-49
Information Technology
And ICT, 49
Boom, 123
Skills, 149

Information, Communication and Technology (ICT), 20, 23, 25, 64, 90, 116, 131, 145
Professionals, 35

Infrastructure, 50, 51, 125
Activities, 25
And Superstructure, 139
Superstructure of Education, 60

Inspection Regime, 52
Institutional
Mechanism, 150
Standards, 46
Structure, 52

International
Labor Markets, 126

Relations, 11
Test Scores, 152

J

Japan and
India, 135, 136
Korea, 64
Job
Market, 86
Oriented Courses, 91

K

Knowledge
And Competencies, 30
Based Economy, 83
Commission, 64, 148
Commission (Sam Pitroda), 19
Industries, 57
Society, 80
Kothari Commission, 1964-66, 11, 19, 89, 146
Report, 143
Kothari, DS, 128

L

Labor
And Employment, 71
Market, 44, 94, 106, 144
Party (UK), 55, 56
Lead College, 114
Leaders/Scholars, 18
CV Raman, 18
Gandhi, 18
Jagdish Chandra Bose, 18
Meghnad Saha, 18
Nehru, 18
Ram Mohan Roy, 18
S Chandrasekhar, 18
Tagore, 18
Leaning Resources, 57
Legacy Applicants, 45
Liberal Education of the British, 18
Liberalization, 60, 81, 85, 131, 135
And Internationalization of Higher Education, 11
In India, 88
Policy, 18
Literacy
Education, 87
Level, 81
Rates, 18, 136
Lohia, 92
Lord Curzon, 146
Lord Macaulay, 60, 136
Lower
Castes, 18
Communities, 72

M

Maharashtra, 87
Madhya Pradesh, 87
Malaysia, 80
Management Experts, 60
Manmohan Singh, 119
Market Rewards, 44
Mathematics—Economics, 53
MCTE, 150
Medical
Council, 73
Courses, 73

- Profession, 74
  - Crises in-, 74
- Meiji Restoration, 135
- Mentally and Physically Handicapped, 88
- Micro Teaching, 62
- Micro-Economic Case Studies, 44
- Mid Day Meal Scheme, 126
- Migration, 134
- Ministry of
  - Human Resource Development, 111
  - Social Justice and Empowerment, 84
- Modern
  - Economy, 87, 131
  - Educated Class, 18
  - Higher Education, 131
  - University in India, 144
- Modernization, 20, 104, 146
  - Projects in India, 87
- Modernizing of Madarsas, 126
- Moily Committee, 46
- Monitoring, 63
- Multiple Intelligence, 30
- Municipal-Panchayat Schools, 89
- Muslim Education of Madarsas, 17

N

- NAAC, 47, 49, 52
- Nai Talim, 127
- Naik, JP, Member of Education Commission, 92, 110, 117
- Nalanda, 18, 29
- Nanotechnology, 53
- NASA, 12
- National
  - Council of Educational Research and Training (NCERT), 57, 127
  - Council of Technical Education (NCTE), 57
  - Education Policies in India, 20
  - Knowledge Commission, 148, 150
  - Policy for Education, (1986), 18, 19, 33, 63, 143
  - Policy for Education, 146, 154
  - Of Education, 1986, 84
  - Of Reform Package, 155
- New
  - Economic Policy, 17
  - Educational Structure (10+2+3), 19
  - Technologies, 25
  - Universities, Establishment, 19
- North Indian University Structure, 139
- Nursing and Pharmacy, 75

O

- OBC, 50, 80, 87
  - Reservations, 12
- Occupational Structure, 73
- OECD Countries, 99, 104, 106, 148
- On-the-Job Training, 119
- Oratory, 15
- Orissa, 87
- Oxford Centre for Staff Development, 63

P

Pakistan and Malaysia, 24
Performance Indictors, 157
Permanent Education Commission,
    (In Place of State Council), 120
Pharmacy, 52-53
    Council, 47
Phooley, Mahatma Jyoti Rao, 87, 92, 146
PL-480, 12
Planning, 128
    Commission, 111, 158
Pod Castes, 25
Poland, 102
Policies
    Of Education, 109
    With Education, 16
    Administrative Policy, 16
    Curriculum, 16
    Financial Policy, 16
    Recruitment Policy, 16
    Changes in Structure of Education, 12
    Formulations, 12
    Of Education in India, 136
    Of Rehabilitation and Settlement, 76
Political Economy, 132, 146
Post Colonial Economy, 11, 12
Pre/Post Liberalization Period, 85
Pre-British India, 17
Pricing Policy, 119
Primary
    Education, 82
    Education Act, 84
Prison Note Book, Gramsci, 78
Private
    Cost of Education, 112
    Foreign Universities, 85
    Institutions, 24
    Investment in Education, 116
Privatization, 91
    And Funding, 24
Process of Promoting Merit, 45
Professional
    And Vocational Courses, 84
    Bodies, 73
    Courses, 74
    Education, Crisis in-, 71-76
Program of Action (POA), 19
Program of Action, 1992, 84
Pseudo Universities, 147
Public
    Accountability, 153-159
    Education, 19, 124
    Examinations, 30
    Expenditure on Education, 122
Pummayya Committee, 110

Q

Quack Doctors, 72
Quality
    And Equity in Education, 47
    And Standards of Higher Education, 47
    Control, 120
    Institutions, 87
    Of Education, 45, 52, 63, 112, 116
    Of Higher Education, 45
    Of Teaching, 64
    Syndrome, 43-54

Quasi-Government Organizations, 30

R

Radhakrishnan, 59
  Commission, 11
Radical Policy Reforms, 21
Rajasthan, 87
Rawls, John, 44
Recruiting
  Agencies, 36
  Boards, 36-37
Reform
  And Policy, 16
  Defined, 16
  In India, 11
Religious
  And Social Groups, 47
  Orientation, 71
Research
  Based Teaching, 57
  Universities, 115
Reservation (s), 76, 80
  For OBC, 21
  Groups, 81
  Of Seats for Weaker Sections, 110
Review Committees, 19
  Acharya Ram Murthy, 19
  N. Janardhana Reddy, 19
Right to
  Education, 111, 128
  Education Act, 20, 123
  Education, 2010, 140
Roemer, John, 44
Rural Colleges, 59
Russian Education, 15

S

Sachar Committee for Muslims, 126
Salary Structure, 106
Sam Pitroda, 146
  National Knowledge Commission, 146
Samkhya and Non-Vedic Agamas, 17
Sanskritization, 20
Sarva Shiksha Abhiyan, 89, 119, 124, 126
SAT (Scholastic Aptitude Test), 32, 33
Scheduled Castes and Tribes, 80, 81
  Commission, 84
  Dalits, 81
  Educational Development, 84
Scheme for Universalization—
  Education (SUCCESS), 125
School
  Curriculum, 58
  Discipline, 55
  Education, 57, 58, 83, 84, 122, 144, 150
  Financing of-, 111
  Problems of-, 111
  Reforms, 56
Science
  And Technology, 12, 26, 37, 103, 104
  Education and Research, 19
Secondary Education, 90
  Commission, 1952-53
Sector,
  ICT, 124, 139
  Indian Corporate, 12
  Manufacture and Service, 86

Manufacture, 58
Secular
Education, 18
VS Caste Procession, 72
Orientation of Education, 20
Professions, 72, 73
Self-Financing, 110
Courses, 87
Sen, Amartya, 44
Short Life Courses, 149
Shortage of Technical Teachers, 126
Silicon Valley, 12
Skilled
Movement, 30
Personnel, 124
Skills, 15
Social
Empowerment, 77-130
Exclusion, 91
Groups, 17, 75, 88
Reform Agenda, 137
Reformers, 18
Phooley, Jothi Rao, 18
System, 72
Socialistic Pattern of Society, 19
Socially and Educationally Deprived Groups, 60
Society,
Indian, 20, 91
Modern Capitalist, 94
Socio-Economic Structure, 131
Technological-, 19
Western, 51
Socio-Economic Inclusion, 79
Soft Skills, 20
Courses, 20
South
Africa, 80
Indian States, 87
Space Science, 53
Sri Lanka, 128
State
Financial Support, 16
Public Service Commission, 36
Structural Changes in Economy and Society, 100
Students Loans, 111
Study Program, 134
Subsidies in America, 145
Subsidization, 112, 117, 119
Sudras, 76
Communities, 75

T

Tagore, 59
Takshasila, 29
Teacher
Education and Infrastructure, 58
Gnandata, 59
Quality Index (TQI), 62
Teaching
And Guidance, 64
Careers, 61
Learning Process (TLP), 64
Technical
Education, 71, 106, 111
Education for Scheduled Caste, 87
Technology, 53, 56, 59
Courses, 74
Supported Teaching, 56

Textbooks, 58
Total Quality Management, (TQM), 49
Traditional
  Skills, 124
  Teaching Methods, 55
  Vedic Education, 18
Traditions of Great Teachers, (TGT), 55
  Radhakrishnan, 55
  Tagore, 55
  Vasista, 55
  Vishnu Sharma, 55
  Vishwamitra, 55
Tribal People, 72
Tropical Agriculture, 35
Twinning Program, 139

U

UCLA Projects, 55
UK, 24, 52, 121,
  Or USA, 64, 152
UN
  Agencies, 78, 80
  Development Program, 43, 50, 80
UNESCO, 22, 25, 35, 99, 100, 109
  Conference in Frankfurt, 12
UNESCO's European Centre, 100
Universal Education, 17
Universalization of Education, 91
Universities, 45, 49, 52-53, 56, 58, 61-62, 64, 85, 115, 139, 153
University
  Education, 17, 90, 116
  Education Commission, 1948-49, 19
  Grants Commission (UGC), 31, 47, 52, 53, 110, 114, 120, 125, 126, 150
  Program, 61
  Regulations, 62
  Of California, 55
  System, 30, 138
  System of Education, 29
UNO's Millennium Development Goals, 123
UPSC, 36-37
USA, 12, 16, 20-22, 24, 33, 38, 45, 47, 80, 116, 125, 127, 128, 133, 134, 137, 145, 148
  And UK, 73
  GMAT System, 32
  Liberal Democracy, 56
USA's Plural Culture, 21
Uttar Pradesh, 87

V

Vajpayee, Atal Behari, 84
Validity and Reliability of Tests, 34
Varna
  Category, 138
  System, 73
Venkataramaiah Committee (Andhra Pradesh), 114
Vocation in India, 71
Vocational
  And Job Oriented Courses, 85
  Education, 71
Vocationalization of Education, 81, 104

W

War in Iraq, 55
Web Based Learning, 56
West Bengal, 87
Western Standards, 29
Westernization, 20
Wikis, 25
Woods Dispatch of East India Company in 1854, 17
World
 Bank, 43, 72, 78, 80, 84, 89, 143
 Indicators to Measure Empowerment, 93
 Development Report, 43, 44
 Trade Organization (WTO), 85, 144

Z

Zilla Parishad, 89